Song For My Father
Ian Clayton

First published by Route in 2014
PO Box 167, Pontefract, WF8 4WW
info@route-online.com
www.route-online.com

First Edition

Hardback:
500 signed and numbered copies

Paperback:
ISBN: 978-1901927-62-7

Ian Clayton asserts his moral right to be
identified as the author of this book

Design:
GOLDEN
www.wearegolden.co.uk

Typeset in Bembo by Route

Printed and bound by CPI Group (UK) Ltd,
Croydon, CR0 4YY

I dedicate this book to three women who have taught me, Miss Mackie at Girnhill Lane Infants, Mrs Taylor at George Street Junior Mixed and Hui Xiao of NENU, the University in Changchun, China. I also dedicate it to Barry Hines, whose story Kes *made me want to write things down in the first place.*

Prelude by Gary McMahon

We were standing on the platform, looking down the track, up around a bend in the past. The future was behind us: even the change two stops up the line at Victoria for Yorkshire, even the terminus, predetermined. Look to yesterday's yonder for what would happen next.

It's an act of faith, looking down the track: a wistful, communal, searching, melancholy, visionary thing to do. Just standing here can turn you into Johnny Cash or Bob Dylan. It can make an expectant father of you, waiting for deliverance. What goes around comes around on the hour, the visitation of what might happen when the past catches up with us out of the haze beyond the trees, under a shiftless sky.

The past can take a long time, and all we could do was meet it half-way. So Ian spoke about his old man, the way Ian is about to tell you about his old man here, and I, fifty-four and there's not much more, spoke about mine. Our fathers remained distant, stalled out of sight.

Mine surprised me long ago with James Bond's Aston Martin DB5 model car. So despite everything, despite wanting to put him in the ejector seat, I remember that. Old fathers mellow with age like old boxers when it's too late to do anything else. Like bad penny blues, estranged fathers will show up down the line, even John Lennon found out, to remind us where we came from before we existed at all, with the startling news that we wound up like they were, or to discover we are what they could have been.

You can't teach an old dog new tricks. My old man read that adage as some sort of triumph for the dog – as if the dog were saying, 'Ho-ho, you can't fox me with your new tricks.' By the time he was seventy you couldn't tell him anything.

Aye, well. The one in these pages comes to life emphatically, redeemed by narrative and not so much by penitence but by the scruff of the neck: riotous, taking his place in a memoir on the immortal continuity of life, the middleman in a grandfather's shaving mirror looking back at you.

Trust is the key to this writing, and trust gives it the courage to face its insights. The consciousness in these pages trusts to time and space to always find a way, and blow me down it does: making tracks through rites of passage from a three-mile walk, four strides to his grandad's one, to the back streets of Changchun, under the same moon.

In the coming year these tracks would take Ian Clayton to the Far East and back; and Indianapolis and back. And always, he takes his sentient prose with him, as portable as a jazzman. Moving fluently to the next synchronicity, making connections with people and places and memory, his writing circulates in anecdotes and an ear for dialogue and thinking every sentence knows exactly when to disembark.

Storytelling runs through the family one way or another: companionable, traveling on free association and legend and real ale. Meandering, like whimsy, the way rural forays wend through Yorkshire townlife; episodic like the turning of the Earth until a direct line to a home-truth swoops to get it straight. This one's got parables and refrains and, in the grooves, a lyric, a telegram, so attuned to the sounds of words; transcendental through the wind on scattered ashes and loose leaf and blown kisses and back pages. There's no time like the present, and immediacy runs through this prose like the past never left town. Any moment can catalyse a life, can pull a disappearing man back from the brink of dementia.

Ian can make a Grade I restoration of any subject, and the real trick, for me, is this: Ian takes a term that's turned callous with the times, 'moving on', and restores it, made poignant and heartwarming and philosophical and loyal. Wherever he goes, he takes the roots of who he is and he disowns nothing. Ian's books – and here comes one now – are the clearest, lyrical, amenable public address system I know.

His train came, a journey beckoned, he waved.

Gary McMahon wrote *Camp In Literature* and *Kurt Vonnegut and the Centrifugal Force of Fate* (2006; 2009: McFarland). Let him through, he's a doctor!

Blood Running Thicker Than Water

I never really knew who my father was. We were only acquainted at the beginning and the end. I lived in the same house as him until I was fifteen but have hardly seen him since. In the final year of his life, I visited him three times and phoned him on half a dozen occasions. In that last year we went from winter through spring and summer and arrived at autumn knowing more about one another than we had in the half century of seasons before then.

I tried to tell him about the middle-aged man that his son had become when he wasn't there. I told him about Heather, my partner of thirty-five years. He asked me, 'Does she still have a Mohawk haircut?' He had met her just once – in the punk years. My dad never met our children. When our daughter Billie died in a canoeing accident, she was nine years old. He sent word with my brother Andrew to ask if he could come to the funeral. I sent word back that he wasn't to bother. There have been times since when I have wished I hadn't been so harsh. All my friends have told me that blood is always thicker than water.

My lad Edward has asked about him once or twice over the years. I don't know where to start. Should I tell him that my dad and mam argued incessantly and that occasionally when he couldn't get the top side of her with words he would lash out with his fists? Should I tell him that he lived most of his life on a whim, improvising everything as he went along like a jazz man, albeit a jazz man without an instrument? Should I tell Edward that my dad seemed to live his life hoping that one day something would turn up? My dad seemed settled forever at a crossroads not knowing which way to go next, so he waited. He waited like a man on a bench at a railway station waits for the next announcement, except the trains aren't running and the public-address system has broken down.

I have an abiding image of my dad. I am nine. We are sitting on a bench at Wakefield Kirkgate railway station. My mother walked out of our house the day before. My dad has decided to look for her and bring her home. His exact words to me before we came to this station were, 'We're going to form a posse, lad, lasso your mam and bring her back.' We sit side by side, not looking at one another. We munch on corned beef sandwiches wrapped in tin foil. My dad has cut his finger opening the tin and he has a piece of rag wrapped round it fastened on with Sellotape. A porter trudges past with a sack barrow full of suitcases, all bearing neatly-written address labels. People get off trains and get on them. My dad stares into space and then looks up at the sky. I sense this and follow his gaze. High up, a little aeroplane moves across the blue leaving a vapour trail that is sharp at first and then thickens until it starts to disappear. I watch the aeroplane until it goes out of my frame of vision. My dad starts to sing a Box Tops song. 'Give me a ticket for an aeroplane; I ain't got time to catch the fast train.' His singing is a peculiar mixture of West Riding Yorkshire and what he thinks is an American accent. I look at my dad, he doesn't look back, just carries on singing and humming when he can't remember the words.

'Are you singing because you are sad?'

He says nothing and still doesn't turn to look at me.

'Are you happy then?'

He carries on singing and humming and looking up at the sky. Another little aeroplane comes into view.

I want to ask my dad all sorts of questions, but I know I won't get an answer. I crumble up the crust of my sandwich and throw pieces of it to some pigeons that have flown down from under the canopy that is over the platform. And that's where this image fades. Over many years I have tried and better tried to recall, but I can't remember what happens next.

My mother used to keep photographs in a shoebox in the cupboard in our sideboard. One day she pulled out every photograph that had my dad on it and started to cut round him with a pair of small scissors. She didn't stop to look at the shape she had cut out, just threw it straight onto the fire. We have photographs that were once family groups that show three boys with identical fringes, a mother looking over us and a hole where our dad used to be. We have seaside donkeys missing a rider and a wedding photograph that shows a young woman outside St. Thomas' Church with part of her arm missing and a hole to one side of her. All that's left is a piece of my dad's lapel and half a carnation. My dad went missing a long time before he started disappearing.

Winter
My Disappearing Dad

'The essence lies not in the headlined heroes
but in the everyday folk who live and die unknown,
yet leave their dreams as legacies.'
Alan Lomax

Cinderella Rockefella

'You're like your bloody father!' My grandmother said this whenever she was angry with me. It's a refrain from my childhood that I have grown to dislike. It makes me shudder when I hear it inside my head, and it has come into my head a lot just lately. My dad rarely had conversations, he just said random thoughts that came to him. He preferred strong tea to beer and smoked one cigarette after another. When he ran out of cigs he chewed on matchsticks or pieces of straw. He had a pair of winklepicker boots but didn't wear them much, he said they made his feet look pointed. My dad only washed in cold water and took his bath on Fridays, whether he needed one or not.

There have been times, especially in the last four or five years or so, when I have smelled my father – a sweetish and sour smell – then I realise it's me. On odd occasions I have said something and reflected afterwards that 'My dad used to say that' and many a time I have been clipping my fingernails and thought how much my fingers look like my dad's. At my Uncle Johnny's eightieth birthday party in a working men's club at Wakefield, my Auntie Marion said, 'Your voice sounds just like Sid's.'

I have hardly known my father since 1975, when he and my mother parted. I've only seen him on about half a dozen occasions since then. For nearly forty years my dad is someone I hear a snippet of news about from time to time. My younger brother Andrew still sees him a lot. They have shared a council flat in Hull on and off over the years. Now and again I bump into our Andrew; he's usually on his way from a betting shop with another dead cert in his trouser pocket. He'll tell me that our dad has been searching for treasure with his metal detector, that he still rages about our mother and that he's taught his Jack Russell dog a new trick. That's about it.

It was through our Andrew that I learned my father was diagnosed with prostate cancer and that it had spread to his bowel. My father's partner, Ivy, was by then eighty-six – or 'nearly ninety' according to my dad's reckoning – and suffering loss of memory. They lived in a grim council bungalow in an even grimmer part of town just off the Beverley Road. Our Andrew decided he would travel backwards and forwards by bus from Castleford to Hull and look after him. Our Andrew is a bit of a lost soul. Of all my mam's and dad's three sons, I think he was the one most affected by their divorce. He's a caring person, though, and had no hesitation in volunteering to look after Dad.

Out of the blue one Sunday, Andrew phoned me.

'My dad says he hasn't got long to live and he'd like to talk to you.'

I was in the middle of preparing some lunch, completely taken off-guard and didn't know what to say. I hadn't spoken to my dad for nearly twenty years and before that only a handful of times in the previous twenty. I think I just said, 'What! Now?' Andrew, calmly and almost distantly, or as distant as a phone call over fifty odd miles is, said, 'Yes, if that's alright.'

It took a long time for my dad to get from wherever he was to the phone. I could hear him asking Andrew, 'Is he right?' and then laughing; he has a laugh that flits between nervous and high-pitched hysteria. The phone rattled, dropped and then was finally handed to him. It sounded like he had put the earpiece to his mouth, his voice was muffled, he was trying to talk to me down the wrong end of the phone, as well as to Andrew and to Ivy, who I could hear saying, 'Is it your son?' I think, finally, Andrew must have put the phone the right way round for him.

'Hello, hello, it's your dad! Turn that telly down Andrew, just a minute Ivy. Hello, hello, it's your dad!'

'Hello.'

'Tha'll have to speak up, I've left my deaf aid somewhere.'

He'd suffered a perforated ear drum as a young man and has been deaf in his left ear for more than sixty years. I said 'Hello' again in as loud a voice as I thought suitable.

He said, 'Nah then, Narrow!'

The phrase catapulted me back to 1972. He called me 'Narrow' when I was a lad, sometimes he called me 'Mouse', sometimes 'Educated Archie' but mostly 'Narrow', I suppose because I was little and slim.

He repeated himself, 'Nah then, Narrow! Is t'alreight?' I told him I was 'alreight' and asked him if he was. In typical melodramatic Sid Clayton fashion he said, 'I'm dying, lad. They've given me three months, but I think I might be able to hold on a bit longer.' I said, 'It's cancer isn't it?' He said, 'Can tha speak up a bit, Ivy pipe down, speak up, lad!' I said, 'It's cancer isn't it?' at the top of my voice, then looked round the room. I was in the house on my own, but still felt self-conscious saying the words at such a high volume.

He said, 'Aye, I'm riddled with it, I've even got it in my arm.'

I didn't know what to say next. I could hear a little dog yapping in the room he was in. 'Andrew, put t'dog into t'passage and shut t'door.' I found myself saying, 'Are you eating alright?' He said, 'I've had it for a bit now, I thought I could get t'top side of it, but it's eating me away.' Silence again apart from the muffled yapping of his dog.

'Anyhow, lad, I'm phoning to say farewell and I'll see thee on the other side.'

More melodrama. I wondered what to say next. 'Shall I come over to Hull to see you?' He said, 'Well don't dawdle, I might not be here.' Then silence again. Our Andrew came on the line. He told me that my dad was crying. I said that I would make a trip over to Hull in the next week or so.

The streets round where my dad lives are a warren of broken fences, dog shit, dumped rubbish, bollards and cul-de-sacs where disenfranchised, unemployed people live and burglars burgle them. I cross a grass verge that is rutted with the tyre marks of cars and stand at the threshold of a bungalow where my dad is seeing out his last days.

On the way here I've been wondering what I will say. I press the bell. I don't hear anything so I knock hard. A dog starts to bark. I hear my brother Andrew's voice, 'Just a minute please.' I wait. I hear muffled voices and a dog being coaxed into another room. A man passes on the pavement with his head down, when he gets in line with me he looks up and says, 'Are you waiting?' Before I can answer, he puts his head down again and scurries along. I hear the sound of two locks being unlocked and our Andrew opens the door, just wide enough for me to squeeze through. As soon as I'm inside, he shuts the door and locks it again. I am shown into a little front room that is full of furniture.

'Do you want a pot of tea?' asks our Andrew.

'No, I'm alright thanks.'

The whole corner of the room across from where I stand is taken up by a fifty-inch flat-screen Panasonic television. There is a sofa opposite, a coffee table, a dining chair that looks like it's been separated from a set, a display cabinet displaying photographs of people I don't know, and another easy chair. Behind the sofa is a folded-up mobility scooter. My dad walks down the passage, he stumbles and stops himself by falling onto me. He says, 'Nah then, cock. Are gooah!' He tries to shake my hand, but misses it and then awkwardly puts his arms around me. He is frail, tiny and his trousers are held up by psychedelic braces. He moves to the sofa and says, 'Sit on this chair, lad, then you're on the right side of me for me to hear what you say.' I sit on the dining chair. 'Andrew, go and make him a pot of tea.' Andrew says, 'I've asked him, he doesn't want one.'

'Speak up, I can't hear you!'

Andrew shouts at the top of his voice, 'I said I've asked him, he says he doesn't want one.'

'Why what's up, is he frightened we're going to poison him?' He looks at me, 'Are you frightened we're going to poison you?'

I say, 'I had a good breakfast and I've had three mugs of tea already this morning.'

'Aye, well I used to like a good breakfast, but I can't do it now. I haven't seen a frying pan for I don't know how long. Look at me, I'm disappearing lad.'

He takes the waistband of his trousers and pulls it outwards. There is a gap of three or four inches between his stomach and where he's holding the trousers. He looks a right sight. He's wearing slippers, a pair of suit trousers and a lumberjack shirt. His psychedelic braces are two inches wide with red and orange swirling patterns and what look like primroses on them. His hair is white, but there are blond highlights. He must have dyed it not too long ago and the blond hasn't quite grown out.

'I've not got long now, lad, but I'm ready.'

He speaks in a strange accent these days. He was born near Wakefield and still has traces of a very old fashioned West Riding dialect, but forty years of living at Hull and trying to mimic the accent has given his spoken words a peculiar sound. He says, 'I'm glad you answered my fern curl lad.'

I say, 'Your fern curl?'

'Aye, when I ferned you the other day I didn't knerr whether you would speak to me or not.'

'Well, I'd heard that you had cancer and I've been wondering myself what I should do.'

'Hey?'

I say, 'I heard you had cancer and I didn't know what to do.'

I feel self-conscious now, I suppose I thought that on meeting my father for the first time in many years our conversation would be conducted in not much more than respectful whispers.

Because he is so deaf, I'm talking to him in a voice loud enough for the neighbours across the street to hear me. And saying the word 'cancer' at such a volume doesn't seem right. People normally whisper that word.

'Don't fret about saying cancer to me, lad. I've been living with it for a long time now. I thought I'd got it beat when I could get out in the fresh air, but since I've been trapped in here, it's eating me.'

He thinks fresh air cures cancer.

I can't ever remember my father visiting a doctor, he cured everything with his own remedies. I recall he swore by a patent medicine called 'Kompo' for colds, drank warm milk and Lyles Golden syrup for stomach ache and put Dettol on cuts. He drank the water left over from boiling a cabbage because he said it was good for the complexion and ate tripe soaked in vinegar for his blood and boiled beetroot to keep his liver working right.

'What do the doctors say?'

'I tell them to fuck off!'

'No, I said, what do the doctors say to you?'

'They've told me I can have that chemotherapy, I've told them I don't want it. They've already been sticking needles all over me, I'm like a bloody watering can.'

All my father's metaphors and similes – and he has a vocabulary comprising thousands of them – are connected to four or five themes. First is allotments, so that when he is full of holes he is a watering can. Second is jobs he has done, from fairgrounds to window cleaning to tannery labourer. Third is nature, he loves birds and animals. Next is western films, or 'cowboy pictures' as he calls them, and old-fashioned gangster movies. He often pretends to be Edward G. Robinson or James Cagney. He also mixes up metaphors, sometimes hilariously, from things he has heard other people say.

He wants to tell me how good our Andrew has been at getting the various benefits for him. 'The lad knows how to take money off the government better than anybody you could meet, he's like bloody Robin Hood.'

I say, 'Is he looking after you well?'

'Looking after me, looking after me, he's been like a gold mine to me.'

I think he wants to say that Andrew has 'a heart of gold', or perhaps he has been 'golden', but doesn't realise the irony of what he has said. My dad doesn't do irony.

'Do you know, lad, the money's flooding in like water, I've even got my own scooter.'

I look at the mobility scooter at the back of where he is sitting.

'No, not that one lad, that's Ivy's, I've got another one in t'bedroom.'

I smile.

'What's tha grinning at, Cheshire?'

I say, 'You don't seem to have lost your sense of humour.'

'Allus have a laugh lad. There's never owt you can't get a laugh out of.'

I think of all the shitty dead-end jobs my dad has had, never any money. The money he has had he's wasted on everything from goats to caravans at washed-up seaside places that stood empty for fifty weeks of the year, the tropical fish tanks that were too big for the front room, the talking parrots and the whippets that would win races for him and make him his fortune.

'How's that lad of yours? Does he want a metal detector?'

I tell him that Edward has never shown any interest in metal detecting.

'I've got a lovely metal detector at my flat, top o't'range model, he can have it if he wants it.'

Another of my father's hobbies. He spent years looking for treasure.

'Did you ever find what you were looking for?'

'Eh?'

'I said did you ever find anything?'

'Oooh! Aye. Roman coins. I was a bugger for digging up Roman coins.'

He drifts off now, then suddenly turns and says, 'I'm not going to talk about your daughter. I never met her, did I?'

I really can't bear the thought of having a conversation about Billie at this moment at high volume, so I say, 'You're alright for money then?'

'Oooh! Aye, all them times when I haven't had ha'penny to scrat my arse with and now it's coming out of my lugs.'

I tell him that I'll have to be off, but that I'll try to come to see him again.

'Aye well, put the past at the back of you, lad, me and your mother had us problems, but we only ever wanted the best for you.'

I could have asked what he thought 'the best' actually was, but I thought better of it.

'Let's have one more cig afore you go.' In front of my dad on the coffee table are two packets of Samson rolling tobacco, some Rizlas and a Bic lighter. We roll cigarettes. My dad blows smoke rings.

'Do you think I ought to have that chemotherapy?'

'I think that is up to you, do you feel up to it?'

'Well, if our Andrew can hold the fort down for a bit, I might be able to get my foot back on the ladder. I don't think I can make it, but I might try. They say it makes you feel sick. I don't want to feel sick all the time.'

He is a bundle of contradictions. He talks about chemotherapy while smoking his roll-up. He says that if he can get out into the fresh air he might get right and in the next breath tells me that he thinks 'it's got him'.

'I want cremating. I've told our Andrew to scatter my ashes. I don't know whether I want to be scattered near my dad or up on Heath Common. If you go up there to fly your kite with Edward, you can tell him I'm scattered there.'

'Edward is seventeen now, I don't take him to fly a kite these days.'

'Why? Is he like thee and thi grandad, supping ale?'

'No, he's a lovely kid, he's got a lot of mates and he plays football and his piano most of the time.'

'Well keep him off that fucking beer, he doesn't want to end up like thee, tha's as fat as a fucking pork pie.'

I look down at my pot belly.

'Aye, tha's some need to look, it's no good for you, you know, isn't beer.' He relights a half-smoked roll-up.

'And look at your hair and beard, grey as a bloody badger, there's no wonder my dog was barking. What happened to all thi freckles? I've got a photo somewhere taken in the sunshine on Blackpool beach and tha's covered in freckles.'

I can't help but wonder what is going through my dad's mind. He is remembering stories about a little lad with freckles who ate ice cream on Blackpool sands. And here he is confronted by a middle-aged man, his eldest son, with a beer belly, greying hair and a whole adult life behind him that he knows nothing about.

'I'm off to China soon.'

'Eh!'

'I said I'm off to China soon.'

'I heard what tha bloody said, lad. What's tha going there for?' He still calls me 'lad'.

'I've been invited to give some talks at a university.'

My dad shakes his head and fumbles for his rolling tobacco.

'Bloody hell! China! You'd think with all them people they'd have their own teachers. Well, Educated Archie, I always said you'd go a long way, but I never thought it would be China!'

I walk away from the bungalow. I hear the door lock behind me. Someone has left a training shoe in the gutter, just one. I kick it like a boy kicking a tin can in the olden days.

★

We're at the Blackpool Tower Circus. Charlie Cairoli – a clown in a black bowler hat with exaggerated eyebrows, a painted nose and a Chaplinesque 'tache – is making my dad laugh like a madman. Charlie's assistant, Paul, a white-faced clown in a conical hat with a clarinet in his hand, stands impassively watching Cairoli's shenanigans. Our Tony hides his face behind his mucky hands. He doesn't like Paul, says he's scary. It's coming towards the end of the show, a show in which they have played various musical instruments, tried to mend a car which has fallen apart, and somehow caught the arse of their breeches on fire. They have run around in circles patting their arses trying to put the fire out, chucked buckets of water over each other, had a custard pie fight and now they're marching off. Paul fingers the clarinet which rests on his shoulder while Charlie marches behind him, blowing the reed.

My dad laughs like a drain and now the circus rings are filling up with water for a finale. He throws his head back and laughs some more then slaps our mother on the shoulder and asks, 'What's up with you, you miserable bugger?' Our mother takes some lipstick and a compact mirror out of her handbag and purses her lips. She paints her top lip into a cupid's bow and says, without taking her eyes of the little mirror, 'I don't like clowns.'

Dad is disappointed. He loves Charlie Cairoli. To see him at Blackpool Tower is the highlight of the year. Charlie Cairoli is up there amongst my dad's heroes alongside Mario Lanza, Audie Murphy, Les Kellett the wrestler, and any amount of cowboys.

I like Blackpool when I'm there. I hate the bus journey to it. I suffer from chronic travel sickness and the indignity of having to board the bus with a small bucket every time we go on our holidays. They give me barley sugar to suck, they sit me on brown wrapping paper, tell me to look out of the window to see if I can be the first to spot the Tower and tell me that, 'We're nearly at the half-way house.' None of it works, I'm always sick before we reach Hebden Bridge, and every electricity pylon in the distance turns out never to be Blackpool Tower. Our Tony always sees the Tower first, I'm usually closing my eyes and trying to stop my head spinning.

I once asked my dad if we might come to live in Blackpool. He said, 'Don't be so bloody daft, lad, people don't live in Blackpool, they come here on their holidays.'

Years later I read that before the war, Charlie Cairoli had been performing in Berlin and was presented with a wristwatch by Adolf Hitler. In 1939, Cairoli was performing in his first summer season at Blackpool when the war broke out. He walked to the end of the North Pier, took off his watch and threw it into the sea. He spent the rest of his life at Blackpool.

My dad lived his life in a few places. At home, he lived in a chair. He called it 'my chair', if anybody sat in his chair he would stand over them and, depending on if he knew them or not, he'd say 'Shift!', 'Have you been keeping it warm?', 'Would you jump into my grave as quick?', or, if it was me, he'd let out a twittering whistle like a chaffinch and make a signalling motion with his thumb. Now and again, he caused havoc by completely forgetting his manners and offended even the most nervous of visitors, like Mr Morel and the vicar in D.H. Lawrence's *Sons and Lovers*.

It's a midweek morning, my dad is out of work. He's been sacked from the cake factory for stealing Swiss rolls. He is spending his weekdays and most weekends in his allotment. My mother's skin has flared up again and she has vivid red spots all over her face. The doctor is paying a visit. He sits on my dad's chair to make out a prescription. I'm playing on the rug with my Johnny Seven gun. My dad comes in like a gust of wind. He kicks off his roll-top wellingtons and hangs his coat on a peg at the back of the staircase door. He is wearing some filthy jeans held up by a fraying snake belt. His socks, that are halfway off his feet, reek of sweat. He stands at the sliding door that separates our front room from the kitchen and announces, 'That bloody goat is shitting through the eye of a needle again.' He looks at my mother, then at me and then at Dr Prasha. 'Has tha got owt in thee bag for goats that can't stop shitting, Doctor?'

Dr Prasha carries on writing his prescription. He then looks up and says, 'Mr Clayton, your wife is not very well, she needs some tonic medicine and a little care and attention.'

'Aye well, I'll see to her when I've seen to me goat!' and he laughs like a clown at Blackpool Pleasure Beach and tilts his head back. Then, just as suddenly, he stops.

'And who told thee tha could sit there? Lift thi arse up and go and sit on t'sofa!'

My mother says, 'Sid!'

My dad says, 'Sid what?' He lifts his stinking foot onto the chair arm. 'Tha's got five seconds to shift, else I'll tell him to shoot thee with that Tommy gun! I'm counting, five, four, three... I'm not kidding!... two...'

Before he can get to one, Dr Prasha stands up. He tears off his prescription, gives it to my mother and says, 'Good day to you, Mrs Clayton.'

My mother shows him to the front door and stands there until he gets into his car. When she turns round, she is crying. 'You're just a bloody ignorant showing up, you're not fit to be let loose!'

My dad sits in his chair and wafts his feet towards me. 'Smell them!'

I pick up the pieces of my Johnny Seven and carry them into the far corner of the room. My mother says, 'Take no gorm of the simple bugger, he's not got the manners he was born with.'

My father pulls off his socks and hangs them on the companion set to dry. 'Put t'kettle on for me lass, I'm spitting bloody feathers here!'

I can see my dad's chair now when I shut my eyes. It had burn holes in it where he had flicked hot ash from the end of his cigarette, various stains from oil to orange juice and an old curtain thrown over the back to be used when he was 'in his muck'. I can't imagine how many hours he spent in it. Every now and again he set about it with a dustpan and brush and tipped it over to find coins that he had dropped down the side. Once he found a brown ten shilling note and sent me up to Rastricks shop to buy a bag of pigeon corn with it. 'And on thi way back, buy thi mam an ice cream.'

When he didn't live in his chair, my dad lived on his bicycle. In the sixties when everybody else went to work 'on an egg', my dad went on a rusty bike. 'A bike is the finest vehicle a man could wish for,' he'd tell you. 'It's like walking with levers.'

I once saw him coming up Girnhill Lane with a dozen cauliflowers in an old orange crate fastened to the front and six lengths of timber tied to the cross-bar. He had our Tony sat on the handlebars, a small sack of hen meal strapped to the seat and he was peddling by standing up on the pedals. I was standing with my gran at the top of our street. She said, 'Just look at this simple bugger, if anybody saw him, they'd have him certified!'

He pulled up outside our house and said, 'Whooah Boy!' and jumped off like Audie Murphy.

My dad had a black Labrador called Rip, it was a vicious animal and he kept it chained to a post. It once bit a dustbin man when he asked it for a paw. When the dustbin man complained, my dad said, 'My dog doesn't shake hands.' He had another dog, a whippet called Skippy, he said that when it was having a shit it looked like a kangaroo. He taught Skippy to fetch his slippers ·and cigarette carton.

He didn't seem to have many friends beyond the top of our street. Come to think of it, he didn't have many in the street, but he took plenty of money off them. He sold eggs and vegetables to all of our neighbours and his prices fluctuated, depending on how skint he was. When door 'flushing' came into fashion, he flushed everybody's doors and then when people replaced their swing doors between kitchen and front room with sliding glass ones, it was my dad who fitted them. He removed pelmets when they went out of fashion and fanlights when they were no longer in vogue. For months at the turn of the 1970s he became a specialist in fitting polystyrene tiles to the living room ceilings of everybody on our row. He never managed to finish a full ceiling without leaving at least three thumb prints in the tiles, so all of our neighbours had my dad's thumb prints in their ceilings, until the time came when Artex was the thing to have. He rechristened himself 'Artex Sid'.

My dad had no interest in anything apart from riding his bike from one job to another, being a handyman and then sitting in his chair, often with his feet in a bowl of salted water. One of his pearls of wisdom was, 'Look after your feet. My Auntie Lil had beautiful feet even when she was an old woman. She put it down to paddling about in duck shit on the allotments and she rubbed them with comfrey leaves every night before she went to bed.'

He swore by the healing powers of comfrey, the medicinal powers of strong tea, cabbage water and soup made by boiling bones.

He liked John Wayne, Alan Ladd and Randolph Scott, but his absolute favourite was Clint Walker as Cheyenne Bodie. He sometimes called me Cheyenne Bodie.

My dad rarely went to pubs, restaurants or clubs, but liked greasy spoon cafés. He once had a steak canadienne in a café when he was on a daytrip to the seaside. He talked about it for years after. He called it a 'snake canadian'.

My mother suffered serious post-natal stress after she gave birth to Andrew. I was just six at the time, our Tony not quite five. I would hear my father muttering occasionally, 'It's her nerves.' He had no idea of how we might help. He bought a budgie in a second-hand cage, I think he thought it might distract her. It didn't. She cried a lot. I heard my dad say to her one day, 'You want to stop crying like that all the time, you're going to make yourself poorly!'

In the year when the Rolling Stones were singing about 'Mother's little helper', my mother was prescribed Librium. My dad, with his healthy disregard for doctors said, 'They're giving bloody tablets out like Smarties and none of 'em work. She'll end up a nervous wreck.'

It didn't help that my dad had found work on the night shift at a foundry driving an overhead crane. He worked all night, then slept all day. My mother was left with three boys, one who had just started infant school, another running around like a whirling dervish and injuring himself all the time, and one still at the breast.

It is just after eight o'clock in the evening. My dad has gone to do his job at the foundry. Andrew will not go to sleep and my mother is feeding him, sitting on the sofa propped on cushions, he is a big baby and my mother struggles to hold him in her arms when she feeds him. Our Tony and me have been told to 'get to bed'. We have ignored the instruction. Tony has fallen to sleep on the rug in front of the fire. I am trying to teach the budgie to say 'pretty boy'. I talk in a high-pitched way, in what I believe is budgie language. There is a play on the television with Sheila Hancock, she lives in a bedsit in London and dreams of a more glamorous life.

Out of nowhere, my mother says, 'When that clock gets to half-past, I am going to die.' I look at her, she is crying again. She lifts Andrew into a cot and then lays back down on the sofa, staring at the clock. I take a handkerchief out of the drawer in the sideboard and wipe her cheek. I go to the clock on the mantelpiece and turn it to face the wall. I snuggle between my mother's stomach and her pulled up knees, take off her glasses and stroke her hair. I don't know how long it takes for the clock to reach half-past. I listen to the ticks. When I am satisfied that the big hand has passed the half-hour mark, I stand up and look at the clock. I turn it back round again so it faces into the room. At some point in the night my mother carries us all upstairs. We all wake in her bed when my dad comes home and announces, 'I've bought us all a goat! We can all drink goat milk, it'll be good for us.'

My mother had treatment at Stanley Royd psychiatric hospital. The 1960s, that decade when England swung and pleasure-seeking young people drove Minis and scooters to pop festivals, didn't really reach our street. My grandfather still laboured underground, inhaling muck in the tailgate at Sharlston Pit, my dad lived on his allotment and my mam had shots of electric-shock therapy. When some people were shouting for 'Peace' and 'Love' and others were cheering on Alf Ramsey's boys at Wembley, my mam was threatening to put her head in the gas oven.

My dad said that it was about time my mother 'snapped out of it'. The catalyst for her 'snapping out' of whatever it was, came when our Andrew fell ill with rheumatic fever and a 'murmur in his heart'. The phrase 'murmur in the heart' I thought was quite a magical one. I didn't really think he could be ill with something like that, it sounded like something that happens to fairies or mermaids. When the doctor inked a cross on his chest in purple dye, I realised it might be a bit more serious. He spent time in a cottage hospital called Ackton, that had once been an isolation hospital for people with scarlet fever and stuff like that. When he got better and came home, our mother started to get better too. By the dawn of the 1970s we started to be a happier family and when Mungo Jerry sang 'In the Summertime' we all joined in.

The joining in didn't last for long. When my dad announced that we were flitting to Hull, I don't think he had any notion of what we were letting ourselves in for. He seemed to think it was a leap forward. For him it was a chance to escape from in-laws who couldn't bear him. For my mother it meant she was much closer to the man she loved much more than my father, his brother Jimmy. I don't think our Andrew knew much about what was going on, but for our Tony and me it meant the clocks went back. I was nearly thirteen, our Tony eleven, and from that moment we started to relive our lives up to that point over and over. We didn't know whether we were coming or going, here or there. We just kept feeling sad about what we had left behind and feeling frustrated about what we had been brought to. Not long out of junior school, we reflected in the way that older people reflect when they are being awarded a clock for long service.

I'm fourteen, a pupil now at Hull Grammar. I'm on my way home from school, I cross Pearson Park, cut through a snicket onto Grove Street and then pass the Old Bull pub onto Stepney Lane. For some reason this part of Hull is named after London streets; there's a Fenchurch Street, a Fleet Street and, the one I live on, Farringdon Street. There's also a series of little cul-de-sacs which the locals call 'ten-foots', I think because they're ten-foot wide. Farringdon Street is always teeming with kids, even when it rains. Girls chalk hop-scotch on the flags and the lads play football in a gap where three houses were bombed in the war. There's always one or two cars up on bricks with a bloke in a boiler suit underneath and the women sit backwards on their window sills to wash their bedroom windows. At the top of Stepney Lane is a tannery. When the wind is blowing in the wrong direction, the stink of the tannery breezes down our street like a gas attack.

Farringdon Street is full of women who put their hands out to see if it's raining, women who wear curlers under nylon headscarves when they set their hair on Fridays. There are blokes here who have 'Love' and 'Hate' tattooed on their knuckles and swallows that fly out of the flesh between thumb and forefinger. There are frying pans full of solidified lard on the back burner of every cooker, stiletto-heeled shoes with straps that need mending at the bottom of every wardrobe and a Swiss roll that wants eating on top of every corrugated roll-front breadbin.

Farringdon Street has a mouth that whistles and blows kisses, it has one hand that will pick you up and wipe your nose and another that will knock you on your arse.

As I get to our front door, I can hear my mother shouting. 'I might as well put my head in the oven.' I go in. My mother and father both look round, my dad is standing in front of the fire, he grimaces, nods his head toward my mother and then puts his index finger to his temple and twists the finger back and forward. My mother is standing at the kitchen door, she has a potato in one hand and a potato peeler in the other. She throws the potato into the washing-up bowl, marches toward my father and screams, 'For two pins I would ram this knife into your eye.' My father pretends to stay calm, thrusts both hands out to his sides and says, 'Go on, I'm waiting.' My mother turns and shouts, 'Well, you can make your own pigging tea. I'm putting my coat on, I'm off out and I might not come back.' My father shouts after her as she rushes out of the back door, 'Throw yourself under a bloody bus while you're at it.'

I don't bother to take my satchel off from round my shoulder. I go to the kitchen, take a tin of sardines out of the cupboard and then look into the breadbin. There is a crumpled Mother's Pride wrapper that is holding one slice of bread, the bottom crust. I put the crust and the sardines into my satchel and follow my mother out of the back door. My mother is standing in the back ginnel with her head on the wall, she is crying. I climb onto the wall and sit there astride it and look down at my mam. She looks up and says, 'Where are you going?' I tell her that I'm off to the library to do my homework. She says, 'Well, come home afore it gets dark.' I drop down on the other side of the wall into the wasteland that is there. Someone has dumped an old settee. I sit on the settee and take the key from the side of the sardine can. I roll back the lid with the key. I empty the sardines onto the crust, spread them with my fingers and devour bread and sardines in about five mouthfuls. I wipe my hands on the settee, pick up my satchel and walk towards Beverley Road. Denise is coming the other way. Denise is the only mixed-race girl in our neighbourhood. She asks me if I've been crying. I say 'No, but my mam is at the back of that wall.' She says, 'That's what my mam's doing as well, she emptied her purse onto the table and started crying.'

A few weeks before, when we were having our Sunday tea, I asked if I might invite a friend round for tea one day. My dad said, 'Why? Is tha courting?' My mother said, 'Stop tormenting him, Sid,' and then turned to me, 'Is it a girl?' I said 'Yes, she's a good friend and she lives near the swimming baths.' My mother said, 'Alright then, I'll get some more boiled ham and we can save the tinned pears and Carnation. You can fetch her round tomorrow.'

On the Monday Denise came for tea, we sat at the table in the middle of the kitchen. I don't think we had enough chairs, so our Andrew shared a chair with our Tony. We ate the boiled ham on sandwiches that my mother had cut into triangles. My dad said to Denise, 'Do you like boiled ham, Doris?' Denise said she did. My dad said, 'Only, I was going to say if you don't you can pass that sandwich over here, because I could eat a rag man's horse.' We came to the pears and Carnation. My mother tried to share the evaporated milk out between six people and realised she couldn't, so reached for a bottle of milk. 'Andrew, you can have the cream from the top of the milk on yours, it's better for you.'

My dad suddenly broke the awkward stillness of the moment by announcing, 'Our Ian's a funny lad y'know, Doris, he likes reading books and going to libraries. Do you like reading books?' Denise said that she liked reading about The Famous Five, but that most of all she liked gymnastics and athletics. My dad said, 'I bet you're a good javelin thrower aren't you?' Then he laughed and spat bits of tinned pear all over us. I said that Denise is a good long-jumper. My dad said, 'Aye well, she will be.'

We all sat in the front room after our tea. My dad lit a Players No. 6 and blew smoke rings to entertain us, 'Look at that! Smoke signals!' he said and laughed at his own joke again.

We sat through *Coronation Street* in silence. My mam called it 'her programme' and nobody was allowed to talk while it was on. Even if a neighbour called round to gossip between half past seven and eight, they would have to stand in silence between the front door and the settee arm until it finished.

Love Thy Neighbour was on next, my dad's favourite programme. He likes a character called Jacko who has a catchphrase in the pub scenes, he says 'I'll have half,' and everybody laughs. My dad also laughs every time Eddie, one of the main characters, calls his next door neighbour 'Sambo' or 'Nig Nog'. Eddie's neighbour, Bill, comes from Trinidad. Denise's mother comes from Trinidad. When the adverts came on, Denise decided she had to be home. I walked with her to the top of her street. I gave her a kiss to say goodnight. She was crying.

When my dad eventually disappeared from my life it came as no surprise. Our mother had been threatening for years to put her head in the gas oven. She said she was sick of looking at four walls and never being taken anywhere nice. My dad shrugged his shoulders, shook his head and muttered under his breath a lot.

When we moved to Hull, for what my dad described as a 'fresh start', I don't know if he knew that not long after we arrived my mam embarked on an affair with his youngest brother, Jimmy. Sometimes when he got home from work he wanted to know why his tea wasn't ready. There were other times when he asked our mam where she had been in her best coat. But most of the time he just carried on as he had done back in Featherstone. He cracked jokes, fed his tropical fish and watched television with his feet up on a pouffe.

When he decided one day to follow my mam, he set about

his youngest brother with his fists and cracked his head on some iron railings round a church opposite the school I went to.

One day when an act called Captain and Tennille were on *Top of the Pops* singing 'Love Will Keep Us Together', our mother announced she was 'going'. Our dad shrugged again and said, 'Well you better take them with you!' he swished his hand at our Andrew, our Tony and me, 'because I can't do owt with 'em.' I didn't see my dad much after that.

★

Two days after I visited my dad with his cancer and psychedelic braces, I was thinking about something he had said. 'Will you ask our Tony to come and see me?' I said I would. 'I'd like all mi three lads to be with me afore I die. I know he's shy, but I'd like that.'

I phone our Tony. 'My car oil light's been flashing, it's alright for just going to work, but I don't want to get fast on the motorway if we break down! If I can get it fixed, we'll go on Wednesday.'

Our Tony knocked on my door at quarter past eight on the Wednesday. I was trying to fix a broken lavatory seat. He laughed at me. 'Every time I come to this house there's something broken. If it isn't your shed roof that needs some bratish, it's your window leaking, your sliding door off its runners or your chuffing gate won't shut!' I grin and ask him if he wants a pot of tea before we set off. He says, 'No, come on, leave thi shit-house seat, let's get going.'

We head for the M62. 'You got your oil sorted out then?'

'Aye, but we might have to keep stopping to push that window on your side up a bit. It's electric, but something's broken off it inside and it keeps dropping down.'

'Bloody hell, Tony, tha's as broken down as me!'

As the Humber Bridge comes into view I say, 'Are you going to be alright about this?'

'How long's he got?'

'I don't know, our Andrew says about six weeks.'

'It feels strange, eh? You don't see your father for all them years, then he wants to see you before he dies.'

We navigate the maze of bollarded streets and cul-de-sacs to get to the bungalow. The dog is yapping behind the door. We hear our father's voice. 'Get down yer dirty rat!' Andrew pulls back the chain, we walk in.

Our dad walks down the passage. 'I have to lock the dog in the bedroom.'

Our Tony asks him why, 'Isn't he friendly?'

'No, lad, he'll bite you. I've trained him to bite anybody apart from me and our Andrew. He's a Jack Russell, a nasty little bugger, if he gets hold of you he'll set his jaw and he won't let go.'

Our Tony looks at me and grins, raises his eyebrows like Charlie Cairoli and shakes his head slightly.

'We've had a lot of break-ins round here, the swines have been in here three times. First time they came they told Ivy to turn t'tap on in t'kitchen and keep watching it. They ransacked the bloody house. She ought to have known better, I told her that the water board wouldn't send four young lads with hoods up to check the pipes, but she's too soft. Then another time they came in the middle of the night and took the bloody window out. They pinched the chuffing flat-screen telly while we were asleep.'

Our Andrew giggles. 'Best of it was, he's forgotten to tell you what they missed. The budgie's cage was on a stand in front of the window. They moved that out of the way to get to the telly. They didn't know there was £500 in tenners underneath the sandpaper at the bottom of the cage!'

My dad looks at Tony. 'Get your hair cut and I'll meet you when the sun goes down!'

Our Tony laughs. He probably hasn't heard that saying for thirty-odd years.

'Can tha remember when tha crashed that tractor? Didn't you end up in a beck?'

Tony casts back through his mind. When he left school at sixteen, he took a job at a market garden place in Cottingham. One lunch time he was pratting about on a tractor that he hadn't yet learned to drive. 'How have you remembered that? I haven't thought about that for ages.'

'What about when I asked thi to look for sandworms on the beach at Blackpool. Can you remember that?'

I can almost see the cogs whirring behind our Tony's eyes.

We're sitting on a tartan rug near the Central Pier. My dad has fetched a pot of tea from a stall, we all drink from white mugs. Our potted meat sandwiches are full of sand and, for some reason, my dad has his flick comb out and is raking through the Brylcream on his hair. 'Look at that, lass!' he announces to our mother, 'Gene Vincent!' He folds up his flick comb and puts it into his arse pocket. Then he takes it out again and flicks it, folds it, then flicks it again. The people on the tartan rug next to us are taking it in turns to sip their tea from the cup on a thermos flask, they probably think my dad has a knife to go along with his turned-up jeans and winklepickers.

My dad is bored sitting on the sand, my mother is fed up with him fidgeting and shuts her eyes so she can't see him. 'Right!' he announces, 'Who's for an ice cream?' Our Tony and Andrew put their hands up like they're in class. I hesitate, I think I know what's coming next. 'No,' he says, 'We'll have one later, it's a bit cold for ice cream.' My mother sits up and looks for her purse. 'Stop bloody tormenting 'em Sid, you'll set our Andrew off crying again. Here, Ian, take them two and go and fetch some ice creams from that van over there and come straight back! I'll have a strawberry mivvy.'

When we get back our mother and father are listening to a tinny little transistor. The Move are singing about fetching the fire brigade. Our dad is singing along and combing his hair again. We eat our ice creams. My dad says, 'Where's the change?'

I give him three warm coins. My mother's hand swoops as he tries to take it. 'That's my bloody change you crafty swine.' She looks at us. 'He's a miser your dad, a bloody tight miser. The first time he ever took me to the pictures he told me to meet him inside! And when I asked for a tub of ice cream in the interval, he told me not to have one because he said that they kept the ice cream that long in the Regal at Wakefield that it had gone sour.'

Our dad announces that he's going to hire a rod and go fishing. 'You three go down near the pier and dig a few holes for sandworms.' We do as we are told. We are gone just five minutes when our Tony looks into a hole and sees something shining. He plucks out a gold ring. We take the ring back to where our parents are sitting. 'I've found a gold ring, Dad!'

'Here, let me have a look at that!'

Dad examines the ring. 'Well bugger me, I never thought I'd see that again. I dropped this last year when I fell off that donkey!'

We look at each other. Our mother says, 'Don't talk so bloody silly, you'll have 'em all growing up to be liars!'

'No! It's true lass. This ring belonged to my grandfather, it's a family heirloom.'

'Arseholes, Sid!'

Our Tony says, 'It's got some initials on it, Q.V. That's not your initials!'

'Aaah! Well, that's where you're wrong! Queen Victoria gave this ring to my grandfather to thank him for what he'd done in the Boer War.'

We all look at one another again.

Our father slips the ring onto his finger. 'It's a bit tight. I shall have to get this ring adjusted, it doesn't fit me as well as it used to.'

From the tinny transistor, Tony Blackburn announces a big hit for Esther and Abi Ofarim, 'Cinderella Rockefella'. Our dad sings along, 'I love your eyes, they're very nice, I love your chinny chin chin' and he tickles our mother under the chin with his flick comb.

'Don't act so bloody stupid, Sid, you'll have everybody looking at us!'

There might have been two thousand people on Blackpool sands that day. Nearly fifty years on I remember looking round to see if any of them were watching my dad pretending to be Abi Ofarim with a plastic flick comb as his microphone.

Our Tony can remember looking in that sand hole that day. 'I wonder what happened to that ring?' he wonders aloud. Then he says, 'Is it alright if I have a cig?'

'Aye, roll me one while you're at it.'

Our Andrew looks to our Tony, 'He still chain-smokes.'

Our dad reaches for his painkillers. Tony, Andrew and I delve into packets of Dutch tobacco.

'I can get plenty of that off the docks if you want any.' Dad crunches on a paracetamol and washes it down with the dregs in a cold tea mug.

It's a strange feeling, to sit with an old man with slight blond highlights in grey hair. A man who is our father, who we only really knew when we were children. All of the anecdotes are about us when we were at junior school and the beginning of grammar school. I left home at fifteen to live with my gran and grandad. Tony and Andrew went to live at my mother's, though Tony wasn't there long before he came to live with Aunt Alice. Andrew shuffled back and forwards between Mam and Dad before he started getting into bother, mixing with a crowd that were no good for him.

Dad always did have a 'couldn't care less' attitude to life, 'I don't give a bugger' was his maxim. He never showed much affection for our mother and thought that 'acting daft' and trying to get a laugh out of anything was the way to go. I never saw him get down about much, he had no interest in politics, society, learning, didn't have many mates, was never one for the pub or going out for meals. I recall an ersatz German beer hall opening in Hull in the early 70s. It was called the Hofbrauhaus and my mother persuaded him to go there once. Not used to drinking, he supped three litres of strong Bavarian lager, jumped on a table, fell off, threw up in somebody's garden on the way home and never went there again.

He enjoyed talking to canaries and observing tropical fish. He liked to listen to old 78 records of the Ink Spots. Whenever he was out walking, he would pick stuff up that he thought he might repair. In a box at home he had bracelets missing clasps, mechanical toys without winding keys, buttons from coats long since thrown away and nails and screws that would, as he put it, 'Come in useful for something one day.'

Out of nowhere, while pulling on a bent roll-up, he announces, 'I know where that lad of yours gets his piano from, Ian.'

I ask him, 'How do you mean?'

'It's in our family's blood. My grandad who lived to be 99 was a beautiful piano player.'

I have never heard him say this before. 'Did he play in public?'

'Oh! Aye. He used to be the pianist at the pictures before they had talking films. He could play owt.'

He then imitates a man playing the piano by moving his fingers quickly up and down the coffee table in front of him. In my mind's eye I see the Keystone Cops chasing Fatty Arbuckle.

'Trouble was, when films started having sound, they didn't need pianists anymore, so he opened a fish and chip shop. Then before the war when nobody had any money for fish and chips he got a job lighting the lamps in the street on a night.'

I ponder on the thought that I have got to the age of 53 before I knew that my father's grandad was a piano-playing, fish-frying, lamp lighter.

'He lived to be 99, but he was lonely. He wouldn't change his clothes, so he started to smell. Folk started keeping away from him, so he sat in a corner at Yates Wine Lodge in Wakefield drinking that strong Australian wine. When he'd had enough he went home and slept in his clothes. In the end they put him in a home and it killed him, he didn't want people washing him and he didn't want to change.'

'What was his name?'

'I can't remember, but he'd some lovely wavy hair.'

I have some family-tree records at home. When I get back I look through them. I phone my dad and tell him that I think his grandfather was called William, that he was born in Staffordshire in 1871 and had three sons and three daughters.

He says, 'Aye, that might be true.'

Now he leans forward and stubs out his tab end in an overflowing ashtray.

'And I bet you didn't know that my mother and her sister were Tiller Girls did you? Kicking their bloody legs up.'

I didn't know that.

'They danced in the music halls all over. Wakefield, Bradford, all over. My mother's sister had an affair with Maurice Chevalier, but when he went to Hollywood he left her behind.'

'Maurice Chevalier was a French actor and singer.'

'Aye, that's right. Thank heaven for little girls...' He sings until he starts coughing. 'And he used to go out with my auntie.'

I don't believe him, but there is a twinkle in his blue eyes.

'Anyroad, I'm pleased you've all come. It's been nice to have all my lads together. Now, before you go, I want you to take me round to my flat, 'cos I've some things you might want.'

Dad spends part of his week at Ivy's bungalow and the rest of his time at his own flat. We drive the three or four streets round to his council flat on the edge of the city centre. 'It's a nice running motor this Tony, do you mend it yourself?'

We park opposite his flat, a three-storey tenement type, the sort built in many cities after wartime bombings and post-war slum clearances. As we cross the road, my dad spots a man he knows tottering from the pub. 'My lads these!' The man smiles and then carries on.

The flat is tidy, but filled with tat and ornaments. A sideboard displays a Toby Jug collection, there's a jeweller's display case filled with thimbles. 'I like collecting thimbles, they look well on show like that.' There are plates featuring world war aircraft on every wall and, in the middle, a table which when opened contains every board game from backgammon to chess to dominoes, as well as five different types of dice. 'I think it's Victorian, I'd like you to have that if you want it.' I want to tell him that it's probably a 1960s reproduction, but I can't. So I make a feeble excuse about not having enough room in our house.

He wants to show us his metal detector. It's in a bag at the back of the settee. The zip is jammed on the bag, but he insists on unjamming it to let us see. After ten minutes of fiddling, I say, 'It doesn't matter.' He says, 'No, no, give us a hand Andrew, you'll like this.' Eventually the zip moves. 'What about that then! She's a beauty isn't she? You'll find some treasures with that! Will it fit in your boot Tony?'

Tony shrugs, I say, 'It's not really something I'm interested in.'

'What are you interested in then? You like art don't you? Andrew plug that waterfall scene in, show him that, he'll want that.'

On the wall near a china cabinet is a glass frame about three feet in length, by two deep. I can see a cable coming out of the side of it that is plugged into a socket on the same wall. Our Andrew flicks the switch next to the plug. The scene lights up, it has a three-dimensional effect. A waterfall pours over some boulders from out of what looks like a rainforest. The sound of the water washes over us and then noises from the rainforest kick in; birds, the breeze in the trees and animal noises that I can't identify. It sounds like the soundtrack to an advert for a shower gel yet to be invented. 'What about that then? Beautiful in't it? I put it on every night before I go to bed. It's very good for your nerves. Do you want it?'

Our Tony interrupts. 'His walls are full of paintings already.' I can sense that Tony realises I am uncomfortable about constantly declining my dad's offers.

My dad says, 'What the bloody hell's up with you? I'm trying to give you all my best stuff and you're turning me down. Follow me then, there's something in that bedroom that you'll want.'

He shows us an old cabinet wind-up gramophone. 'Wind it up gently. As soon as you feel it going tight, stop, else you'll snap the bloody spring.' He blows the dust from a Deanna Durbin record of 'Ave Maria'. It sounds terrible. I don't know whether it's the worn-out record or a sprained spring. 'Don't tell me you don't want that either, what the bloody hell's up with you, lad? I thought you were supposed to be educated!'

He looks at Andrew. 'Don't you let them house-clearance men have that for nowt when I've gone. It's a chuffing antique that, make sure you get the right price.'

We come down the steps from the flat, my dad tries to dance on the landing, uses his walking stick as a cane and then nearly falls over. He knocks into a planter filled with flowers outside of his neighbour's front door. I remark on how nice the display of flowers look. My dad turns to me and in a loudish whisper says, 'Aye, but him who lives there is a bloody pouffe, he answers the door before he's dressed on a morning.'

'Just because he likes flowers, doesn't mean to say he's a pouffe!'

'No it doesn't, but he is, a fat pouffe an'all.'

We reach the middle landing. A lady in a head scarf with a child of about three is unlocking her door.

'Good morning, love, are you right?'

The lady says good morning and speaks to her child in a middle eastern voice.

'These are my sons, love. This one's going to China.' She smiles.

When we reach the bottom of the stairs, my dad checks for

mail and raises his eyes to the floor above. 'Nice young woman her... Iraqish, but they're a good family.'

'Iraqish!' I say.

'Aye, Iraqish, but there's nowt wrong with 'em. They're better than them bloody drug dealers that lived there before.'

We drop our father off with Andrew at the bungalow. He puts his arms round our Tony and kisses him on his forehead. He tries to do the same with me, but manages to poke me in the eye with his thumb and get my zip tangled in his cardigan. He ruffles my hair. 'You know what to do if they bite don't you? Squeeze 'em tight, then they won't come another night!' He laughs while he remembers his rhyme about bed bugs from a long time ago.

We drive off through the maze of streets. At the window of one house is a curtain made out of a quilt cover. It is blue with space rockets and moons on it. Next door someone has thrown a pair of underpants onto an outhouse roof. We stop to ask a woman directions. 'Can we get back onto the Beverley Road this way?' She looks at us as though we might be trying to steal her shopping bag and then carries on walking without replying. We stop further down to ask a young man with headphones on. He lifts one headphone and says, 'I don't know, I don't live here.'

When we get to the Beverley Road I ask our Tony if he has time to visit our old street. He nods. We drive to Farringdon Street and park outside our old house. It's for sale. We don't stay long. As we drive back up the street, Tony points to a house on the corner, 'The Savilles lived there, can you remember them, three daughters and a son.'

I can remember them. 'The lad was called Edward, he broke his arm when he fell off the wall at the back of our house.'

Tony nods, then points to a gable end across the street, 'Just look at that.'

Someone has painted an emulsion warning: 'Do not throw shitty nappies into my wheelybin'.

Our Tony is a bit quiet on the road home.

'What do you think, Tone?'

'I don't know. He doesn't seem much different to the last time I saw him and that must be twenty years ago.'

We move from the A63 to the M62, not quite knowing what to say to each other.

To break the silence I point across the fields at the tower of Howden Church. 'It's a big church that, eh!'

Tony ponders the word Howden. 'Can you remember when we all nearly got killed by that train at Howden station?'

After we first moved to Hull in 1972, we came home to the West Riding to visit our relatives by train; this involved a journey from Paragon to Goole and then the local train from Goole to Pontefract Monkhill. The tiny village stations along that second line are imprinted on my memory like a brand. Rawcliffe with its Victoria post box on the platform, Hensall, Whitley Bridge, Knottingley and Monkhill. I guess that when Beeching was axing his lines, the folder for this one must have dropped down the back of the filing cabinet. How this line stayed open and does so to this day is one of the great railway mysteries of the world. In 1973, a big barge on the Humber crashed into a railway bridge to the east of Goole and damaged it so badly that it was out of service for months. On our trip to our gran's that year we had to change trains at the unfamiliar Howden station. We crossed the line in front of what we thought was our train coming. But it wasn't, it was a fast express that wasn't stopping and only at the last minute did we realise.

Tony says, 'Auntie Alice was the last to get across, can you remember what she said?'

'By, that's a strong breeze, it nearly took my coat off.' We say this simultaneously and then laugh at the memory.

We were lucky. And the whitened face of the porter who showed us to the warmth of a little waiting room with a pot-bellied stove told us how lucky we were. The porter shook his head, removed his cap and said, 'You have a guardian angel on your shoulder, but you're still stupid!'

The cooling towers and big chimney at Drax Power Station come into view through the windscreen when our Tony starts to tell me how he came to leave home.

'After my mam and dad parted I went to live with her and Jimmy.'

My mother set up home with Jimmy after she and our father decided to separate.

'When I left school I got that job at the market garden place in Cottingham, I think they paid me about a tenner a week, I was sixteen. By then Heidi had just been born.'

My mother gave birth to the girl she had always wanted; Jimmy and my mam called their daughter Heidi, it had been one of my mother's favourite storybooks when she was young.

'Jimmy and my mam made it clear that as soon as I left school and was earning I'd have to start fending for myself. They didn't really want me there. Our Andrew had started senior school, but they weren't bothering much with him either, they were doting on Heidi.'

At this time I had been back at my gran's for a couple of years and had started at an engineering works in Pontefract.

'One morning when I was getting ready for the market garden place I could see Mam was in a foul mood. In the end she turned round to me and said, "Don't bother coming home tonight, I want you out," just like that.'

Tony then told me how he traipsed up and down Newland Avenue and Princess Avenue, the student district of Hull, looking in post office windows for rooms to let.

'I phoned a number and a woman answered. I asked her if she still had a room to let. She said she had and I could look at it straightaway. It was somewhere round the back of Pearson Park, a big house converted into bedsits. There was a shared kitchen and a shared bathroom for six. She showed me the room, there was nothing in it apart from a spring mattress and a bed frame leaning up against the wall. She gave me a bed spanner and said, "You know how to put it up don't you?" I started to fix up the bed. She said, "How much money have you got?" I told her that I had nineteen pounds, but that was all I had to my name. She looked at me, laughed and said, "Nineteen pounds eh! Well that's exactly what this room costs." She took every last penny off me and went out laughing.'

'What did you do for clothes and food?'

'I went back to my mam's for some stuff, she just stood and watched me, she didn't even say a word.'

Tony spent six weeks in that bare flat in the middle of one of the coldest winters we'd had for years.

'I can't remember now what I used for bedding. The landlady might have given me a blanket. I had a good mate and his mam worked afternoon shifts at one of the factories. He let me go round to his house for chip sandwiches and fish fingers, but just before his mam got home I came to the bedsit and it was bloody freezing. I got sacked from the market garden for crashing the tractor and it took ages to get some social security sorted out. For some reason I had saved all of my wage slips and brown paper wage packets. I put them one at a time onto the fire grate and lit them and held my hands over the flame. There was a bloke next door, he only had one LP, Simon and Garfunkel's *Greatest Hits*, he played it over and over again. I know every word on that album still to this day.'

We turn off the motorway and head towards Pontefract and home. I look across at my brother. He's concentrating on the road as we come past the race course, but I can see painful memories in his eyes.

'Auntie Alice was my angel. She came over to Hull on the bus and brought me back with her. She was in her sixties then, but she didn't half look after me. I got a job at the pop factory and there was a warm fire, a good dinner and a comfy bed to come home to every night.'

We get back to our house. I put the kettle on. Tony says, 'What did you do with that shit-house seat. Let's see if I can mend it for you.' We mend it together, sip our tea. We talk about children. Tony's daughter Kelly will make him a grandfather soon, she is expecting twins. We talk about that and inevitably about us losing Billie. Tony forces himself to join in, though I can see the pain when he mentions her name. He still says 'Our Billie' and it makes him want to cry. After that, we remember when we were children.

The Day Gordon Banks Saved Pelé's Header

Up on the Coal Board estate past Mafeking Street there was a big old tree. It stood on the edge of a field high above the haw and black thorn bushes that formed the boundary between the fields and Girnhill Lane. We called it The Big Tree and it was our meeting place, as it had been for the generation before us who ended up as mods and rockers sipping coffee in The Hideaway Café, and the generation before them who worked days at the pit and put their best clothes on for a dance and a fight at The Welfare Hall. The tree had been struck by lightning at least twice, and it's limbs and trunk were tattooed like the arms of a gnarled old fairground boxer. These tattoos were carved with penknives; love hearts with names inside them and an arrow passing through, RIP Jimmy, and Kilroy had been there of course. Someone had painted the words 'Don't leave me Jennifer' in mid-Brunswick green gloss on the trunk. The Big Tree sheltered us, taught us how to climb and how to burn our hands on a rope swing. It was just The Big Tree and it was always there.

In the summer of 1970, beneath its branches, we collected the names of the players who were to represent their countries in the World Cup. We had a particular fascination for the Eastern European teams. Paul Hickman became Hristo Bonev of Lokomotiv Plovdiv, the Bulgarian striker. Pete Cross was Ladislav Petras of Czechoslovakia. Brighty was Florea Dumitrache of Dinamo Bucharest and Romania, though we hoped he wouldn't score because they were in England's group. Neil Allington, our bravest goalkeeper, was the Russian hero, Lev Yashin. One day Mark Greenhalgh turned up at the tree wearing a white vest with a red sash arranged diagonally across his chest and announced he was Héctor Chumpitaz of Peru. Mark always had a taste for the exotic and became more and more excited as Peru unexpectedly progressed to the quarter-final and fought valiantly in a 4-2 defeat to the Brazil of Jairzinho and Pelé and Rivelino.

In the George Street schoolyard, Lev Yashin, in the portly shape of Neil Allington, prepares to face a penalty. Someone puts four fingers in their mouth to blow a whistle. Gerd Müller, in the shape of John Parker, hits the ball hard and low. Neil Allington dives full length on the concrete and punches the ball away. There is a spontaneous round of applause, even the girls join in. Neil stands up, both knees grazed and bleeding, shakes himself like a dog that's climbed out of a park lake and pumps a fist. 'Lev Yashin!' he shouts and glares at the penalty taker.

On the day England are to play Brazil, my dad announces that we are all going for a walk. It is a Sunday and after our dinner we start to get ready. Our mam tells us to put our best clothes on and the Hush Puppies shoes our gran bought us for Whitsuntide.

Dad says he's going to take us to Heath Common and show us where he played when he was a lad. Our mother says, 'I don't know why we can't go on the bus, you know our Andrew has had rheumatic fever, it's a bloody long way and it might be too much for him.'

'It's a lovely day, a walk in the fresh air will do us all good,' says Dad 'I've asked Fred Hickman if he wants to come as well. I'll show you all a goldfinch's nest.'

Mam can't decide whether she wants to wear her sandals or her boots. She has a pair of white vinyl boots that zip up the sides and come up to just below her knee. She wears them with a mini-skirt on the rare occasions that my dad takes her to the club on a Saturday night.

'Put your sandals on Pauline, your feet will sweat in them boots,' is my dad's advice.

'When I want your opinion on how I ought to dress, I'll ask for it, but it won't be before they put me in a box!' Mam puts the boots to one side, 'I'll never get to bloody wear them anywhere nice!' She picks up her sandals, spits on the leather and rubs them with a yellow duster. 'I've been wearing these since we went to that boarding house at Blackpool and the bloody World Cup was in London then.'

We walk together down Mafeking Street and knock on Fred Hickman's front door. Fred answers. 'Our lass isn't ready yet, she's always the bloody last. I've told her, if she doesn't come out of that kitchen mirror before I count to three, she's stopping at home.' Then he looks over his shoulder, 'And I'm bloody counting, three, two...' Madge comes to the door pulling her cardigan on. Her son, my mate Paul, and his sister Diane are alongside her. She looks at us in our clothes and then at Paul, 'I told you to wash your bloody face and neck, come here you mucky little sod.' She spits on her hanky and rubs it round Paul's face.

'Gi o'er, Mam.'

Dad says, 'Are we going or what? It'll be bloody dark before we get where we want to be.'

We all set off. Fred and our dad at the front. They both wear Wellingtons rolled over at the top, like they're going up the allotments. My mam and Madge are behind us kids, I hear them telling each other that they have got nothing to wear and about how badly they have felt all week. We reach Wakefield Road and pass the Mill Cottages and then the Lin-Pac packaging factory. My dad reminds everybody that he's recently got his 'compo' from the factory owners after he was crushed when a roll of paper fell on him. We pass Snydale pit where our neighbour John Tom Hope works and carry on through Streeethouse, over the level crossing that bisects the village. A coal train comes through just after we cross, so us kids run back and lean on the gates to watch it. At Sharlston I point to the pit headgear and say, 'My grandad goes down there, I've been with him to collect his wage sometimes on a Friday.' Dad points across the road at the Kibble, the Sharlston Welfare working men's club and says, 'Aye and that's where he spends the bugger.' Then he laughs like a madman and Fred laughs like a madman as well. Neither of them like my grandad, and he doesn't like them. He says they're both soft.

We come to some stone cottages near the edge of Heath Common. Dad says, 'Go and knock on that woman's door and ask her for a drink of water and bring some for us.'

'Dad!'

'How's tha mean *Dad*!'

'I don't know her.'

'It doesn't matter. I do. Now go and ask.'

I knock on the door of one of the cottages. A lady lifts the curtain at the front window and then comes to the door.

'Can I have a beaker of water please?'

The lady brings a pint pot full of water. I sip some and then offer it to my mam. My dad's hand swoops down and he takes is straight out of my hand. He drinks nearly half of it in one go and then passes it to Fred. He takes a big gulp, gargles and spits on the pavement. The pot is passed to my mam who wipes the rim with the back of her hand. 'You greedy swines, there's hardly any left.' She wets her lips and passes it to Madge.

Fred says, 'Don't drink it too fast, you'll get colic!'

I take the pot back to the lady.

'What do you say?'

'Oh! Sorry, thank you.'

'Good job.'

On Heath Common we sit on the grass and watch some people flying kites. Dad says, 'When I was a lad I had the best kite in bloody Wakefield. A big red and yellow one it was, I made it myself. It had a tail on it as long as a rattlesnake. They used to come from all over to see me flying it. I bet they could see it

from as far away as Halifax when it went up into that breeze.'
Dad lays on his back. He picks up a blade of grass and puts it into
his mouth. 'There's summat about Heath Common that makes
me feel like I've come home.'

Madge takes off her cardigan and lays on her side, propping
herself on her elbow. She says, 'Oooh, in't it warm.'

Fred shouts at her, 'Get that bloody cardigan back on, we
don't want to see your flabby arms.'

Madge looks embarrassed and hurt. I didn't realise that other
men talked to their wife like that, I thought it was just my dad.
Dad cuts through the tension by singing the song by Mungo
Jerry that's climbing up the charts. 'In the summertime when
the weather's fine, you can stretch right up and touch the sky.'

My dad is lost in reverie now, his thoughts scattered across
the rough grasslands of Heath Common.

'Look at them piebald horses chomping over there. They
belong to t'gypsies, they've been bringing their horses here for
hundreds o' years. When we used to come with the fairground
we used to race the horses to the top o' that hill.'

We follow his finger to the top of the hill. 'We were like
bloody John Wayne and Gary Cooper.' He stands up and urges
an imaginary pony onward, slapping his backside with the palm
of his hand, 'Go on Ned, Gerrup theer! Now whoah! Whoah
boy!'

He's revelling in his fairground days. 'We made some bloody
money at Easter time and it used to be snowing sometimes, but
they still come. We had their money off 'em afore it had chance
to get warm in their hands.' He then goes into a long stream of
consciousness of things he's seen on fairgrounds; tattooed and
bearded ladies, chickens with four legs, lambs with two heads
pickled in jars, strongmen who could lift blacksmiths' anvils
with their ears.

'Did I ever tell you about the time when I met Prince
Monolulu?'

Our mother tuts and says, 'Here we bloody go again! Prince Monolulu was walking down Lock Lane.'

'He was walking down Lock Lane in Castleford. He used to lodge at a boarding house down there when he was at Pontefract races. And he said to me, "I'll give you a tip, Sid. God made the bee, the bee made the honey, the labourer do the dirty work and the bookie takes all the money." And that's why I don't back horses, not like your grandad who'd bet on two flies going up a wall! Watch your pockets! Always watch your pockets.'

We decide to take the bus home. The bus driver and his conductor are listening to a little wireless. England are playing well but Brazil are winning 1–0.

A lot of people will remember 7 June 1970 as the day when Gordon Banks made the save of the century from Pelé's downward header, the day when Pelé and Bobby Moore exchanged shirts and embraced each other. I will always remember it as the day our dad took us to Heath Common to show us somewhere that made him happy.

England were eventually knocked out of the Cup by West Germany. Everybody under The Big Tree blamed Peter Bonetti, the second choice goalkeeper. Paul Hickman said Gordon Banks had been poisoned by the Germans in revenge for Wembley in '66.

During the miners' strike in 1972, somebody cut The Big Tree down for firewood. Everybody on the coalboard estate barrowed home logs from it. After that we couldn't all meet there anymore. Our days of juvenile gang meetings had come to a close anyhow. Some of the lads had passed for the grammar school, some went to South Featherstone School and prepared for a life at the pit and others, like me, had gone to Pontefract Boys, their mams and dads hoping that they might learn enough to get them an apprenticeship.

Now You're An Apple Tree

My left foot is heavily bandaged and it's resting on a little stool. A few days ago I had been splashing about in some dirty water at a paddling pool in the Valley Gardens at Pontefract. Someone had thrown a broken bottle into the pool and I had managed to stand on it. When I brought my foot out of the water, I had the base of a milk bottle attached to my heel.

I can date this memory to the late summer of 1964. I started my first day at Girnhill Lane Infants School with the bandage still wrapped round my foot, fastened with a safety pin from my grandmother's sewing box. I can't get my shoe on, so my father has fashioned a kind of slipper from an old moped tyre and laced it over the bandage.

We're lucky to have Girnhill Lane School at the bottom of our street. It's one of the new stream of West Riding Schools set up by Sir Alec Clegg since he became head of the Education Board just after the war. Clegg's mission is simple, he believes even the scruffiest child from the most impoverished neighbourhood can be creative if only given the opportunity.

The school is just three years old. The headmistress is Miss Mackie, she wears floral patterned dresses and horn rimmed glasses. I like her straightaway. She is one of Sir Alec Clegg's front-line troops bringing education to the sort of kids who wipe snot on their sleeves. Kids like me who sell eggs from their father's allotments, sit on lavatories at the bottom of the yard while reading comics by the light of a tilly lamp. Kids who share freezing back bedrooms with their siblings, kids who eat crusts of bread and dripping on their way to school.

I can't remember too much about that first day. I remember

Miss Carlyle turning up on a Lambretta scooter, and I recall my teacher, Miss Mogg, trying to coax me out from under her desk. When my gran came at lunchtime to take me home for my dinner she said, 'When he goes under the table at our house, I push him out with a sweeping brush.' On the second day, I went under Miss Mogg's desk again. She gave me some wooden blocks to play with. By the end of the morning I had used every wooden block in the school and built a town from them. I surrounded this town with books opened enough so that they would stand on their fore edge, their covers like the sloping roofs of terraced houses, their spines like ridge tiles. Miss Mogg sent for Miss Mackie and two other teachers. They stood over me, Miss Mogg said, 'Tell them what you have done.' I thought I was in trouble, so I started to knock my wooden blocks over. 'No, no, Ian, build it again and tell us the story about it.' I looked at them, Miss Mackie said, 'What have you made, young man?' I pointed at the books, 'Well these are our houses and these towers are where we are going to live after they knock 'em all down.' Miss Mackie sent for the school secretary to come with a camera. They took a photograph. 'Who told you this story?'

'Mi dad says that the government have run out of land and seeing as they're not making land anymore, we shall have to live up in the sky and we'll all have a machine apiece to fly about in. And he says that them who work down the pit might have to start living underground.'

For weeks after I was allowed to design things with the wooden blocks and tell a story about it.

Nearly fifty years later, I bump into Miss Mackie near Marks and Spencer's. I say, 'Good morning, Mrs Mackie.' She corrects me, 'No, Ian, it's still Miss.' She has a huge shopping bag full of vegetables and strawberries and raspberries. I offer to carry it for her and say, 'You eat well.' She agrees and adds, 'But I still get lots of visitors, so it's not all for me.' She then tells me that she has been following my writing career with interest. 'I'm pleased to know that you were listening all those years ago.' We stand talking while we shelter from the rain in Tesco's doorway. 'I have a book for you, it's the book Alec Clegg wrote after visiting us. I will pass it on to Nora Carlyle and she can give you it. We'll call it a long term loan, but you must look after it.'

Two years before I started at Girnhill Lane in the early 1960s, Clegg himself had visited while researching his book *The Excitement of Writing*. In the book, Clegg talks about how much the children at this school enjoy telling and writing stories and how they are encouraged by the teachers to write about their own experiences. Clegg gives examples of some of the writing. There is a piece called 'Our Jane' written by a boy aged six. I love this story.

'Our Jane is two
She plays with a boy and
She has white hair and
She has blue eyes and
She has a runny nose and
She can't talk and
She eats biscuits and
She's fat and
She pinched my biscuits and
She's got a bike like an old cronk and
She plays with my train and
She's a monkey when t'telly's on.
She plays about.
She plays up and down.
They let her.'

The next time I see Miss Mackie she mentions the piece called 'Our Jane'. She asks me to tell her what I think the most important line in that piece is, but before I can think, she says,

'No, I'll tell you. It is the last line, "They let her".' And I nod in agreement.

At school we have a reading card, every now and again the teacher brings out the card and points to words in succession. The card starts, 'Tree, Little, Egg, Milk, Book' and moves onto a last line that includes the words 'Idiosyncrasy' and 'Bibliography'. I pride myself on being the first boy to reach the end of the reading card. On this day I can't wait to tell someone about it. When I get home my dad is mending a puncture on his bike. He has the washing-up bowl full of water and he is dipping his inner tube into it. My mother is laid on the sofa because, according to my dad, she has had 'one of her funny turns'. I start to tell him about the reading card test. He says, 'Aye, well, afore tha does owt else, take a cup of tea in to your mother and ask her if she's coming to make us something to eat.' My mother is looking into her sideboard mirror and brushing her hair. I give her the beaker of tea and say, 'Mam, we've been doing the reading card at school.' She sips her tea, 'Bloody hell, it's clap cold, don't you know how to boil a kettle at your age.'

'My dad says are you going to make some dinner.'

'Tell him he can arseholes.' Then she changes her mind and asks me to fetch her purse from the kitchen drawer. 'Nip to the shop and fetch a packet of Burdall's gravy salt and a few potatoes.'

We sit in silence eating boiled minced meat and gravy with mashed potato and a cabbage from the allotment. My father is sitting no more than two yards from my mother. He says to me, 'Ask your mother to pass me some salt will you, lad.' I say to my mother, 'My dad says will you pass him the salt pot.' My mother says, 'Will you ask your mother to pass the salt pot *please*.' I turn back to my dad, 'My mam says you should say will you pass the salt pot please.' My dad says, 'I heard what she bloody said, now pass that bloody salt pot and don't be so cheeky else you'll feel the back of my hand.'

My dad finishes his dinner by wiping a slice of bread around his plate, he belches loudly and wipes his mouth on the dish cloth. 'I could eat a bowl of Angel Delight, ask your mother if there's any in the cabinet.' Before I can say anything, my mother says, 'Will you ask your father if he can uncross his legs at the table, ask him if he can take that tyre inner tube off the back of that chair, ask him to take his spanners off the draining board, tell him he can shove his Angels Delight up his arse and when he's done tell him he can drop dead for all I care.'

My dad goes off to feed his rabbits, he keeps half a dozen in pens in the back yard for breeding and for the pot. My mother starts to plump up the cushions on the settee and hangs up the coat she has been sleeping under in the afternoon. She throws a shovel of coal onto the fire and tells me to go to the coal house and fill the bucket. Our Tony and Andrew, who have said nothing in the last hour, go to play on the floor with a toy fort. I take my bucket to the coal house. As I go past my dad, he mutters under his breath, 'She's nicked!'

In the snicket between our back yard and Girnhill Lane I can see a girl I know called Pauline. She is holding a kitten. The kitten has had diarrhoea and the shit is all down the front of Pauline's gabardine coat. She says, 'This kitten is poorly, I want to take it to the RSPCA, but I don't know where the RSPCA is, do you know where the RSPCA is?' I tell her that I don't, but my dad might know what to do. My dad is still tinkering about with his rabbit pens.

Pauline asks him what we ought to do with the kitten. My dad says, 'I'll tell you what to do with that bloody thing. Take it up the gardens, find a rain barrel and chuck the bugger in.'

Pauline starts to cry, 'It's my kitten, not yours.'

'And when you've done that, take that bloody coat off and chuck it on the fire, you bloody stink.'

Pauline stops sobbing enough to say to my dad, 'When I find out where the RSPCA is I'm going to report you!'

I walk to the top of our street with Pauline. I tell her that I have managed to finish the reading card at school. She smiles and says, 'You can stroke this kitten if you want.' She then walks off down the hill. When she turns round, I wave.

In 2011 Girnhill Lane School celebrated it's fiftieth birthday, I was invited to come and tell stories to an assembly of the whole school.

I walk the route I once walked while holding the side of our Andrew's pram. The school layout is exactly the same; an entrance lobby from which radiates three corridors of classrooms. There is a caretaker's bungalow, in our day it was the house of Mr Hutchinson who wore a navy blue overall and had a built-up shoe. We called him 'Hutchy Wa-Wa'. The assembly hall doubles as a gym and dining room and the children here still get homemade food. One of the dinner ladies tells me that I should sample her coconut sponge. Miss Carlyle is there alongside mams, aunties and grandparents. I estimate that she will have taught 99% of the people in the hall. I sit on a tiny wooden chair in front of children cross-legged, whose voices rise and fall like a wave. They look like the children who went to this school with me. In many cases they are the grandchildren of children who went to school with me. My dad was wrong. They didn't knock our houses down and send us to live in the sky. They knocked some of our houses down and moved us into houses they built on the fields we once played in. Perhaps somewhere in a filing cabinet in this school is a fading black and white photograph of wooden towers in a city that never got built.

Before she died, Sir Alec Clegg's widow, Lady Jessie Clegg, acted as a warden in a little church near Tadcaster, a tiny place of worship in the middle of a field. I met her there once when I was making a television programme about it. Lead Church is teeming with history, it is where many of the wounded and dying from the Battle of Towton sought sanctuary after the army of the future Edward IV and his Yorkists faced that of the Lancastrian Duke of Somerset on some ploughed fields on Palm Sunday 1461. They say it was the bloodiest battle ever fought on British soil and that the nearby Cock Beck ran red with blood for days after.

Today, a lady comes to arrange flowers on a table next to the visitors' book. At this time I don't know that she is Lady Clegg, the woman who was married to one of this country's most visionary educationalists. I see a sweet old lady faffing over some carnations and roses. She tells me that this church is known as 'The Ramblers Church' and the walkers come here from all over. She says, 'You are welcome here any time, the door is always open.' This is a timeless place, apart from a pub called The Crooked Billet over the fields that advertises the 'World's largest Yorkshire puddings' and the occasional car, there's not much to tell you that you are in the 21st century. The Cock Beck still flows by on its way to join the River Wharfe near Tadcaster, the church in Saxton where Lord Dacre was buried in 'the Long Acre' is just over the hill. It's easy to imagine the Yorkist arrows flying on the breeze to pierce Lancastrian armour.

A school teacher friend of mine called Mel Dyke knows Lady Clegg and has told her that I have been giving talks about what Sir Alec's vision for education has done for me. Mel takes me to her house in Saxton. Lady Clegg, in her nineties now, is like a little bird; quick, bright and full of inquisitiveness. I recognise her as the lady who arranges flowers at St Mary's Chapel, Lead, and tell her she was once there when I visited. 'Oh! I meet so many people at that chapel, you wouldn't believe it in such an isolated place, but it gets quite busy at times.'

Lady Clegg has arranged for us to have lunch at a posh golf club nearby. She recommends the guinea fowl with an asparagus bundle and mashed swede. I take her recommendation and between mouthfuls washed down with an Alsace Pinot Gris she talks about the need to get children, particularly boys from what she calls the working-class estates, reading from an earlier age.

Just before he retired in 1972, Sir Alec Clegg made a speech at Bingley College. He mentioned that when Michelangelo was going to Rome to see the Pope, prior to his being employed to build the great dome of St. Peter's and to paint the Sistine Chapel, he took a reference with him which said:

'The bearer of these presents is Michelangelo the sculptor, his nature is that he requires to be drawn out by kindness and encouragement, but if love be shown to him and he be treated well, he will accomplish things that would make the whole world wonder.'

He also mentioned a poem in a frame on a wall at his aunt's house. The poem read:

If thou of fortune be bereft
And of thou earthly store have left
Two loaves, sell one and with the dole
Buy hyacinths to feed the soul.

Sir Alec rounded off his speech with four things to remember when teaching children. There is good in every child, however damaged, repellent or ill-favoured he may be. That all children matter. That the life of a child can be enriched by the development of his creative powers. That encouragement is far more important than punishment.

About five years before he made this speech, I was on my way to Junior School. Sir Alec's vision hadn't quite reached George Street Junior Mixed in Featherstone yet, but it was about to.

George Street School is different to Girnhill Lane, it's not modern, in fact it's so old that my grandad's dad went there. There is a big stone shield on the wall that says 'Endowed 1884'. This school was built for the children of the first influx of coal miners. My grandfather came here in the early 1920s, he told me about a headteacher called 'Bulldog Watson', a red-faced man with big chops who liked to drill his boys like a sergeant major. In the middle of the 1960s when I came here they still did a morning drill on the playground. The boys lined up on the side near the wall that overlooked the beck. We put out our right arm perpendicular to our body and touched the shoulder of the next boy. Once the distances were measured we put our arms by our side and stood to attention in silence until a whistle blew and we turned to march to our classrooms, a gaggle of coal miners' sons with scabby knees and mucky necks.

We had an old teacher called Mr Burke who had fought with distinction in the war. He was an avuncular sort of chap with a lined face, a stickler for good grammar and a believer in gentle punishment for those who stepped out of line. His favourite form of correction was the 'jungle drums' which involved boys bending over while he beat out a rhythm on your backside like a tom-tom percussionist. Some of the other teachers favoured the slipper, which was in reality a rotting tennis shoe missing its laces, though the headmaster still wielded a stick with a certain amount of glee.

The lavatories at George Street School were still outside ones. There were three closets for sitting down, but the urinals were in the open air, separated from the playground by a red brick enclosing wall. One day Pete Goodfellow, Mel Fletcher, Dave Goulding and I decided to have a pissing competition to see who could wet the wall the highest. I can't remember which one of us it was now, but one of us managed to piss right over the wall and sprinkle a passing dinner lady. She wasn't best pleased and reported us to the headmaster. He lined us all up in his office, told us to hold out both hands and went down the line giving us three strokes on either hand. I recall the swish of the cane as it passed through the air. I was last in line and was filled with so much fear before he got to me that I moved my hand as he struck. The end of the cane caught me like a whip on my thumb and for my pains I got an extra strike. Outside the office we compared notes. Pete said he'd had it hardest because he was the first in line. Mel said, 'It didn't hurt much,' but he was holding both hands under his armpits. Many years later Featherstone Rovers beat Hull in the final of the Rugby League Challenge Cup at Wembley. As the final whistle blew everybody in our vicinity on those famous terraces celebrated by hugging and shaking hands. A balding man in front of me turned round and shook me warmly by the hand. I recognised him as my old headteacher from George Street. I remember thinking at the time, 'the last time that hand touched me, it was holding a wooden cane.'

George Street School started to change as we entered our third year there. Mr Burke told us that the old sloping desks with ink wells in the top right hand corner and a groove for your pencils were to be thrown out and that in future we would sit at tables of six. He told us that there would be a carpeted area where we could sit to read books and a tiled area for modelling clay and splashing paint. He gave us all a platinum pen apiece with a squared off nib and introduced us to 'italic' writing. When I told my dad he said, 'What the bloody hell have they got you learning Italian for?'

Some trainee teachers started to come, I recall one of these was Mr Manship, a man from Sheffield with a gingery moustache and jam-jar bottom glasses. He wore a paisley patterned tie and a buttoned-up, mustard-coloured waistcoat.

'Now boys and girls, tomorrow we are going to do some creative writing and I'd like you all to bring two objects from home that you might like to write about.'

In a box at home I have an interesting shell that I picked up on the beach near Flamborough Head and a little brown First World War diary that my Auntie Alice gave me. The diary had been carried in the trenches by one of her uncles. I decide to bring these two items to Mr Manship's class.

Scattered on the tables in front of us are an assortment of

broken dolls, toy tractors, Thunderbird rockets and the cards that come in packets of Brooke Bond tea. Mr Manship surveys the jumble and starts to choose things he seems to want to examine in detail. Pete Goodfellow has brought in a blown Song Thrush egg. 'Tell me something about this egg, Peter.'

'I got it out of a nest wi' four in a bush up near t'park.'

'And what do you see when you look properly at it?'

'Well, it's blue wi' some speckles on it.'

'That's right, but look closely, what else do you see?'

I put my hand up. 'It's got some black zig-zag lines on it, that looks as though somebody has splattered their ink on it?'

'Yes, that's right young man, the lines do look like splashed ink. Let me see that shell in front of you. What do you see when you examine the shell?'

'Well, it's mainly dark brown and dark grey, but it's got some light grey flecks in it and if you put it to your ear you can hear the sea.'

'Wonderful! Now, tell me what it's like.'

'Well, sir, I think this bit looks like an old man's beard and this hole is his mouth. It might be a pirate and when I put his mouth to my ear, he's whispering some secrets about where he's buried his treasure.'

Julie says, 'He's a romancer, sir, he's allus making stories up!' Everybody laughs.

'Well that's a very good story, now tell me more.'

'I can hear the waves and the wind and this bit of rusty colour is like a scar. He might have got stabbed wi' a cutlass.'

'Very good. Now, when we say something is like something else, for instance "a rusty mark like a scar", that's called a simile. And when we say something is something else, "the hole in a shell is a mouth", that's a metaphor. Put your hands up and give me an example of a simile and a metaphor.'

Mel Fletcher puts up his hand and says, 'My mam thinks I am as daft as a brush.'

'Yes, Melvin, that's a simile. Now someone give me a metaphor.'

Everybody is laughing again.

Neil Allington puts his hand up. 'This school is a milkman.'

Laughter again.

Mr Manship smiles under his 'tache. 'Why is it a milkman, Neil?'

''Cos it gives us a bottle of milk every morning.'

Everybody nods.

At the end of the lesson I hang back to show Mr Manship my World War I diary. He carefully turns the loosened pages. 'Look here, Ian, your ancestor has written down the days when he took a bath. A bath must have been a very important event for the soldiers who were up to their eyeballs in muck and mud.'

I asked Mr Manship if he wouldn't mind writing his autograph on one of the back pages. He tells me that he doesn't want to spoil such an ancient document. I insist, so he writes *Terry Manship* in his best italic writing.

Another young teacher comes not long after. This time a lady, who we all fall in love with. She is Miss Price, she wears beads and mini-skirts and a flower in the side of her hair. I thought she had been sent from paradise. She hadn't, she had come from a teacher training college at Hull. Alec Clegg had sent her. We do dance and movement with her. One morning in the school hall she says, 'Ian, pick up a green beanbag and a red one and now... you're an apple tree!'

I raise my branches and start to sway.

'Keep still Ian, trees don't move.'

'There's a stiff breeze, Miss!'

More laughter.

Another morning she says, 'Form a crocodile children, hold hands, boy girl, boy girl, we're going to the library.'

At the head of this crocodile are me and Julie Harper, the only girl in our class who has private piano lessons. We set off up Station Lane, past Evans' shop where hares and rabbits hang by their legs dripping blood onto the pavement, past the Gospel Hall, where a sign proclaims, 'He that goes forward bearing precious seeds, shall come back rejoicing, bringing in the sheaves', past The Railway Hotel where the smell of lunchtime drinking and tobacco blow through the front door and on up to the pit yard. A loco shunting coal passes over a bridge marked 'NCB 1954' and we all wave to the driver. He waves back with an oily rag. We could place our Clarks Commandoes into the mucky footsteps of all the colliers who have trodden this path up to the pit before us, but when we get to the pit gates we don't turn left, we carry on up to the Miners' Welfare Hall and the library which is built onto the side of it.

I have never been to a library before. The lady behind the counter asks us to show our hands. When I show her mine, she asks me to turn them over. 'Your hands are black bright! What have you been doing with them? Go and wash them and use some soap and make sure they're clean before you use the towel!'

I don't bother to tell her that before I came to school I had 'mucked out' my dad's rabbit pens and filled two buckets with coal at the coal house.

The library is a wonder. It smells of must and polish and old paper. There is a sparkling parquet floor and rows and rows of oak shelving.

Miss Price says, 'Choose any book you want and the lady will stamp your page and let you borrow it.'

I spin round and round on the parquet floor until I make myself dizzy and then lurch towards the nearest book case. I put my finger on the spine of the first book I can reach and randomly decide that this book will be the one I borrow. I take it to the counter. The librarian lady puts on the spectacles that hang on a silver chain over her jumper. 'Emmeline Pankhurst! You can't borrow that, it's too old for you.'

'Our teacher says we can borrow any book we choose.'

Of course I had never heard of Emmeline Pankhurst, but having made my choice I am determined to stick with it.

'Well, what do you know about Emmeline Pankhurst? If you can tell me something you can borrow it.'

'She once got arrested!'

I can't remember the cover exactly now, but in my mind's eye Emmeline Pankhurst is being carried a foot off the ground by a big copper with a handlebar moustache. She is wearing a large Edwardian lady's hat with a pheasant's feather in it and the green, white and mauve tricolour sash of the suffragette movement diagonally across her chest.

The librarian tuts and stamps my book.

I carry that book home like I carry our elderly neighbour Mr Hope's mantle back from the shop. Gently. When I get it home I don't know where to put it; people who don't have books in their houses don't have book shelves. I slide it between my pillow case and the pillow and fold over the cotton flap. I sleep for three nights with my head on the book.

On the Saturday I bring my book downstairs and into our front room. My dad is laying on the settee with his legs resting on the arm, he has one slipper on, the other has dropped off. He has a pint pot half filled with tea next to him on the floor. On the television Eddie Waring is commentating on the second half of a match from Huddersfield.

'Poke that fire up a bit lad and throw a shovel full on, then make me a fresh pot of tea, this 'un's gone cold and afore tha does owt else, nip t'shop and fetch me twenty Players No. 6 and what's that in thi hand?'

'It's a book.'

'I can see it's a book, what's tha want a book for?'

'I thought I might read it.'

'Aye, well, tha might read it, but tha won't be able to eat it will tha?'

He was wrong. I devoured it. And I devoured the next book

I borrowed as well, and the one after that and then I found out that you could borrow three books at a time, so I started feeding on three at a time.

At some point in the 1990s this library is closed and all the books are shipped to a new library and community centre at the corner of Albert Street. The shelves are left in the silence and dark that envelopes a municipal library when it becomes redundant. A firm of funeral directors buys the empty building. One day I'm having a pint in the Featherstone Hotel across the road and I watch it snowing through the taproom window. Then I see some men in overalls bringing out oak shelves and stacking them against the wall in the snow. I can't bear to see these shelves lying lonely in the wet, so I phone my mate Wayne who has a trailer for the back of his van. We rescue the shelves and put them into storage at an old school that is partly occupied by Yorkshire Art Circus. Over the weeks we strip down this shelving and fashion some smaller book cases out of the carcasses. As we pull off some of the outer planks, pencilled handwriting comes into view. 'These shelves were made by William Sykes in 1921.' The library was built by subscription in the years after the First World War, miners having pennies stopped off their wages to fund a welfare building. Then further pennies to furnish the library with shelves and books. The furniture was fashioned by local joiners who left their names in pencil.

'What is your name, son?'

'Ian Clayton, sir.'

I am standing in front of a panel of examiners at a school in Pontefract, about to take the interview part of my 11-plus exam.

I have my heart set on a grammar school place. I've been having a dream for some time now that I am walking down the snicket from Girnhill Lane into our backs, my mother is waiting at the gate by the rabbit pens. I tell her that I have passed my 11-plus. She tells me that she can't afford the uniform, but then my Aunt Laura comes to the rescue and takes me to a shop in Pontefract called Albert Lee's and they measure me for one. The dream carries on to me coming home from college to say I have a place at university and then to a breezy day when I return from university with a striped scarf blowing behind me in the breeze up the snicket. None of the dream comes true. I failed the 11-plus.

My mate Mick passed his exam and thought that it was because he had done well in his interview. 'What did you tell that panel?' he asked me some months after.

'How do you mean?'

'Well, when they asked me where I went for my holidays I said that I'd been to Spain and when they asked me my hobbies I told them that I collected stamps, that I liked to identify the flags of the world and that I had an interest in visiting historic buildings.'

'I told them that I went on the working men's club trip to Blackpool and that my hobbies were helping my dad to build scratching pens for his hens in the allotment and milking the goat.'

I ended up at the Secondary Modern at Pontefract because my mother said South Featherstone School was too rough. I never understood that logic, I was on free dinners at George Street, always in bother for fighting with David Stanley and Stephen Brightmore and I once heard one of the dinner ladies say, 'He can't help it, he's from a rough family.'

On the first day at Pontefract, or Carleton School as everybody called it, a big lad took my Beech Nut chewing gum, my sixpence piece and my pencil and compass off me. When he turned round I jumped on his back and pulled him onto the floor. I was holding handfuls of his long hair, but before I could start banging his head on the concrete he said, 'Alright, I submit,' like Jackie Pallo, 'Don't hit me and I'll give you something.' He gave me back my belongings and Led Zeppelin's second LP.

After just one year at this school my father announced that there was going to be a revolution.

This revolution involved us flitting from our house in Mafeking Street that we rented from a solicitor in Leeds, to a house in Farringdon Street, Hull, that my dad decided to buy with the compensation money he got after being crushed in the cardboard box factory.

I think my dad was paid £1000 in compensation after his accident. He couldn't wait to sign the paper and be handed a cheque. He actually asked for cash because he'd never had a bank account.

He bought the house in Farringdon Street in Hull for about £700. It was exactly the same as the house we lived in already in Mafeking Street, two-up-two-down, hot water from a geyser, no bathroom, outside toilet and a kitchen with black mould on the wall that led to a little back yard. It was, however, fifty miles away from my mother's parents and the threat of a bloody good hiding from my grandad every time my dad did something they didn't like.

There is a little man with a goatee beard who lives at the bottom of the street. He walks right fast. Sometimes we imitate him and walk right fast behind him. One evening he turned round, looked at us kids without saying anything, and then walked off even faster.

Another man who lives up near the corner shop likes to read Sven Hassell books. They all have pictures of Nazi storm troopers on the cover. We're playing hide-and-seek in the passage at the back of his house when we see this man going out. We sneak into his back yard and peer through his kitchen window. On the far wall beneath a cuckoo clock is a pennant with a swastika on it and underneath that is a bayonet hanging from a piece of ribbon. A woman who lives across from us who we call Auntie Rita tells us that if ever that man offers us sweets, we have to come and tell her.

Another old man who lives up near The Bull pub carries a walking stick with a worn out ferule on it. He swings his way up and down Stepney Lane like a rusting gate in the wind. He always seems to be angry about something. He stinks of last night's beer, has flecks of spit at the corner of his mouth and his teeth are browner than the pipe he has clenched between them. He coughs and hacks like a tiler's hammer and swears and spits at all the kids in the neighbourhood. Auntie Rita says that we're to keep away from him when he starts, but we're not to tease him. I heard her telling my mam and dad that his son had been a trawler man who drowned near Greenland.

After the summer holidays of 1972 I am enrolled at Brunswick Junior High. I come straight into contact with a bully called Jackson, who claims he's related to a supermarket chain that is popular in Hull at the time. One morning, on the way to class, and for reasons known only to himself, he comes smiling up to me then knees me straight in the knackers. That night, I cower in the bath as my mother pours in a panful of boiling water. She notices the large purple bruise that has appeared between my inner thigh and cheek of my backside. When I tell her how I came by it, she says, 'Well, you have two choices, either you give him some of his own medicine or I go up to that school and I'll do it.' I was terrified at the thought of my mother showing me up by attacking a school bully, so I told her that I'd get my own back. 'Good lad,' she said, 'Make sure you make his nose bleed!'

Next morning in the school playground I walk straight up to Jackson and headbutt him in the face. He runs away. One of his henchmen stands with his back to a wall. I take hold of him by the front of his jumper and bunch it up into my fist. 'Go and tell him that is nothing to what he is going to get after school.'

For a whole year after that Jackson steered clear of me, but I kept my eyes up my arse whenever I saw him, I never trusted his smile.

A year on and I moved up to Hull Grammar School; one of the oldest grammar schools in England, it traces its roots back to

1330, but was endowed by Dr John Alcock, the Bishop of Ely, in 1479. Notable old boys include the poet Andrew Marvell, William Wilberforce and William Gavin who founded the Boxing Association in America.

By the time I get here in the autumn of 1973, the school is no longer a grammar school, but an all-boys comprehensive. It still hangs on to some of its old traditions, the school's alma mater 'Floreat Nostra Schola' is sung with gusto on special occasions, '500 years have been and gone on Humber's swelling ti...ide'. The floppy fringed boys in the upper-sixth swagger about in black capes and sip coffee in their common room with their feet up on chairs like something out of Lindsay Anderson's film *If*. The First XV rugger team sing filthy songs on the way back from games on the back of the bus, while games masters who stuff pot bellies into tracksuits turn a blind eye.

Oh! Sir Jasper do not touch me
Oh! Sir Jasper do not touch me
Oh! Sir Jasper do not touch me
As she lay between the lily white sheets
With nothing on at all.

Some of the masters sneer at the idea that the school is now a 'Comp' and a lot of the pupils – the sons of old boys who are now businessmen in Hong Kong and doctors in West Hull – sneer at the boys who, like me, have come from the streets with factories at the end of them.

After the first year, boys are put into forms according to academic ability and I find myself in the top stream. A boy, who later became head boy, comes up to me and says, 'I say, what are you doing here?'

'Well, I've been put here.'

'Oh! I see!'

Later, on the rugby field, I sling out a pass to this boy who is idling on the wing. He is not expecting the pass, nor the clattering he gets from the lad that tackles him, and ends up winded on the touchline. I trot over and stand over him.

'What are you doing down there?'

I see the venom in his stare.

When I am fifteen I get picked for the First XV, by default, but picked nevertheless. The regular choice scrum half has an ankle injury and the one for the second team isn't up to much. In the first minute of the game I collect the ball in front of my own posts, put my head down and charge, I sidestep the forward bearing down on me, run diagonally towards the touchline, dummy their centre and then go for the posts. I make fifty yards before I'm brought down in a tackle by someone much quicker than me. A ruck forms, I get caught under the chin with a flying boot and stepped on by some of my own players. I still come up smiling, pleased with myself. Our captain comes jogging over. 'Look here! You're not playing that fucking yobs game they play in the West Riding now, next time kick the ball or pass it to one of us.' He points to three or four lank-haired upper-sixth formers, the Jeremys and Wills.

I don't get picked after that one game. The regular scrum half recovers from his ankle strain and his kicking game is nothing short of splendid.

At the second General Election in '74 when, according to a man called Karl Douglas, 'Everybody was kung fu fighting', Harold Wilson clawed back power from Ted Heath. The National Front fielded nearly 100 candidates, including one at Hull Grammar School. The school had decided to have a mock election and boys from the upper years were encouraged to enter into the debate. There was a long-haired Labour candidate who I knew to be a fan of the blues guitarist Rory Gallagher; a Tory who I suspect liked The Osmonds, they were number one at the time with a song called 'Love Me For a Reason'; and a Liberal, a thin freckly lad in jam-jar glasses, a sad sweet dreamer if ever I saw one. Representing the National Front was a lad with a mop of hair like something off a candyfloss stall at Hull Fair. This was Walter, a popular boy, in the way that boys who are made fun of can sometimes be popular. Walter had highly polished shoes, trousers with a crease that would cut you like a blade of grass and a face so scrubbed that it shone like Bardolph's. There came a point in the campaign when the polls were suggesting that Walter might even win. There was a fair deal of consternation amongst some of the geography teachers and downright panic among some of the young bearded staff who were freshly graduated from the more radical universities. I recall Mr Bradshaw taking me to one side and saying, 'It might be a laugh now, but it's not very funny if people like him do get elected. Have a word with some of your mates and let's make sure he doesn't win!'

Why he picked on me to round up the posse I don't know, though I had once told him that my grandad used to come picketing at Sculcoates Power Station during the strike in 1972. In the end Walter got well beat. On election day the Labour lad prevailed. The headmaster announced the result through clenched teeth.

In all my time at school, my dad never did pay any attention. I was once asked to read a story from the Bible at our school's Christmas carol service in the chapel at Wilson Street. All parents were invited and everybody's came except mine. My mam was poorly and didn't want everybody to see the nervous rash on her skin and my dad said he was too busy. That 'too busy' was yet another puncture that wanted mending on his bike tyre and wiping 3-In-One oil off the lino on our kitchen floor.

Another time I made it to the final of a public-speaking competition and my parents were invited again. My mam came in her new coat, but my dad said it was too hot to be sat inside a school assembly hall.

Then, one time I was in bother and in danger of being expelled from school for violence on the rugby field. The headteacher demanded to see my father and summoned him in a strongly worded letter. My mother read it to him and said, 'You'd better go and see what's up.'

My dad turned up for the meeting in the headmaster's study in rolled-over Wellingtons and bib-and-brace overalls. I don't think he listened to a single word the headteacher said, but as he was going out of the door he said, 'Don't worry headmaster, he's going to get the best good-hiding he's ever had when I get him home.'

At home, my dad pretended to loosen his belt. I stared him down. He started to laugh and said, 'Nip t'shop and fetch me twenty Players No. 6 tipped and don't have me traipsing to that school ever again. Tha knows I can't stand fucking teachers!'

Spring
In Search of a Father Figure

'So long as we learn it doesn't matter
who teaches us, does it?'
E.R. Braithwaite

Homing Pigeon

On my father's allotment sometime in the middle of the 1960s I fell face down into a muddy pool of water while being chased by a mad cockerel. The cockerel jumped on my back and started pecking my neck. I was crying and frightened, panicking as the mud clogged my nose. Something came over me. I jumped up and kicked the cockerel. It ran away to hide under some hawthorn bushes. My dad arrived with his spade, accompanied by an old bloke from the next plot who had a lump of wood in his hand. My dad held his spade, he swung it in the air and said, 'I'll chop its fucking head clean off.' I stood there, covered head to toe in mud and hen shit, defiant, glaring, waiting for the cockerel to come out of hiding so that I could kick it again. The old bloke rested on his lump of wood, he looked at my dad and then at me and said, 'By go, Sid! That little apple didn't roll very far away from the tree did he?'

The old man on the allotment planted a seed, but I never really saw it grow. I may have been an apple from my dad's tree, but I don't know where that tree was. My dad rarely talked about his roots and, when he did, his stories seemed so far-fetched it was difficult to believe them. He told me that his own father had been killed on his way home from a pub in the middle of the night during the Second World War. He didn't go into detail, but sometimes when he was that road out, he would draw his forefinger across his throat to suggest that he'd had his throat cut. My dad's mam, Joyce, who I saw from time to time, lived to be in her nineties. She was still a young woman when she lost her husband and was left to bring up four lads who were running wild. The eldest was Johnny, then my dad, third was Colin, and then there was Jimmy who my mam fell in love with. Johnny lived all his life in and around Wakefield. At some point both Colin and Jimmy drifted to Kingston upon Hull. Joyce herself had a relationship with a man who worked as a chauffeur for the Needler's chocolate factory over there.

I don't know much more than that, because my dad never told any stories apart from made-up ones improvised on the spot. Add to that the repeated warning from my grandmother to 'not believe a word that man says, because he's a born liar' and I had a recipe for something that would never get made.

In this way my dad was always a clown, a cowboy, a damned liar, a laughing stock or a twister. He was my dad in name only. I didn't know who he was apart from that and I certainly didn't know where he came from, even how he got here, except that he bumped into my mam at a seaside fairground and not long after that I was on my way and my grandad told them that they better look sharp and get married.

I once saw a photograph of that wedding day. Neither my mother nor father are smiling. My mother looks startled and pale. She holds a bouquet of flowers in front of the bump in her belly. My dad looks half-soaked and distant. He has one arm casually linked to my mother's and his other hand in his pocket. He stares out of the photo like a mask, like someone in a police station who ought to be holding a series of numbers up.

I want my dad to be my hero, but his mask never falls. I want him to help with my school work but, because he can't read or write properly, he can't. I want him to watch me playing rugby, but he doesn't like sport. When I'm collecting stamps and I ask him where Tanganyika is he says, 'Oooh! It's a long way from here.' And when I read about Oliver Cromwell and I want to know more he just says, 'You don't need to know about stuff that happened before the war!'

All the while I look for the father I never find, so I end up searching for a father figure. I decide that my father is in history and, because I don't know my father's history, I look on my mother's side and to some extent I find a lot of fathers, though these fathers are wishes, fathers to my thoughts.

I'm drawn to my mother's dad. He is strong and noble, a coal miner with political opinions, a reputation for hard drinking, and a hard-working one as well. Despite all this tough exterior, when he holds my gran to him, he does it with real tenderness, like a man holding a small bird. Then there's old Johnny Hope, a neighbour who seems to be full of wisdom and nous about nature. Another neighbour, Frankie Parr, a studious, learned and gentle man who has good manners and a gentle speaking voice that draws you in.

After that come people I don't know who I look up to; sporting heroes like Bob Beaman, Stevie Nash who plays rugby for Featherstone Rovers, and picture book heroes like Captain Kidd. I wished for a while that Captain Kidd was my dad instead of the pirate I had foisted on me.

As I grow I am inspired by artists, musicians and writers. When Barry Hines writes *A Kestrel for a Knave*, I become Caspar because his mam is like my mam. She spits on her shoes and wipes them with her hankie before she goes out and she's fed up all the time like my mam is.

I want to follow some of the footpaths that my ancestors took. The great Islamic mapmaker and scholar, Al-Masudi, once wrote in a book called *Meadows of Gold*, 'He who has never left his hearth and has confined his researches to the narrow field of the history of his own country cannot be compared to the courageous traveller who has worn out his life in journeys of exploration to distant parts and each day has faced danger in order to persevere in excavating the mines of learning and in snatching precious fragments of the past from oblivion.' I agree with that, but I think that sometimes our history is much closer to home. I like what the poet Richard Monckton Milnes has to say on this.

'A man's best things are nearest him
Lie close about his feet.'

In his book *Songlines*, Bruce Chatwin examines the aboriginal notion of 'Dreamtime' and how this had laid down patterns of life before and after a person exists. The songlines are paths that lead us to our ancestors and help us to realise that people and the land they come from are the same thing. A rock or a tree or a stream exists therefore because someone once sang it into being. I like this notion, I'd often thought that people like my neighbour Johnny Hope and his dog Rex were as much of a landmark of my childhood as the Wesleyan Chapel at the bottom of Station Lane, the working men's club on Girnhill Lane or the dairy at the top of the snicket that led from the corner of our backs. In some ways this all helps me to understand how my mind and memory work. I tell stories because I cannot separate them from the journey, and I tell stories in order to retrieve the information that would otherwise be lost or forgotten.

I like to follow these paths into memory, but I want to follow the real ones as well. I want to follow the ginnels and snickets that my ancestors once trod and try to connect to a lodestone. I don't know what that lodestone is but, like a homing pigeon that comes tumbling through the air, I'm trying to find it. Old Bill Larkin, our next door neighbour, told me that the earth is full of magnets and that pigeons have pieces of the same magnet in their heads. They come home, not because they always want to, but because they have to.

Johnny Hope, a veteran of the First War who lived three doors down from my gran, looked after racing pigeons all his life and kept pigeon corn in sacks in his back bedroom; the neighbours were always on to him about the mice that they could hear scratching behind the skirting boards upstairs. Mr Hope could touch his nose to make one of his eyes close and then open it again when he twisted his ear. He fastened his boots with different coloured laces and kept his trousers up with braces and a thick belt. If anybody teased him, he took his belt off, doubled it and said, 'Come on, I'm ready.' He wore a flat cap three sizes bigger than it needed to be that sat like a pancake on his head. He wore a waistcoat which was seldom washed and in the waistcoat pocket was a watch on a chain. Sometimes he span the watch around his finger and dropped it straight back into its pocket, never missing.

It's a Saturday morning and I'm standing outside of my favourite shop, Evans. I like this shop most of all when it's the season for seagulls' eggs to come. They are displayed in huge wicker baskets with straw in them for protection and small breast feathers fly about on the breeze. The seagull eggs are fawn or brown coloured with brown and black blotches and speckles. I love the markings. I think they are the eggs of the black-headed gull. They are cheaper to buy than hens' eggs and a lot of old coal miners like to eat them.

Mr Hope comes up with his dog, Rex, trailing behind him. He says, 'Nah then young 'un, what's tha doing admiring them eggs.' I tell him that I like to see all the different colours and patterns. He says, 'Reight oh, lad, well pick two and me and thee are going to have a treat.' I stand staring at him. 'C'mon wi' thee, pick two of them eggs afore they go off.'

I select two of the eggs, picking what I think are the best patterns and hand them to Mr Hope. He closes his ancient hands around them and takes them into the shop. I follow on behind. The shop smells of celery with soil and tangerines. There are vats of peas steeping in water. Mr Evans takes the eggs and says, 'Do you want them in a bag, Mr Hope?' Mr Hope, quick as a flash, says deadpan, 'No, chuck 'em on t'floor, I'll dribble 'em home!'

Mr Evans places the eggs into a brown paper bag. When we

get outside Mr Hope whistles to his dog. 'Here Rex,' he calls, then places the top of the bag into Rex's mouth, 'Now don't you drop 'em or there'll be bother.' We walk the half mile from Station Lane to Mafeking Street, slaver and foam spill from the corner of Rex's mouth, but he doesn't drop the eggs.

Old Mr Hope pushes open the front door of his house. The front room smells of gas. It is 1968 and he still hasn't converted to electricity, he sees by gas mantle. Open corned beef tins stand on his table with their key still hanging down the side and there are three or four Fray Bentos pie tins full of milk for the cats. His room is full of stuff. He uses old copies of the *Green Final* for a tablecloth. When you sit down you can read how Sheffield Wednesday got on against Preston North End the previous Saturday. This evening, just as it is getting dark, a man called Jack who lives at Hunslet near Leeds, who has only one tooth and the blackest fingernails in Yorkshire, will come and bang on doors. He will shout, 'Greeeen! Fi...nil!' On Monday if I come back to Mr Hope's he will have a new tablecloth on.

Mrs Hope isn't very well. She has a deep chesty voice and says just one word at a time before she gets out of breath. Her and Mr Hope have celebrated their emerald wedding anniversary. She tells Mr Hope to make tea. He picks up a blackened kettle from the hearth and goes to fill it at a dripping tap in the kitchen. He comes back and puts the kettle back onto the hearth. He then lifts his boot and starts to tamp down the coals on the fire. The room is filled with the smell of rubber burning. Mrs Hope says, 'I've... told... you... about that... you'll have... us... afire!' Satisfied that he's flattened the coals, Mr Hope places the big old kettle directly onto the fire. When the water starts to bubble and spit he says, 'Rex, fetch them eggs.' Rex picks up the paper bag again and brings it to the fireside. Mr Hope drops the eggs into the kettle. After a while waiting, listening to the clock on the mantle and Mrs Hope's breathing, Mr Hope picks up a rag and takes the eggs out of the water. He hands me one. It burns me and I chuck it from one hand to the other. Mr Hope scolds me, 'Don't drop the bugger, lad, blow on it and get it peeled.' I watch him peel the shell from his egg and copy. 'Now, lad, what tha does is this.' He bites a piece off the top of the hard boiled egg and then reaches into a saucer on top of the mantelpiece for a pinch of salt, which he makes a big show of sprinkling. I do the same and with a flourish that involves a wind-milling of my arm I sprinkle my egg with warm salt. 'Aye, lad, that's it. Now get it down thi.' The taste is a shock, it's like the cod roe that my gran sometimes fries for my grandad's tea. We sit hunched like two old mates eighty years apart munching on the hard boiled eggs of the black-headed gull.

'When I was in the first lot in them trenches we used to eat raw eggs.' He mimes the act of breaking an egg, then pretends to tilt back his head and swallow the contents. I see his big old Adams apple move up and down. 'Now what we need to swill these down, son, is a nice pot of tea.' He replaces the kettle on the fire and we wait again for it to come back to the boil. Mr Hope puts his hand inside a caddy that says 'Indian and Ceylon' on the side and scoops half a handful into a brown pot. 'Go and swill these two beakers under the tap, lad, and look on that dresser for a cup and saucer with a pink rose on, Mrs Hope likes hers out of that.' I did as I was bid. Mr Hope hasn't got a hot tap, just a cold one that hangs off a bracket on the wall with sacking fastened round it to stifle a leak. I put my fingers inside the beakers and try to clean off the brown. 'Four sugars for me lad and two for Mrs Hope. And she likes plenty of milk.' We sip our tea, it is very strong, I put four sugars into Mr Hope's and four into mine as well. The milk leaves little white spots on the top of the tea. Mrs Hope says, 'Lovely,' and then turns to Mr Hope, 'but... I... think... milk's on... t'turn.'

When I come out of Mr Hope's I see that there is a knife sharpener at the top of the street. He is peddling his bike on a stand to turn a grinding wheel and sharpening Mrs Minnie's scissors. I stand watching. He smiles and says, 'Do you like to see them sparks fly, lad?' I say that I do and then tell him, 'I like seagulls' eggs an'all, I've just had one at Mr Hope's.' He laughs at me and ruffles my hair. 'Bloody lovely! You've done well there though, I've never known him to invite anybody in.'

Mr Hope once gave me some pigeons. The first time I let them fly they circled round and then flew off to perch on some gasometers near the Girnhill Lane club. I thought that they wouldn't come home and I started to cry. Mr Hope said, 'What's up with thee?' I told him that my pigeons wouldn't come back. He gave me an old Ringtons tea tin and put some corn into it. He said, 'Shake that magic corn and see what happens.' I shook the tin and shouted, 'Come on, come on then.' The tin sounded like an old instrument for making it rain. The pigeons came out of the sky and landed in front of the coop. I shoved them in and dropped the latch. 'You see, magic corn, lad.'

'Mr Larkins told me that they had magnets in their heads.'

'Magnets my arse! It's corn that brings them home.'

For a lot of my life I've followed the trails of corn and been pulled along by magnets.

In a Broken Dream

If you're interested in real ale, as I have been since I bought my first CAMRA *Good Beer Guide* in 1978, you're aware that one of the 'holy grail' pubs of Britain is one called Ma Pardoe's in Netherton, near Dudley. I had always thought that I'd like to visit it but, for one reason or another, I never got round to it.

One spring day my mate Colin Tetley, a former collier at the Prince of Wales pit, decides that he'd like to have a day trip to Netherton to look at Ma Pardoe's. Since his redundancy, Colin has collected 'breweriana' souvenirs from long-gone breweries. We park the car in a space overlooking the pub and a statue to 'Jumping Joe' Darby, the finest athlete ever to have come out of Netherton. The beer at Ma Pardoe's is still brewed in a cobbled yard at the back of the pub, as it has been for two centuries. It's lovely beer and I tell the man in the apron at the back of the bar so, as I wipe the froth off my 'tache after the first sip. I blurt out, 'I've been longing to come here, because this is where my ancestors came from.' The barman seems interested, puts down a tea towel that he has been forcing inside a pint pot, wipes his hands on his front and says, 'And what did they call your ancestors?'

I tell him 'Fletcher' and he smiles.

'Aye, well that'll be right then, this town is full of Fletchers. Just walk a hundred yards up this hill young man,' the barman points at the window, 'and you'll see a man called Fletcher who runs a shop selling wild western gear and line-dancing outfits.'

I order another pint of Ma Pardoe's finest, then I walk around the pub. The walls tell the pub's history. There is a photograph of a team of twenty shire horses pulling an anchor out of a foundry.

This is the anchor for RMS *Titanic*. The anchor was cast by the firm of Noah Hingley and towed through the streets one sunny Sunday in August 1911. All the townsfolk turned out to wave their handkerchiefs as the horses, two abreast, and the anchor passed by on its way to Dudley Station. There were boys in flat caps, girls in their Sunday-best wide-brimmed bonnets and clean pinafores and dads back from the pub with their hands thrust deep into emptied pockets.

I drink off my beer and decide to visit the wild western shop. On the way out of the pub I smile at three old men in flat caps, who look as though they might have been there since the *Titanic*'s anchor went by. They smile back and then one of them says in an almost impenetrable Black Country dialect, 'We're just the flat-arse gang, son.'

'And why might you be the flat-arse gang, lads?'

'Don't you know, son, we're bloody famous round these parts.'

I tell them that I have no idea why they might be called that. Then one of them says, 'If you'd been sitting here for as long as we have on this wooden form, you'd know,' and they all start laughing and coughing up years of hard work.

I find the shop. It is called 'Ranch House'. I suppose a cowboy outfit shop on the Halesowen Road in the West Midlands ought to look out of place, but for some reason, this shop doesn't. It is full of cowboy hats, leather chaps, holsters, whips and bandanas. There are native American headdresses and dreamcatchers hanging on fishing lines from the ceiling. A tall man behind the counter with his back to me hears the shop bell go and, without turning round, says, 'Hello, can I help you?'

'I'm just looking,' I say.

The tall man behind the counter turns round, he's polishing the buckle on a belt.

'Well, actually I was looking for a man called Fletcher, but I think I've found him.'

'My name's Fletcher,' he says.

'I can see that.'

'How do you mean?'

'You look like my grandad and every other Fletcher I've ever seen on a photograph.'

He doesn't seem to know what to say, so he shows me a belt with a scene of a buffalo hunt on the buckle. 'These are on special offer at the moment if you're interested.'

I feel at the leather and tell him that it seems to be of a fine quality, but I've only recently bought a belt from an ex-miner on Pontefract market, who started making leather goods after he took his redundancy from the pit. 'Have you ever tried to trace your family tree?'

Mr Fletcher seems more interested in selling me something. He shows me a tasselled buck-skin jacket that wouldn't have looked out of place on the back of Buffalo Bill. 'No. I've never tried to trace my family tree.'

'A lot of Fletchers left Netherton to travel up to West Yorkshire to find work in the pits.'

'Oh! I see. I don't think I've been told that before. I've got some beautiful dreamcatchers over here if you're interested in that sort of thing.'

'I like to catch my dreams,' I say. 'I'm going for a walk round town and another pint in Ma Pardoe's and I might call back later.'

Mr Fletcher nods and goes back to his buckle polishing. He holds his mouth in a straight line, in the way my grandad did when he was pulling a pipe cleaner through his pipe. Every few seconds he flicks his eyes upwards to look at me. I guess he is weighing me up and wondering if I might be a long-lost relative.

I rejoin Colin in the pub. He's on Coke and laughing along with the flat-arse gang. I fancy another pint. Colin says, 'Well, I can't have any more if I'm driving, so I'm going to go back to the car and have a squint at my *Daily Mirror*. I might have forty winks 'cos I've been up since half-past four.' Like a lot of retired miners, he still gets up at pit time.

Colin goes back to the car for his squint and winks. I finish my pint and go to look at the statue of Joseph Darby 'the champion jumper of the world'. There is a plaque that describes his feats.

He was born near here in August 1861, originally a maker of nails and horseshoes and then a blacksmith, his physical prowess led him to become the greatest Victorian 'spring jumper' (a long jump without a run up, often using weights). After retirement he kept The Albion pub on Stone Street, Dudley. He died in 1937.

Some of his feats: one forward spring jump, 14 feet 9 inches, Sept. 1890; one backward spring jump, 12 feet 11 inches, Sept. 1891; in Boston USA, he twice bettered G W Hamilton, the champion jumper of the world. His trick jumps included: clearing a canal in two jumps, appearing to make the second leap from the water's surface; jumping on some eggs without breaking them; jumping on someone's face without hurting them; clearing half a dozen chairs after jumping from a glass of water, without spilling any.

On his plinth, Joe Darby stands, knees bent, fists clenching two dumbbells, he is about to spring.

I walk back up to the car. Colin is gently snoring with the *Daily Mirror* on his stomach. I sit at the side of him and close my eyes. In my reverie, I see my little Billie, she is looking at the dreamcatchers hanging from the ceiling in Mr Fletcher's wild western shop. She touches the feathers on them. I remember a time when we stroked a barn owl. I told her that the feathers on its breast were so soft that if you close your eyes and move your finger slowly towards its breast, you won't feel the feathers when you touch. She shut her eyes and tried it. She opened them and realised she was touching the feathers without knowing.

I'm daydreaming now about Jumping Joe Darby. He holds open the door to a working men's club full of layered tobacco smoke and men clenching clay pipes between their teeth. There's a billiard table in the middle of the room and the men with pipes have formed a funnel on either side of it. Jumping

Joe acknowledges the crowd who are hushed now. He then sits on a wooden stool and removes some work boots. He starts to unfold a parcel wrapped in newspaper as though it were a fish-and-chip supper. He takes out a pair of worn plimsolls and makes an act of pulling the plimsolls onto his bare feet, like a Music Hall turn doing a mime. He ties a double bow in the laces and, satisfied, he stands, looks down at his feet and then does a little leap into the air and clicks his heels together. The crowd of men cheer. Joe now takes a deep breath, expanding his chest to take in lungsful of the working men's club atmosphere. He stands barely five-foot-three in his pumps, but has a chest like a kilderkin. The funnel of men breathe in too, then cough and hack and spit phlegm like gobstoppers onto the sawdust on the floor. Someone hands Joe a pair of iron dumbbells and he swings them, increasing the arc on either side of his body as he does. The crowd are completely silent now, save for the occasional rattling cough. Joe leaps into the air from a standing start, clears the length of the billiard table and lands on the other side like a cat jumping from a midden roof.

The men cheer and slap each other on the back, spilling pints of ale. In the corner stands my great-great-grandfather, 'Jack' Fletcher. He's impressed by what he has seen, but doesn't join in with the cheering. He stands quiet, with a gone-out pipe and an empty glass. Jack has other things on his mind. Tomorrow he has to make a decision. He has heard from some cousins that there is money to be made in the coal pits of Yorkshire. They have walked north some months before and have settled in a village called Royston, near Barnsley. They have told him that he can make more money in these new coalfields than he could ever make hand fashioning nails here in Netherton.

Jack wants to set off, but at the same time he wants to stay with what he knows. He can't make up his mind. He relights his pipe and puffs out sparks.

Joe Darby is still receiving the backslaps, sticks out his chest like a bantie cock, and then holds his biceps out for folk to feel. He raises a finger like a farmer testing the wind, then holds out his arms. From between the jostling bodies in the throng comes a little girl, she is about seven years old. Joe calls for silence and excitement turns to anticipation. 'I will now perform a most dangerous feat for you, I would appreciate it if you will give the best of order.'

Knowing looks and nudging elbows greet this announcement. One old man turns to Jack Fletcher and says, 'He's going to jump onto his daughter's face.' Jack tightens his teeth around the stem of his pipe.

Joe Darby springs onto the bar top. The barman throws a tea towel over his shoulder and clears away empty pots. The little girl lies down amongst the wet sawdust and waits, while Joe asks for a piece of billiard chalk. He rubs the blue chalk onto the instep of each of his plimsolls and again asks for silence. He pulls himself up to his full five-foot-three, twists the edges of his moustache, as though taking a piece of chewing tobacco, and closes his eyes. He now cocks his head to one side like a robin does on a wall, but Joe seems to be listening to something, maybe a far-off drum roll. Then he leaps into the air. He seems to hang in the layers of blue tobacco smoke, a flying squirrel of a man, caught in flickering lamplight like a silent film and then he comes down.

Back in the car park, Colin stirs when his *Daily Mirror* slides into the footwell. He makes the smacking noise of tongue on top palate and says, 'I'll just have another five.' He doesn't know, but he has broken my reverie. I close my eyes again and try to get back to the film show I have going on at the back of my eyes.

Joe Darby falls in slow motion. His daughter doesn't flinch, lying stock still. Joe lands on the floorboards, one foot either side of her face and in one more leap lands on the side of the billiard table, from where he bows deeply. The crowd erupts again and Jumping Joe lifts his daughter, throws her into the air then catches her. He points to two blue marks on either cheek and then rubs them off with his thumb. The little girl smiles before doing a curtsey, holding the edge of her pinafore. The crowd clank beer pots together, roar their approval and throw their caps into the air.

Jack Fletcher has seen all he wants to see. He tries to drink the dregs from a long empty glass, puts it onto the bar and steps out into the night air on the Halesowen Road. Tomorrow he will make his decision. He sleeps on and off all night, under an overcoat, on a mattress he shares with two younger brothers.

At dawn he wakes to the sound of clogs on the street. He pulls on a coat and a cap and steps outside. He still hasn't worked out what he wants to do. He decides to toss a coin, but when he feels inside his pocket, he realises that he hasn't got one. He takes off his cap and tosses it into the air, the cap swirls about in the breeze, long enough for him to say under his breath, 'Heads or Tails'. He decides if it comes down with the outside up, he will set off walking to Yorkshire to find work in the coal pits. If it comes down lining side up, he'll stop where he is, making nails and earning a few extra bob labouring for a farrier down the street. On the toss of this cap, the entire destiny of our family over the next century and a half is decided.

The cap comes down to land in a gutter... right side up. Jack lifts it, squashes it back onto his head and goes back to poke his head around the door of the house in King Street, Upper Netherton, where he was born on a stone kitchen floor in the summer of 1867.

He tells his mother that he is going 'to see a man about a job'. He kisses his mother on the cheek. A little tear glistens down the side of her eye. He rubs it away with his thumb. She shoves a piece of bread into his pocket. He sets off to walk the 120 miles to Featherstone in Yorkshire, leaving the town of his birth for one he doesn't know.

At the corner of King Street, he turns. His mother waves and shouts, 'A merry wind to thi arse, Jack.' Jack kicks the toe of his boots onto the gable end of the last house, to move the little stones from near his toes. He lifts one boot and then the other. He can see the skin on the soles of his feet through the holes at the bottom. He wonders how far these boots will carry him.

Two days after this he carries his boots to the bottom of Station Lane in Featherstone. He has walked the last miles in his bare feet with just toe rags for protection. His feet are bleeding. Jack finds lodgings for that night at Dobson's Lodging House near the rabbit fields.

Colin stretches his back in the driving seat, picks up his *Daily Mirror* and tosses it onto the back seat of the car. 'Right lad, we'll get off, we'll stop somewhere nice on the way home, this Tom-Tom says it's…'

'120 miles,' I say.

'How do you know that?'

'My great-great-grandad, Jack Fletcher, once walked it.'

As we drive back down onto the road near Jack Darby's statue, I look up at him. In my mind's eye he winks at me, leaps into the air and clicks his heels together.

The morning after he arrived in Featherstone, Jack Fletcher went to see about a job at the Featherstone Main Colliery. This pit was then on its way to becoming the biggest, most profitable pit in the Empire. He got his job and that's where he laboured for the rest of his life. And his son, my great-grandad, Edward Fletcher, followed him into the pit and that's where he laboured for the rest of his life, apart from a stint in Russia at the end of the First World War. And his brother, my Great-Uncle Oliver, followed him into the pit, only he didn't work there for the rest of his life, just until one day a big stone fell out of the roof in the tail-gate and severed his leg. And Edward's son, my grandad, followed him into the pit and that's where he laboured for the rest of his life, apart from the Second World War when he rode a motorbike, taking messages across the front at El Alamein for

General Montgomery. Then I broke the chain and I didn't go down the pit because my grandad didn't want me to, and my son, Edward, won't go to the pit either... because there aren't any left now.

My great-grandad, Edward Fletcher, was born in the same year as the future King Edward VIII. Just before the First War he married a woman called Ethel Bull, the daughter of Alf Bull, a coal hewer from Sharlston. She died of peritonitis when she was still in her twenties. My grandad told me that he could remember her, he was five at the time. He said that she had appendicitis, but thought that it was no more than belly-ache or colic. She tried to cure it with milk and Indian Brandee. My grandad told me that by the time they sent for a doctor to look at her, his mother's appendix had burst and she died on the sofa. His father was left with three children under school age, he had not long returned from a stint in Russia during the First War and couldn't cope. The kids were drinking out of 'titty' bottles and eating 'pobs' out of jam jars, running about with no shoes to their feet and the old man was drinking himself into a stupor in the Central Working Men's Club. 'Pobs' is dried bread soaked in warm milk with sugar sprinkled on it. It's funny how some things stick. More than fifty years later when I came back to live with my gran and grandad, my grandad teased me whenever he saw me eating porridge for breakfast. 'I see tha's got thi pobs, where's thi titty bottle to go with it.'

Ethel Bull died in 1922. Her younger sister, Edna, was just 21 at the time. She moved in with my great-grandfather to look after him and his three children. She married him in 1928 and, by all accounts, had a life of drudgery. She possessed just one dress, a rough sleeveless smock. If ever she was taken out, which according to my grandfather was once in a blue moon, she sewed sleeves onto her smock. Her husband drank beer, laboured underground, raged about his experiences in Russia and gambled away what spare money he had. My grandad told me that his dad had a beautiful baritone singing voice and had once sung at Wakefield Cathedral, but most of his singing was done when drunk in working men's clubs. His favourite was an old song called 'Le rêve passe' or 'The Soldier's Dream' written during the First World War by Armand Foucher. If he wanted more beer and he hadn't the money to pay for it, he would sing the first few lines and then stop. The other miners in the club would egg him on and take up a collection. As soon as his cap was filled with pennies he would stand up swaying and find his key. 'Come on Eddie sing about the famous white horse.'

'See them pass by!
There they go, what a show!
Those guardsmen!
All hearts beat high
At the sight of this grand array
Cheers fill the air
They are blazing a trail to glory
Heroes are there, who will live in song and story.'

Josef Locke, the drunken Irish tenor, became synonymous with the same song many years after.

In 1936, Featherstone Main Colliery, where my grandad and his dad worked, was shut down. They said because of cheaper imported coal from Poland. My great-grandfather raged again, got drunk more and sang his song most nights. My grandfather found work as a conductor for Bullock and Sons, a local bus company. One day my gran was coming back on the bus from Tadcaster to Castleford. My grandad was the conductor. He took my gran's bus fare and said to her, 'By hell lass, them eyes of yours would fetch ducks off the water.' My gran smiled. My grandad then told her that he could get tickets to see George Formby at Castleford Theatre Royal. They made a date.

My gran told me that my grandad's house was a disgrace, but that she felt sorry for his stepmother. 'The poor old bugger hadn't a pot to piss in. They didn't even have enough plates, so they used to take it in turns to have something to eat.'

When I was a lad I liked to sit on a little stool at our back door and listen to my grandad telling the tales. My grandad knew his grandad, Staffy Jack, who walked from the Black Country in 1890. He was still living in Albert Street in the 1930s, in fact his daughter, my Great-Aunt Charlotte, still lived in the same house in the 1970s.

'My old Grandad Jack was always skint. He was a proper Staffy and talked like they do from there. He used to say, "How yam today? Yo look clemmed." He used to leave what he owed the travelling salesman on a book in the window bottom and stand back from the curtain until the bloke had been. This salesman – they called him a 'packy man' – sold dishcloths and towels. He'd go on his way down the street and tell the neighbours, "Mr Fletcher isn't in again, but I know he's an honest man, because he's left his money out for me." What he didn't know was that Jack would wait until he had gone and put the money back in his pocket.

Once, there was a funeral going up Station Lane. The packy man took his hat off and said, "Who are they burying today?" to a man standing with his cap in his hand. This man was Staffy Jack, but he was still black-faced in his muck from the pit, and the salesman hadn't recognised him. "Oh! don't you know, it's poor old Jack Fletcher." The packy man threw his hands in the air and said, "Oh dear me and he still owes me some money!"'

My grandad laughed loud in baritone every time he told that story. I must have heard it a hundred times, but never tired of it. 'And when he knew he was dying he asked them to bury him near the cemetery wall. He said, "If ever there's a resurrection I want to be first out."'

The year after Featherstone Main Colliery closed down, King

Edward VIII married Wallis Simpson. My gran said that Mrs Simpson had 'sweaty feet'. I don't know how she knew this, but she repeated it every time her name was on the news or in the papers. On 24 April 1986, Mrs Simpson died at her home in the Bois de Boulogne. On that day we were at my gran's council flat at the back of the fire station. Gran had baked a cake to celebrate the joint birthdays of her sister, my Auntie Alice, and Heather, my partner. When the news came on about Wallis Simpson, my gran said, 'She had right sweaty feet her y'know.'

Spilt More Ale Down My Waistcoat

My mother always looked nice in her clothes. She didn't have many, but made the most of what she had. The sticking point came between her smoothing her frocks in front of the wardrobe mirror and getting taken anywhere to show them off. My dad, having settled in his chair to watch *Alias Smith and Jones*, never wanted to get off his arse to go out. He didn't like drinking alcohol. He kept a bottle of dry sherry in the china cabinet and made a flourish of taking it out just before Christmas every year, putting it back again after the new year with the slightest change in its level.

One Saturday night my mam persuaded him to take her to a pub called The Junction, a well-known local that sold barrel after barrel of Tetley bitter to thirsty coal miners and rugby-league players.

My dad didn't really want to go, but was persuaded to put a collar and tie on and some new shoes he had been given. I can't imagine what they drank or what they talked about while they drank it, but I know there must have been a fall out, because I heard them shouting in the backs as they came home.

'You show me up everywhere we go!'

'I was having a bit of fun.'

'Well it's not bloody funny! We can't go anywhere.'

They carried on rowing when they got in. I heard the kettle being filled and banged onto the stove. My mother brought a hot-water bottle up to bed and my dad slept under an overcoat on the sofa.

At breakfast time we could all see he was worse for wear. We ate our porridge, he kept his head under the coat.

'The simple pig has thrown my new kid gloves onto the chapel roof.'

It turned out that on their way home from The Junction, my mother dropped her gloves. My dad picked them up, but instead of giving her them back, he threw them onto the roof of the Wesleyan Chapel at the bottom of Girnhill Lane.

After her breakfast my mother went to the front door and shouted across the street, 'Mam, Mam!' My grandmother's ears were well attuned to this distress call and came straight over. She looked to where my dad lay on the sofa with his head still under the overcoat.

'Get up you stinker!'

My dad peered above the coat collar.

'Get up, get dressed and get in that back yard and unchain that window-cleaning ladder, you're going to find that lass's gloves if it's the last thing you do! You've got until I count to five and if you don't shift yourself by then I'm fetching Eddie and he'll give you a bloody good hiding on top.'

My dad staggered into the kitchen and rummaged through a cabinet drawer to find a padlock key. He unchained his ladder. The chapel goers were still filing into the building when my dad leant his ladder up against the wall. He climbed while my gran footed the bottom rung and us kids looked up at him. To everybody who asked her what she was doing my gran said, 'It's just that simple bugger up the ladder, if I aren't blessed.'

My dad never did find the gloves. He never went to The Junction again.

Every Saturday for many years my grandfather liked to get the dust off his chest by walking the three miles down a country lane to the village of Wragby. He loved the Spread Eagle and the Tetley's they served there. He had three mates, two other miners and a farm labourer who formed a school to play fives and threes. From the age of about five, when my little legs needed four strides to keep up with his one, I went with him. I learned more about nature, life, gambling, rugby, boxing, being a man and good manners on that walk than anywhere I've ever been.

'Look in the bottom of that hedgerow there, lad. Can you see them purple flowers with the yellow in the middle, that's what they call the Bittersweet Nightshade, you'll have seen them shiny red berries like little rugby balls? Well don't eat them; they'll poison you. Now look on this bit of wasteland here, this is called Good King Henry, some people call it Poor Man's Asparagus and you can eat that, there's more vitamins in it than a cabbage.'

'Can we take some home to cook, Grandad?'

'Can we bloody hell, it tastes like shit!'

We come to a bridge where the road bends over the River Went. Every time we come here, he tells me the same tale. I don't mind hearing it over and again and I'd be disappointed if he didn't say it.

'You see where that pipe comes out the wall, lad, when I was about fourteen before I started at t'pit, I used to jump off there onto that banking at t'other side.'

'It's a long way that, Grandad, you must have been a good long jumper.'

'I was like Jesse Owens, lad. Now then, them long plants on the other side of this beck, them's called Teasels, if you get scabies, you can itch your skin with them. They use 'em to comb billiard table cloths as well.'

We walk up the hill to the farm they call Owlet Hall.

'When I was a lad they called this Dog at t'Wall.'

'There might have been a dog that sat on t'wall, Grandad.'

'Aye, there might have been. Now look across there where they've had that fire. Can you see them bees buzzing round that tall plant? That's called Rosebay Willow Herb, some people call it Fireweed 'cos it likes to grow on land where's there's been a fire. Bees love it.'

They keep pigs at this farm. I love to look over the half barn door to see the mother feeding her piglets.

'Do you know, lad, pigs like to eat coal.'

'Coal! Why do they eat coal?'

'It might sweeten their breath a bit.' He pauses and gives me the sort of look that says, 'And if you believe that you'll believe anything.'

I never know when to believe my grandad and when not to. I'm not sure that anybody could ever leap over the beck like he claimed he could, though I know he was a very quick sprinter because I once heard Sam Lowe the barber telling one of the customers in his shop that 'Ted Fletcher was an even timer over 100 yards'.

Perhaps my own children were less naive than I was at that age. When my twins were six or seven, I took them on this same walk and passed on my grandad's plant wisdom and, though the piglets no longer lay on straw in the barn at Owlet Hall, I did describe my grandfather's leap. Our Billie looked incredulous. 'What! He jumped right over to the other side? I think he might have been kidding you, Dad.'

'Come on, lad. Pigs don't really sweeten their breath with lumps of coal. But I think they might eat it to help their indigestion. I used to suck a piece of coal down the pit when I had heartburn.'

'How did you know to do that?'

'When I first went down the pit I used to drive ponies pulling tubs out of the hole. There was a lot of old blokes working with picks and shovels and they stunk of ale in their sweat and farts. I used to see them sucking coal to cure the wind. I copied them.'

My grandfather celebrated his fourteenth birthday on 2nd January 1929. He left George Street School a few days after that and followed his father's boot steps to Featherstone Main Colliery. For the first few weeks he was on a different shift to his dad, a good job, because he shared his boots. His first job was pony leading.

We're now more than halfway to the Spread Eagle pub. We come to a wood we know as 'The Bluebell Wood'. My grandad says, 'Come on, we'll have a little rest on this grass banking.' I ask him to tell me some more about the ponies in the pit.

'The ponies only came up on bank holidays. They had stables in the pit bottom for them. The ponies worked two shifts to the men's one. You should have seen them when they let 'em out on holidays. They'd run into the fields kicking their legs up behind them, just like us running down the beach at Blackpool to the sea on the first day of our holidays.'

My grandad had a favourite pony called Blackie, when I rode my first donkey at Blackpool on the beach, I secretly christened him 'Blackie' in honour of my grandad's favourite.

'That Blackie could pull some full tubs, lad. No matter how many you fastened onto him, he'd try. There were times when I've seen him nearly on his belly pulling. But I worked sometimes with another one called Major and he was as stubborn as a mule. He was crafty an'all, he used to count the jinks of the chain and if he thought there was too many he wouldn't pull, choose what. I've hit him with chocks of wood until my arms were aching, but he wouldn't budge.'

'That was cruel, Grandad.'

'It was, but if I didn't get them ponies pulling, the old colliers I worked for didn't get paid, then they'd set about me with their belts. I've seen me hit that Major, then get down on the floor and cry at what I'd done.'

I'm always surprised when I hear my grandad admit that he was crying. Big tough men like my grandad don't cry, they just bite their lip and carry on.

'Now, lad. I'm going to show you something, but you're not to tell anybody.'

We walk to the edge of the woods near the barley field. My

grandad uses his big hands to part some grass and reveals a nest on the ground filled with olive coloured eggs.

'That's a partridge's nest. They lay a lot of eggs does a partridge.' He folds the grass back over. 'Now, I don't want you to go telling your mates about this nest.'

We reach the Spread Eagle pub. For years my grandad has said the same thing to me as we come to the door. 'Now you sit on this bench and I'll fetch you a bottle of ginger beer and some crisps.' Today he says, 'How old are you now, lad?'

'I'm coming up to sixteen next month.'

'Right then, it's time I let thi have a pint.'

The taproom is dark, full of Park Drive smoke, the rhythm of the triple thump of darts in a cork board and an occasional rattle of dominoes on a wooden table. The conversations rises and falls like a poor signal on a wireless, but then is lost as I walk in.

'This is our Ian.'

There is the scrape of a chair.

'Come and sit here wi' us, kid. Have you walked it?'

My grandad's mates make room in the corner by the window. My grandfather fetches five pints to the table, the glasses have handles and he can carry five at once.

'Get it down thi, lad, it'll do thi good.'

Over a period of about an hour and a half, in between games of fives and threes that I watch but am not invited to join in with, we drink four pints of bitter. Each man takes his turn to go to the bar. I watch the levels of beer going down and as we get to the bottom of the fourth pint, I say to my grandfather, 'Is it my turn to get the beer?'

He says, 'Well, we haven't come for a bloody look round.'

He then taps my legs under the table and presses a pound note into my hand. I fetch five more pints in three journeys to and from the bar.

On the bus on the way home I start to feel dizzy and sick. The

South Yorkshire bus from Wragby via Ackworth to the stop by the Travellers at Purston takes ages, it seems to pull up at every bus stop. My head is swirling by the time it comes for us to get off.

'Tha looks a bit pale, lad.'

'It's just me and buses, I always feel sick on buses.'

We step off the bus and we haven't gone more than twenty yards when I have to bend to be sick in a grate. My grandad rubs my back. 'Get it up, lad, it'll do thi good!'

It was the first time. I promised myself as the hot sick came down my nose that there wouldn't be another. I haven't kept my promise forever, but I nearly have, I hate being sick.

I'm hanging about outside the front door of the Blackmoor Head in Pontefract. John Southall has told me that we can get served in here. He has been in twice already, but then he does look a bit older than me, he's already got sideburns.

'Do you know what to ask for, John?'

'I had Double-Diamond last time, but that beer out of the wickets tastes a lot better, I had some of Dad's at the Cross Keys last week.'

We hear the hubbub of pub conversation, a tinny jukebox is playing a song called 'How Long (Has This Been Going On)'.

A bloke in a trilby hat and overcoat walks past us and pauses before he goes in. 'What's up, lads, are you waiting for somebody to bring you some crisps?'

'Err, no mate, we're just on our way in.'

'Right then, what are you dawdling for?'

We follow him in. He shouts out his order before he gets to the bar, 'Pint of best Ethel and look sharp, me stomach thinks me throat's bin cut!'

He gets his pint and throws a handful of coins onto the bar. The elderly barmaid, who looks like my Auntie Doris, picks up some coins and before turning to the till looks at John and me and says, 'What can I get you, lads?'

I cough, deepen my voice and say, 'Two pints of best please Ethel.'

'Speak up, lad!'

'Two pints of best please.'

Ethel narrows her eyes. 'You can have half apiece and then bugger off before you get me shot.'

The two halves cost a total of nineteen pence. John said, 'That landlord in the White Hart serves you as well! How much have you got to spend? And leave enough for a packet of Stimorol, my mam smelt beer on my breath last week and I had to tell her that I'd nicked a bottle of my dad's home brew to try.' We walk out of the pub buzzing.

That was perhaps the cheapest, most refreshing beer I ever tasted. I don't know what it is about pubs that appeals to me, the beer obviously, but there is something beyond the beer and the effect it has, and this is the pub I always return to in my mind: the Blackmoor Head, in the late 1970s. The pub was a clash of ideas like no other I've seen. There was a 1920s fireplace blazing away merrily in the front room opposite a jukebox that was stacked with classic rock music, so, on the one hand, you'd have a retired miner warming his arse and, on the other, a bloke in patched up jeans nodding his head and playing air guitar to the opening bars of 'Honky Tonk Woman'. There was flock wallpaper in the snug and leather seating with little bell pushes left over from the days when blokes in white coats delivered beer on trays to your table, while in the back room psychedelic lighting accompanied two lads from Barnsley who played Jefferson Airplane records every Sunday night.

The people in here on any given day are like a parade in a Tom Waits video. There's early punk rockers with the beginnings of Mohawk haircuts asking Ethel, the landlord's mother, to see if she can get some Lurkers records onto the jukebox, old blokes playing dominoes who wear suits that they might have been demobbed in, and out-of-work Scottish labourers who came south for the coal standing with cues at the ready for anybody who is daft enough to risk a stake of fifty pence on the pool table.

Big Frank Duncan is always in the taproom. Frank is well above six feet tall, but likes to squat on his haunches. He has a half-smoked Rothmans between his fingers with the lit end pointing towards his palm, smoke curling from a chimney formed by the gap between his thumb and forefinger. In his other hand he clutches a box of Swan Vestas. Frank once told me that his father was in the Black Watch and that the other part of his family were Romany gypsies. He writes poetry in a spiral-bound notebook which is usually peeping out of the side pocket in his sports jacket. Nobody messes with Big Frank, some people call him Mad Frank and will talk about a fight he once had with some other big men outside the newspaper shop that involved motorbike chains and knuckle-dusters. Frank knows hundreds of folk songs. I like to hear him sing 'The Lakes of Pontchartrian' and 'Three Score and Ten'. When he's too drunk to remember the words he does a weird sort of scat singing, slurring his syllables to make a kind of jazz folk music that I have only heard him do.

One New Year's Eve in the 1980s, Heather and I decide that we would take up an invitation to attend a party in London. It's late in the afternoon when we make our minds up and we have no idea how we are going to get from a pub in Pontefract to London. We decide to splash out on a taxi. As we tumble out of the pub to the car waiting outside Big Frank is on his way in. He asks us where we are going. When we tell him 'to a party in London' he decides, without a seconds thought, that he will come with us and plonks himself down in the back of the taxi. The taxi driver is about nineteen years old. He rarely gets a fare beyond the railway station at Wakefield. Heather and I have already had a few beers and Frank is looking dishevelled from the night before, his supper stains the lapel of his jacket. The driver says, 'Where to?' Frank booms out from the back seat, 'London!' The driver looks into his rear view mirror. He surveys Heather in a cheesecloth blouse and long Indian skirt covered in bangles and beads and sporting an Afghani skull cap, then Frank in a foisty sports jacket with leather patches on the elbows, then he looks at me, 'Are you fuckin' serious?' Frank barks out again, 'A1 south, quick as you like and we'll direct you once you get to Cricklewood.' The taxi lad picks up his radio, 'Car 9, can you hear me? They want to go to fuckin' London.'

'Well make sure they pay up front, it's going to be a hundred quid.'

Heather gives me twenty quid towards the fare and Frank donates a fiver and tells me that he'll give me some 'on top' when the 'pancrack' opens again after the holidays. The driver says, 'You'll have to help me, I've no fuckin' idea once I get past Doncaster.'

He has just one cassette tape. A very grubby homemade copy of Iron Maiden's first album. As we cross the Wentbridge flyover, Maiden are singing 'Running Free' and Frank is joining in with his jazz–folk scat singing. By the time we are near Stilton the tape is about to play for the third time and Frank shouts, 'Turn the bloody thing off, I'm going to sing.' And he is well into 'Three Score and Ten' before the taxi driver has chance to press his finger on the eject button.

And it's three score and ten, boys and men
We're lost from Grimsby town
From Yarmouth down to Scarborough
Many hundreds more were drowned.

The taxi driver shakes his head. He is still shaking it as we come to the outskirts of London. Frank informs us all, 'The crack is good in Cricklewood.' The taxi driver has his hands firmly on the wheel, his knuckles as white as someone holding the bar on a dodgem. 'Fuckin' hell, there's cars on both sides o' me!' Somehow we manage to navigate ourselves to South London to a house in New Cross going up towards Telegraph Hill. The driver pulls up outside the house and says, 'I don't know how the fuckin' hell I'm going to get back home.' We invite him in for a drink and a bite to eat. It's eight in the evening now and he tells us, 'I haven't had owt since my breakfast at seven o'clock this morning.' Our host tells us that she has just brewed a pot of camomile tea and that there are crudities on the table through in the kitchen. I see the taxi driver wince. There are batons of carrot, celery and little tomatoes and some hummus, guacamole and cream cheese with chives in little pot bowls. The taxi driver sips his camomile, winces again and asks for milk and sugar. He picks up a samosa, takes a bite and whispers to Heather, 'What the fuck is this?' She tells him it's an Indian savoury. 'Fuck me, I don't like curry and that.' Frank is offered wine. 'Yes please, I'll have a bottle of red.'

We draw a map for the taxi driver and wave him off. Many years later, I took a taxi to work, it was the same lad. He reminded me that he had once driven us to London on New Year's Eve. I asked him if he had found his way back alright. 'Did I fuck!'

Frank sang 'Auld Lang Syne' with great gusto and then squatted near the fireplace to talk to an opera singer who had been performing that night at Covent Garden. The singer was called Russell, Frank thought he was called Raffles and kept addressing him by that name. It was very funny, but we didn't have the heart to correct him, and Russell was too pissed to tell what Frank was saying.

In the early hours Frank tried to chat up a young Chinese woman who he had decided was from Mongolia. I overheard him say to her, 'When I look into your eyes, I can see history. I can see that your ancestors swept across the steppes behind Genghis Khan.' The Chinese woman said to Heather, 'I don't know what on earth he is on about, I'm from Camberwell.'

We slept until noon the next day. Frank was nowhere to be seen. I caught up with him a few weeks later in the Blackmoor taproom. He told me that he had hitchhiked back and for some reason ended up in Warrington, where he sheltered from a rain storm in a big steel pipe in a goods yard. When I asked him for a contribution towards the taxi fare he told me that I would have to wait as he was currently barred from the social security office for setting fire to a poster on the wall when he got bored with waiting.

Frank once took a bet in the Blackmoor Head that he wouldn't dare dress up as a chicken for a week. The bloke who bet Frank a hundred quid didn't know Frank very well. Frank dressed, not just as a chicken, but as a six-foot-four-inch blue chicken with a fine red comb, made out of a blown up rubber washing up glove. He did his shopping, his visits to the council office and to the pub in costume. One night he climbed to the top of a lamppost and cock-a-doodle-dooed into the early hours.

He spent his winnings in the Blackmoor Head Inn.

I'm sitting nursing a pint of Tetley's with Bert, Sean, Rasta and Pete Simpson. We watch a man called 'Chivvy' Linnet arguing with a bloke called 'Dicky Bow'. Two pensioners with nothing better to do. Chivvy is going through a well-practised and surreal stream-of-consciousness routine to entertain anybody who is listening. 'Bruce Forsyth said to me, it's nice to see you, to see you nice and here is Anita Londesborough in slow motion,' he mimes the action of a breast-stroke swimmer while puckering and opening his lips like a goldfish in a bowl. 'Now we see, Lester Piggot in slow motion,' this time he bends slightly at the knee and holds imaginary reins, urging on an invisible horse.

Dicky Bow, resplendent in white frilled shirt and spotted bow tie, says, 'Chivvy, tha's stupid. Nobody's listening to thi nonsense.'

Chivvy urges his imaginary steed to go faster and then slows him up over the line. 'Whooaah! Boy.' He reckons to climb down from the horse, pats it on the withers and strolls over toward Dicky. He pretends to take a stethoscope from his jacket pocket and places it onto Dicky's chest. 'Mr Richard Bow. You need to lose some weight, either that or your child will be due at any moment.'

Dicky looks down at his huge pot belly. He says what he always says when the attention goes to his stomach. 'They don't put bay windows on shit-houses you know.'

Quick as a flash Chivvy Linnet says, 'I didn't realise you were a shit-house, sir.'

Ethel shouts at the top of her voice from behind the bar. 'That's enough now. Pack it in or you're barred... again!'

Chivvy waits until she turns her back, reaches his fingertips to the fireback and with the soot, paints an Adolph Hitler moustache onto his top lip. He clicks his heels, gives a Nazi salute and says, 'Ja wohl.' As Ethel turns, he changes his stance, goes bowlegged, twitches his nose and walks down the room swinging an imaginary cane like Charlie Chaplin.

We all laugh, our conversation about the finer points of Scott Gorham's guitar playing on the new Thin Lizzy album waylaid by a septuagenarian nutter.

In the corner sits old Bill. His trouser waistband finishes just below his chest. He walks with two sticks and has one leg. He told some of the more gullible lads that he was bitten by an alligator, and others say he was shot in the trenches. If ever you ask Bill how he is, he will say, 'Ask me forty years since! Black patent leather shoes, black trousers, white shirt, dicky bow, Bobby Dazzler. I'm fuckin' knackered now. Aye, Palais de Dance, gliding up and down with a sweetheart.' Then he will twang the pair of braces that hold his trousers up to his chest and have a swig of his ale. 'Do you know, lads, I'm as dry as a witch's tit,' he'll say, then take out a bookie's pencil and lick it.

Bill has said nothing while Chivvy has been creating. Bert looks over, 'How are you today, Bill?'

'Ask me forty years since. Black patent...', but before he can go any further, the door swings open, 'Tricky Mickey', who sells sheets and pillow cases on the market, strides in. He looks at us laughing, at Chivvy with his soot moustache, and at Dicky trying to hold in his belly.

Tricky announces himself with his own routine. 'I don't care if your daughter's been turnip cutting, tatey scratting or pea pulling. Come and feel the quality of this flannelette. If you buy it in green, she'll think she's a queen, buy it in pink yer feet won't stink, buy it in blue yer dreams'll come true and buy it in white, you'll be at it all night. And if you don't want sheets or pillowcases this week I've some lovely towels, madam. Here, feel the quality of these. And if you're going to Pontefract Races later on, I can tell you the winners, the riders, the horses and the jockeys... can I have a pint of your finest bitter please Ethel and can you put the froth at the bottom.'

That's how it was in the Blackmoor Head then. A mad parade of characters that turned taproom into theatre. At some point in the eighties, the brewery in its wisdom decided to modernise. They knocked out all the little corners and made it 'open plan', pulled out ancient fireplaces and chucked domino tables into the skip. All the old blokes who had fought the Nazis had nowhere to go anymore. If we are to look for what caused the decline of the English pub, we need look no further than the point where eccentricity was no longer welcome in ale houses.

In my mind's eye I still see a bizarre game of fives and threes in that bar. The lead singer of The Monkees, Davy Jones, has returned from a visit to Pontefract Races. He is drunk and has pockets overflowing with winnings. Chivvy Linnet and Dicky Bow and a drunken pot collector called Flanagan have involved him in a game. Davy Jones staggers out of the pub even drunker, looking for a taxi to Leeds. I doubt whether he had enough left to pay for it. Flanagan winks at Chivvy and says, 'He looked a bit worse for wear.'

Chivvy sups his Tetley's, draining the pot in one go, belches loudly and announces, 'I've spilt more ale down my waistcoat than that bugger supped toneet!'

My Grandfather's Shaving Mirror

I'm standing in front of a mirror on my bedroom wall. I'm about a foot away from it, but I feel as though I'm a long way from home. This mirror I'm standing in front of is my grandfather's shaving mirror. It's a very old one and I think he inherited from his own father; for all I know his father inherited from his father. It came to me from my grandmother a few years before she died. The mirror is small, it measures just short of six inches across by eight inches in length. It's chunky and heavy. The glass itself is a quarter-inch deep and the wood it's backed with is nearly twice that thickness. The wood is probably oak and the clips, one in the middle of each side, are rusted iron held in place by old screws. It's a very fine quality glass, the reflection is as clear as a bell, though the edges of the glass have tarnished over the years and the mirroring appears as little black waves. I like to look in this mirror and picture the faces that have reflected in it over time. If I want to be anywhere now, I guess I'd like to be somewhere inside this mirror connecting again to those who have looked in it.

That's where I want to be; back to my roots, to a back yard where I feel secure. This place I want to be is a story, a story between the glass and the oak backboard of my grandfather's shaving mirror.

My grandfather is having a shave. His mirror hangs on a nail that has been knocked into the wall just beside the kitchen sink and next to the Ascot geyser that gives us hot water. He has lathered his face with an old ivory-handled shaving brush and Imperial Leather soap. My grandad looks down at me looking up at him.

He paints each side of my face with shaving lather and then blobs some onto my nose. 'Do you know what this shaving brush is made out of, lad?'

I tell him that it was once an elephant's tusk.

'Aye, that's right and do you know where the bristles come from?'

I do, but I know he's going to tell me because he always does and then laughs.

'A badger's arse, lad!' and then he laughs a rattling laugh that is half a measure of coal dust, a quarter Woodbines and the rest amusement.

I watch my grandad's lathered face looking into his mirror. A big man with his mirror too high up on the wall for anybody else to look into. My grandmother is listening to *Housewives' Choice* on the BBC Light Programme. My grandfather picks up his razor and starts to scrape. He stretches his cheek by opening his mouth to an oval, moving his jaw to one side and holding the skin with the tips of his fingers. His whiskers are like iron filings. I don't need to look at my grandfather to know he is shaving, I can listen to him. Today he catches himself and blood from the cut starts to mix with the white lather. He unscrews the handle of his razor, takes out the blunted blade and places it on the window sill. The sill is marked with the rusted remains of previous blunted blades. 'Hilda, have I got any new blades?'

My grandmother comes to the kitchen and looks into the cupboard beneath the sink. On a shelf in this cupboard are stacked blocks of green Fairy soap, Izal disinfectant and a starch called Robin. She looks up at my grandfather, 'Have you thought of growing a beard?'

My grandfather wipes his chops with a flannel and throws the flannel into the pot sink. 'I'll look like creeping Moses woman! Young 'un,' he looks down at me, 'Nip up to the shop and fetch me a packet of Wilkinson's Sword blades and tell Mrs Johnson that your gran will pay her for them on Friday.'

He tears a corner from last night's *Evening Post* and sticks it to the cut on his cheek. I put on my coat and open the back door. 'Climb over the wall you'll be quicker, and fasten that coat and look both ways when you cross the road and look sharp.'

I have my first shave in that same mirror on my seventeenth birthday. I can't see myself in the mirror, so I try to stand on tiptoe and hold the front of the sink with one hand. This doesn't work. There is a small stool with a wicker-work seat, I stand on that and start to work the razor. The whiskers have only grown on my chin – what my grandad calls 'bum fluff' – and by the corners of my top lip. I make a cack-handed job of it and then sting myself with some Brut 33 aftershave. The Brut is a birthday present from Aunt Laura. I've heard that Elvis Presley uses it and if it's good enough for Henry Cooper, well then! When my grandad gets home from the pit he wants to know who has been using his razor. My gran sarcastically tells him that she has decided to do away with her moustache. He looks at me, 'Why didn't tha just open t'back door and stand in t'yard?'

I look at him, I know he's already got a punchline and that I'm about to get knocked down with it.

'Well, there's enough breeze today to blow that bit of fluff off!'

Twenty years later and my twin children are watching a TV programme called *The Bear in the Big Blue House*. The bear has lots of friends, Billie my daughter likes Treelo the lemur, Edward is fond of Ojo the baby bear. They haven't learned how to walk yet, they're a bit late getting upright and they're nearly two years old. My grandfather, who they know as 'Old Grandad' though they never met him, has been dead now for ten years. My grandmother still lives in the council flat they moved into not that long before he died. When the kids' TV programme finishes I put them in the twin pushchair and wheel them the two miles down to my gran's house. I turn into St Martin's Close and I can see my grandmother lifting her kitchen curtain. She waves. I tell the children to wave back. By the time we get to the door, my gran is outside wiping her hands on her pinny. 'Come on, come on, let me have hold of them babbies.' She lifts Edward from the pushchair. 'Come on, Edward, eeeh! thi grandad would have eaten thee!' She's very proud that we named Edward after her husband. I lift Billie from the buggy. 'Give her here, come on Lily,' for some reason she thinks Billie is called Lily.

My grandmother at eighty is still very strong, she balances one child on either hip. 'Come on, let's see what we've got for you.' She takes us all in and places the kids onto the settee and puts two cushions onto the carpet in front of it. 'There, if you tumble off you won't hurt yourselves.' She turns to me and says, 'It's about time they were bloody walking, there's nowt wrong with their legs is there?' I sit on my grandad's chair and pick up the *Daily Mirror* to read the sports pages. I notice my grandfather's pipe still rests on his ashtray by the side of the fireplace. My grandmother is fully central heated, but misses having a fireplace. Her solution was to buy a wooden fire surround with a 'log-effect' plastic fire in it. It's lit by two red bulbs and two thin metal wheels above the bulbs turn when they get warm to give the effect of a glow. Above the fire surround is a plate held on a plastic plate grip. The words on the plate say 'To celebrate the Saphire Wedding of Edward and Hilda Fletcher'. The word 'sapphire' is missing a 'p' because the engraver didn't know how to spell. When I pointed this out at the time, my gran said, 'Don't worry Educated Archie, I've been p'd off many a time in my life, don't tell above a dozen.'

Above the plate is a photo of Gran with Edward and Billie taken on their first birthday. A studio photographer came to the house to take it. He spent ages trying to arrange and compose the picture. In the end my gran said to him, 'Shake your feathers, love, I haven't written my will yet!' There is a lamp in one corner of the room with a snow-covered cottage on the shade. When the bulb is lit the leaded windows of the cottage light up. In the other corner is a telephone that sits on a telephone seat. You sit sideways on it to make a call. Also on this seat is a wooden money-box on which is written 'A present from Blackpool'. Between the lamp and the phone, almost the length of the back wall is a sideboard. The sideboard came from the old house and it's far too big for this council flat, so much so that my gran had to saw the antlers on her models of wooden stags to fit them between the top shelf and the ceiling.

My gran comes from the kitchen with two glasses of Kia-ora orange squash for the kids. 'Do you like meat and potato pie, Lily?' Billie looks at my gran, 'I say do you like meat and potato pie? I bet you like it Edward don't you?'

I tell her that they've never had meat and potato pie. 'What! There's no wonder they're still shuffling about on their arses! What do they have then?'

I mention that they like spaghetti. 'Spaghetti! I'm not giving 'em tinned stuff, anyhow I haven't got any, I wouldn't give it house room.'

I want to say proper pasta but I know my gran won't know what I'm on about so I turn to the kids and say, 'Old Granny's mashed potato is the best in the whole wide world.'

We sit at a table that is far too big for the kitchen when the flaps are up. The kids devour a huge plateful of dinner apiece, I have never seen them eat so much before. A few years later when Billie decides she will become a vegetarian I ask her if there is anything she will miss. She smiles and says, 'No, not really.' Then she thinks again, I can see in her eyes an attempt to remember. 'Well there was once a dinner at Old Granny's,' then she smiles again and stirs a frying pan filled with mushrooms, courgettes and tomatoes with her favourite wooden spoon.

Before we leave, my gran reaches under the kitchen sink. She takes out three bottles of Domestos, a dozen bars of Fairy green soap, an enamel jug, a plunger and some packets of Brillo. She finds what she has been looking for. She holds up Grandad's shaving mirror. 'I've been saving this, I don't know why. If you can make use of it take it, else I'm going to give it to t'binman.'

I tell her that I would be delighted to have it. She wraps it in a tea towel and places it into a shopping bag. 'You can keep that bag an'all, I've got one of them shopping trolleys now, it's a fast model, I can't keep up with the bugger.'

She then starts rooting through her cupboards. 'There's some semolina here that wants eating, do you like semolina, Lily?' She places it into the bag. 'Do you want any light bulbs? I've got plenty.' She opens a top cupboard to reveal a collection of various bulbs. 'If I leave them any longer the buggers will be sprouting come Easter.'

There are 40 watt, 60 watt and 100 watt, orange ones to light up the windows of snow-covered country cottages and red ones that pretend to be a glowing log fire. 'Oh! and here, take this blackberry jam, an old man off the allotments gave me it, but he's a dirty old bugger and I don't think he washes his hands so I'm not eating it.'

When we get back home I unwrap the mirror. The tea towel has a picture of the jolly fisherman on it and the slogan 'Skegness – it's so bracing'. I look in the mirror at a beard that's turning grey. I show Billie and Edward their faces in it. I start to tell them some stories about their Old Grandad.

I take the mirror to our bedroom and nail a hook in the wall at the height Billie and Edward are when sitting up straight. 'When you both start walking I'll move this mirror up the wall and when you start growing I'll keep moving it up.' I draw a pencil mark in line with the top of the mirror.

A few days later, Billie and Edward are watching *Teletubbies*. Edward is sitting on the step between our kitchen and living room, Billie is in front of the telly, with Heather and me behind her on the sofa. I say to Edward, 'Don't sit over there on your own, come and have a cuddle on the sofa with me and your mam.'

Instead of shuffling off the step on his bottom like he usually does, he tries to stand up. He surprises himself and just stands there wobbling, but he doesn't fall. I go down on my knees and put my hands out, 'Come on, son, you can do it.'

He takes a step and then another and still doesn't fall. He tries another step, then another and then wants to run. He reaches my arms just before he tipples over. 'Good lad, there's no stopping you now!'

Heather encourages Billie to have a go. She's more interested in Tinky-Winky and Po, but with a bit of coaxing she's up and then straight down. Heather stands behind her and puts her hands beneath Billie's arms. Together they walk and stumble around the room. Within a few days Edward and Billie are chasing each other around the coffee table. I move the shaving mirror up the wall and draw a new pencil line. Edward stands in front of the mirror and blinks his brown eyes. Billie sticks out her tongue.

On the day before the aeroplanes flew into the Twin Towers, my grandmother died in Pontefract Hospital. She had fallen down in her bathroom a few days before. I inherited her handbag and shoebox full of photos, her Richardsons of Sheffield knives and forks, a lovely vase which had stood on her sideboard for many years and an ancient Ringtons teapot. I wish she had left me some words.

After my gran's funeral we tell stories around our kitchen table and eat sausages. Billie has insisted that we all try Linda McCartney's' vegetarian ones. Then after tea Edward mentions that he and Billie haven't been measured against Old Grandad's mirror for a bit. We trip upstairs and they take it in turns to look into the mirror. Billie is slightly taller, Edward wants to know if, when he grows, he will be as tall as the man he is named after. We move the mirror up a few inches and draw another pencil line.

Billie was four feet tall when she was killed in a canoeing

accident in the spring of 2006. The people dealing with the funeral told us that when they measured her for her coffin.

We stopped moving the mirror up the wall after Billie died, drew no more pencil lines. Edward has now grown as tall as me. Out of the blue, one day when he came home from school, he decided we should move the mirror up to our height.

Handbags and Shoe Boxes

When my gran died I thought that I knew everything there was to know about her. I thought that she had told me all of her life in stories and anecdotes. I even knew that she hid money from my grandfather under the flour and tea in tins on the pantry shelf.

One day, a woman who had been a neighbour and had spent a lot of time in my grandmother's kitchen, asked me something that astonished me.

'Did you know that your gran bathed with Chanel soap?'

I was walking to Pontefract at the time, this lady Jenny was walking back from town. We came across each other halfway, near where some geese graze in a farmer's field. It was spitting with rain.

'Well she did. When we first flitted and had a bathroom inside for the first time, we used to invite her to use our bathroom. She used to come with a spotless towel over her arm and her soap and say, "It's Fairy Snow here". She had the soap sent up from London to the chemist at the bottom of the lane.'

I didn't know my gran bathed with Chanel soap, I can't begin to imagine how she even knew about Chanel soap. I thought that she had told me most of her secrets, little things like how to make gravy, how to sew on a button so it doesn't come off, how to make a fire in a hearth with just a copy of the *Evening Post* and a shovel full of coal. She told me big secrets too and earthy things that made me laugh. I can hear her now. 'I nearly died on the day your mother was born, it was touch and go. The doctor told me that I mustn't under any circumstances have any more children.'

Most families round where we lived were full of children.

Women from the square joked, 'He's only to hang his bloody trousers on the bedstead and I'm in the family way again.' I wondered how my gran and grandad coped as a young couple who had a baby when they were twenty-one years old and then prevented from having children all the time after.

One day she told me in the middle of cackling laughter with a group of women neighbours. 'We used to buy a ticket to Leeds and get off at Hunslet.'

My gran's sister, my beloved Auntie Alice, never had any children. She lived on her own for her entire adult life, my gran told me that she had a boyfriend once, a man called George. I found a photograph of him. He was a tall, handsome, curly-haired man in blazer and Oxford bags. 'It's a bloody mystery,' my gran said, 'as to what happened to the pair of 'em, but they parted before he could ask her to marry him. Nobody knows why, but I do!' She never went further than that. If my gran really did know why one day her older sister suddenly chucked her handsome boyfriend and then never bothered with another man from 1934 until 2010, she never let on. And whenever I tried to mention 'George' to Auntie Alice she asked me if I wanted a mint or a glass of pop or a walk to the cricket fields.

She kept a 'bottom drawer' though, a steel trunk called The Warwick made by the Jones Brothers of Wolverhampton, a very robust one with a hinged lid and carrying handles. It came to Heather and me just before Auntie Alice moved to the sheltered housing from 14 Mafeking Street. Before then, a series of items that had once been saved in it came to us; two pairs of the most beautiful white cotton sheets, some pillowcases, towels and tea towels. She must have started putting them away in the 1920s and after curly-haired, Oxford-bagged George disappeared from the scene, there they lay, pristine and untouched.

Auntie Alice worked at a munitions factory during the war, on her first day there was an explosion when she handled a faulty detonator. She ran out of the factory and caught the bus home. 'I was deaf on the bus and still deaf when I went back there the day after.' After the war she moved to her house on South View overlooking the cricket field. She had a laburnum tree in her garden and a next-door neighbour called Miss Ponds. In the 1960s she worked at Dunhills Pontefract Cake factory in the cream room. She wore a white turban and travelled to and fro on the steam train from Featherstone station to one called Tanshelf. She brought home sweets; mushrooms, japs, mint imperials and 'spanish' liquorice sticks. In her long cupboard in an alcove by the kitchen fireplace there was a big white tureen filled with sweets. I stayed with her every weekend then and on Fridays she would tip all her sweets out of a pocket in the front of her pinny into that white pot tureen. 'Do they let you have spice for nowt at where you work, Auntie Alice?' She would wink and say, 'No, lad, but sometimes they fall into my pinny pocket.'

On Saturdays we used to go to watch the cricket match. My Auntie had no interest whatsoever in the cricket, but she liked to sit in the sunshine and knit or read romantic stories in magazines like *The Red Star*. On the way back to her house we bought fish and chips. She tipped vinegar from the pickled onion jar onto them and cut doorstep slices of brown bread.

In the evening she took me to the pictures. Her favourite cinemas were in Castleford; the Albion and the New Star. The Albion had been a lovely cinema, with a white-marbled facade and perfumed foyer. When 'Mighty Joe Young' played there in the 40s, they drove around Castleford with a life-sized model of him on the back of a lorry. By the time I started going there, The Albion was a bit worse for wear. The New Star, as far as I could tell, had always been a bit of a flea pit, by the late sixties it was clinging on to life on a diet of 'Carry On' films and Hammer horrors.

Auntie Alice missed the theatre. Every time we got off the bus she would point across to Grandways Supermarket and tell me, 'That used to be the Theatre Royal. By, it was a grand little theatre. I saw George Formby there and Hylda Baker.' Then she'd go into a routine. 'Eeeh! She knows you know. Oooh! I must get a little hand for this watch. Have you been, Walter?' And at the top of Wilson Street she would always stop to remember. 'See that house over there, Ian, they all stayed there, Roy Dotrice, Roy Castle, Gus Aubrey, he was Frank Randle's stooge, the seven dwarves from Snow White, they stayed there. And a bloke who had some seals. I saw the sea lions coming into the back of the theatre, they were balancing bloody beach balls on their noses.'

I saw *Zulu* and *Charge of the Light Brigade* and Rod Steiger in *Waterloo* at the Albion with Auntie Alice and I think we went to see *The Railway Children* three times.

One Saturday we walked down to the New Star. They were showing the Hammer horror *Twins of Evil* with Peter Cushing. It was an 'X' film. Auntie Alice marched up to the box office and asked for 'one and a half'. The bloke behind the glass said, 'Can I remind you, Madam, that this film is for those over eighteen only.' Auntie Alice drew in a breath. 'Well young man, I'm very flattered, but I was born before the First World War, so I think I'm old enough don't you?'

'I'm not talking about you, Madam. I'm talking about him.'

I'd probably be twelve at the time and not long out of short trousers.

'Ohh! Don't worry about him, love. I'll tell him to shut his eyes if owt comes on that I don't think is suitable.'

We didn't get in, so went for some more fish and chips at a café called The ACME. We sat at a formica table with a plateful of bread and butter in front of us. Auntie Alice pulled out a mirror from her handbag. She held it up away from her. Then she took out some rouge and put a bit on. 'He might have thought I was your sister,' she said and winked again.

After she retired from the liquorice factory, Auntie Alice

moved from South View to Mafeking Street, to a house just across the street from my gran. In her sideboard she had an old handbag full of photos. Every now and then we'd get them out and go through some of the older ones. Every time she came to the photos of her brothers, Edwin and Fred, she took out her hankie and dabbed her eyes. Before the war, Edwin had been a check weighman at Glass Houghton Colliery. This means he was the man elected by fellow miners to check the findings of the coal owners' weighman, where colliers are paid by weight. He supped his bitter in the taproom at the Royal Oak and liked greyhound racing. Auntie Alice told me that in the 1926 strike he described himself as a 'Bolshevik'. I once mentioned this in front of Auntie Laura. Auntie Laura was married to a civil servant, my Uncle Ray, they lived in a nice semi-detached 1930s house in Dorchester Avenue, read the *Daily Mail* and went to Bournemouth for their holidays. Auntie Laura said, 'Our Edwin was not a Bolshevik and I'll thank you very much for not mentioning the word "Bolshevik" in this house again.' Once, when I was in my teens and going to left-wing meetings at the Turks Head, I tried to tease my Aunt Laura by asking, 'Were there any Bolsheviks in the Royal Oak at Glass Hougton?' She looked straight through me, tutted and started to polish the banister rail with her hankie.

Auntie Alice holds up Edwin's photo like a compact mirror. Tears fall onto her cheeks. 'He was a very kind brother, he used to take us boating on Pontefract Park lake. In them days some of the greyhound men were cruel to their dogs, they used to slit their pads with a blade to make them run slower and then bet on an outsider. If our Edwin caught anybody doing it he'd give them a bloody good hiding.'

Auntie Alice went on to tell me how Edwin took her to a cinema at the bottom of Wilson Street called The Crown. 'He used to go there to see films starring Pola Negri, the Polish actress who was in love with Rudolph Valentino. But he took me to see Pearl White in *The Perils of Pauline*. She was always fastened to a railway line or something and you had to go back next week to see how she got away.'

Auntie Alice kisses the photo of Uncle Fred. 'Look at him, Ian. He always parted his hair nicely. And do you know he never went out of the house without polishing his shoes. He even polished underneath them, in the gap between the sole and heel.' She places the photo carefully back into the handbag.

Alice wants to put her handbag of photos away, but then finds a couple more pictures that she wants to reminisce about. 'Look, this is your granny when she's about eleven. She's feeding the geese on our auntie's farm at Barmby Moor. In the school holidays she used to go there and help out. It was her job to look after the geese and pump water from the well.'

In close order next to each other filed in the handbag are three more photos of young men in military uniform. These are Wilf, Harry and Arthur Ellis, the three and only sons of Thomas Ellis and Hannah Palfreyman of Pocklington, and brothers of Eliza Annie, Auntie Alice's mother. They smile at the camera in the formal set-up of a photographic studio just before they are waved off to the trenches of the First World War. They look like boys. 'My grandad never got over losing them,' Auntie Alice says, 'They're all in Belgium and France.'

The last photograph Alice shows me is a tiny one. It is of an old man in a battered trilby hat. He wears a dirty looking jacket and his trousers are held up with frayed string. There are four young boys on the photo with him, dressed in long shorts, jumpers with holes in and knee length socks and boots without laces. They are playing conkers.

'Grandad was a right character. He had a cart for carrying sacks of coal. When he'd done his delivery he used to get drunk on beer and then let the horse bring him home. It used to stop outside of his house and he'd be flat out on the back of the cart.'

Auntie Alice told me so many stories about my ancestors that helped me to make sense of who I am and where I'm from. She was a vegetarian a long time before it became a lifestyle choice. She seemed to live on Marks and Spencer's currant tea cakes and ground rice tarts. She thrived on Camp Coffee, the brown liquid that came in a bottle, onto which she poured boiled milk. She had two mattresses on her bed and a front room that was freezing cold. She only ever went into it on Sundays. And she told story after story.

I loved Alice all my life. I last saw her just a couple of weeks before she died.

I wake up on Boxing Day morning in 2009 with Auntie Alice in my half-dream. I don't know what the dream is about, it's just a series of images: Auntie Alice sitting on a park bench in a floral pattern frock with her arm around me and our Tony; Alice by the back window at my gran's house lifting a net curtain; on holiday with her friend Amy at the Spalding flower show; standing in the corner of her kitchen washing her legs, lifting one at a time over the pot lip of the sink. Maybe I have made this up, to explain what I do next, but I'm sure she was calling to me. The next day my friend Colin drove me to the nursing home on the other side of York where she had been living for about a year. I hadn't been to see her there yet. I don't know why. She had been taken there when the sheltered housing place she had lived in at Featherstone had become too difficult for her. She was 95, had become lost in her world and was swearing at everybody who tried to help her. She didn't seem to know or recognise people and was repeating herself using just the same few words.

At the reception desk at the nursing home, a young girl looked up from her mobile phone and said, 'Can I help?' I said, 'Yes please, I've come to see my Auntie Alice, Miss Barker.' The girl ran her finger down a sheet. 'Do you know that your Aunt isn't very well and she might not know who you are?' I smiled, 'Just tell me which room she is in please.' I had arranged to meet my half-cousin Angela, my Aunt Laura's daughter and her husband, Martin. Angela and Martin are very close to Auntie Alice. Martin came to the reception to greet me and led me down a series of corridors through a number of locked doors. He told me to prepare myself, because Aunt Alice was very confused. Angela greeted me at the door to a little breakfast room, I could see Aunt Alice sitting in a high-backed chair staring into space.

Angela turned to her. 'Look who's here Auntie Alice. You've got a visitor.' Auntie Alice carried on staring into space.

'Is that my lovely Auntie Alice,' I said in a loud voice.

'Is that our Ian?'

I leaned over to kiss her on the cheek.

'Are you busy, lad?'

'A bit, but I wanted to see you, did you have a nice Christmas?'

'Are you working? Where do you work these days?'

'I'm still writing and doing a bit of teaching.'

'Are you teaching 'em how to box eggs?'

We all laugh. Angela tells me that she hasn't lost her twinkle and sense of humour.

'Are you working, lad?'

'Yes, Auntie Alice, I'm working.'

'Are you busy?'

'A bit.'

'What're you doing here?'

'I've come to see you.'

Auntie Alice stares into a space somewhere beyond the prints of bowls of fruit on the wall.

'Is it nice?'

'What?'

'Here! Is it nice here?'

'It seems to be.'

'Are you working?'

'Not today.'

'Did you ever see that film with Tom Mix in it?'

'Which one?'

'Cement!'

'What, Tom Mix in cement?' Then I realised what I had said and laughed. And Auntie Alice laughed and I'm sure she winked at me in conspiracy for a joke that she once told me fifty years ago when we queued up outside the New Star Cinema on Aire Street in Castleford.

'Are you working?'

A young girl comes with a beaker of warm tea. The sort of beaker with a lid and spout on it that toddlers tumble around nurseries with. Auntie Alice picks up a ground rice tart, chews a bit of it and spits a piece at the girl. It hits the girl on the cheek. Angela says, 'Oh! That's naughty, Auntie Alice. Don't do things like that.'

Auntie Alice chews some more and shapes up to spit again, then looks at me and winks again. 'Shit Pot her!'

I try not to, but I laugh.

The girl scowls, tuts and walks away.

'Shit Pot!' Auntie Alice says again.

This time Angela tuts a bit. I put my hand over my mouth to disguise my laughing.

'Are you working, lad?'

'Can you remember Heather, Auntie Alice? She sends her love.'

'You never got married did you?'

'No.'

'No. I didn't either.'

Hanging on the Old Barbed Wire

My father is nursing half a pint of mild and my mother has a Babycham in one of those glasses that look like a chalice. Our Tony, our Andrew and me are playing 'tig' with a stick and rushing around the tables in the garden. My mother occasionally shouts at us, 'Go steady with that bloody stick, you'll have some bugger's eye out!' Some customers are tutting and trying to ignore us. We are staying in a bed and breakfast on Marshall Avenue in Bridlington. Every morning my dad has gone to wash his face at the sea's edge and every evening we have come to this beer garden so our mam can have a Babycham or two. In the corner of the garden beneath a tree, a young man with very long hair is laid down with his head resting on a rolled-up sleeping bag. He wears glasses like John Lennon's, has a beard like Jesus and his jeans are a patchwork of different materials sewn together. My dad declares, 'He's a bloody hippy looking for somewhere to get his head down for the night.' My mother shushes him, 'Leave the poor bugger alone.' I start to stare at this man. I walk over to where he is laying. He looks up at me and smiles. His teeth are brown, like pieces of wood in his mouth. He pulls on a roll-up. 'I've got a stick,' I say.

He looks at my stick. 'Where did you find that?'

'I found it in the sea this morning.'

He thinks for a little bit and nips his roll-up, then puts it behind his ear. 'I think it's a pirate's stick.'

I look at him again. He smiles with his wooden teeth. 'Are you a pirate?'

He scratches at his beard. 'No, man, I'm just a wanderer, just a wanderer.'

I go back to our table. My father asks, 'What did Creeping Moses want?'

'Nowt.'

'Well keep away from him, you don't know where he's been and you might catch summat. Did he ask for any money?'

'No.'

'Well don't give him any, he's a beggar!'

My dad then shouts across to the man with the beard. 'Get your bloody hair cut and I'll meet you when the sun goes down!'

My mother just says, 'Sid!'

The man with the beard gets up and strolls off towards the cliffs. I catch up with him and tap him on the arm. 'Here, I want you to have this stick.'

He takes the stick and carries on walking, tapping the stick on the ground like Blind Pew. I watch him slowly disappear until he goes out of sight.

I have often thought about what road he would take and where my stick would go. For as long as I know I have spent time wondering where things go; objects that I've found or had given to me. These things might just be simple stuff like that stick or important things that I treasure like my Uncle's First World War diary. I like to travel backwards and forwards in time this way.

In 2009, my lad Edward went on the school history trip to the First World War battlefields. Before he went we had a look on the Commonwealth War Graves website. I wanted him to see if he could find the resting places of his three uncles; Wilf, Harry and Arthur Ellis. We established that Wilf's name was on the Menin Gate in Ypres. Eddie wrote the name down on a scrap of paper and slipped it into his wallet. Wilf had been born in Stamford Bridge, the village on the Yorkshire Wolds where nearly a thousand years ago King Harold had fought his brother Tostig Godwinson in the weeks before the Battle of Hastings. He died in the mud near Ypres on 21 June 1917.

While Edward was touring the trenches with his classmates, Heather and I took the opportunity to spend a few days in Florence. As we were queuing outside the Uffizi Gallery my mobile phone rang. It was Eddie, 'I've found my Great-Great-Great-Uncle Wilf, Dad. I've taken a photo on my iPhone of his name on the Menin Gate. He's on Panel 21!'

'I bet it was a bit moving, eh? Did you see the band play?'

'Yes, I did. I won't stop on. It's expensive to phone from Belgium to Italy and I've hardly got any credit left.'

Heather and I were standing in the queue next to a young woman from Korea. I told Heather the story and the young woman said, 'If there are two more brothers, you should search for them too.'

I made a promise to myself at that moment, that one day I would track down the last resting places of Wilf's brothers, Harry and Arthur, and lay some flowers on behalf of my Auntie Alice.

I'm on my way to the First World War battlefields, with a strange fantasy in my head that I might be able to track down my great-great-uncles' final resting places. I had absolutely no idea of how to start, or even what this kind of project would entail. I was happy with the thought that I could see the final post being played at the Menin Gate. I was also thrilled that my companions on this trip would be my old mate Tony Lumb, who had done years of research of men from Featherstone who had fallen in the First World War, and his mate John, who told me that he had become interested in the First World War after his alcoholic brother had sold his grandad's medals 'for some ale'.

John told me that his grandad was one of a wave of coal miners who were conscripted to dig tunnels at Passchendale. 'They promised the coal miners six bob a day to sign up for the Royal Engineers and a lot from round here went. When they got to the trenches, they found they'd been tricked and they were put on two and a tanner. So they went on strike. Imagine that! Going on bloody strike in the middle of all that lot.'

John is interrupted by an announcement over the coach's PA system. 'Good morning ladies and gentlemen, I hope you will all have a good trip...' The microphone fades and the man making the announcement taps it with his fingers, 'Testing... testing... one... two... come on you bloody thing... Hello. Hello, can you hear me?' It's like a Norman Collier sketch. 'Yes, right, well, we will be selling teas or coffees if you prefer... we have hot chocolate... we have got some hot chocolate haven't we, Peter? Yes, tea, coffee and chocolate also horange and happle juice.'

Tony nudges me. 'Just to let you know, we'll be having this cabaret all the way to Belgium.'

I smile. I had been thinking that this might be a solemn trip, but I could see now that I needn't have worried. '...and on Saturday ladies and gentlemen, we shall be having our lunch at the Old Blighty tea rooms near the Somme. In a moment my assistant will come round with a menu. Please tick your preference. You can have ham, cheese, paté or tuna with mayonnaise and sweetcorn. Please don't change your mind or forget what you ordered as last August when we came some people who ordered ham took cheese and the vegetarians ended up with paté.'

The whole coach starts to laugh. John nudges me and says, 'Serves the buggers right!'

'...and on Sunday I shall come round and ask you what you would like for lunch at the Three Pigeons pub in Albert. I must warn you, they have a limited menu there with it being a pub, so if you don't like ham you can have cheese. Now in a moment I shall be putting on a film about Captain Noel Chavasse who won two Victoria Crosses, one at the Somme and one near Ypres. I shall be showing you his grave at Brandhoek when we get there. It is the only gravestone in the world with two Victoria Crosses on it. Thank you.'

In Ypres they sell chocolate, abbey beers, tobacco and 'over the top' tours to people from all over Britain who are searching for their ancestors in beautifully kept war cemeteries with manicured lawns. Nearby, at a place called Sanctuary Wood, a huge fat man sits on a stool behind a counter sweating. This is 'Fat Jacques', John tells me he is one of the richest men in Belgium. He looks like he needs a change of clothes and a good bath. His swollen ankles are heavily bandaged and he waits to take a tenner from First War tourists. In exchange you get to see the trenches at the back of his bungalow, uniforms, piles of shrapnel, and weapons of various sizes that lie in rusting piles all over the shop.

He will tell you that his grandfather opened this 'tribute to the brave heroes' in 1924, when everybody else was trying to forget the war.

'The government want to take it all off me, but I am a tough guy and they will never get it,' he tells me when I ask him about his 'museum'.

Fat Jacques' scrapyard reminds me of a woodyard my dad bought from a dignified old-timer called Dave. This Dave used to sell bundles of firewood door-to-door, for a lot of years. When Dave retired, my dad made him an offer out of an interim payment on his compensation.

The woodyard was really an overgrown allotment lined with rotting fence posts that looked like sore thumbs sticking out. There was a big shed with an earthen floor, and in the centre of this shed was an ancient circular saw that terrified me every time it was cranked up. Hanging from the walls on rusting nails were even more ancient saws of various sizes, planes, adzes and other woodworking tools that had gone out with the ark. There was a work bench with three or four vices bolted to it, one was like a round clamp with a long steel handle attached to it. You put freshly chopped sticks of wood into the round clamp, pulled down on the handle to clamp them and fastened the bundle with lengths of thin, bendable wire. My dad showed me how to do the firewood bundles and, once I got the hang of it, I could do sixty an hour. We were like a conveyor belt, my father and me, when we prepared firewood. He sat on a low stool with a sharpened axe and chopped the sticks on the end of an old tree stump and I gathered them for bundling.

'Make sure you wind that wire tight, lad, they'll be no use to nobody if they don't stick together. And watch your bloody fingers!' He said this every time I tried to take the sticks from too close to where he was chopping. 'Tha'll be no good to a piano wi'out them.'

On Saturday teatimes I filled a homemade barrow with bundles and went knocking on doors. I sold firewood to people who built hearth-grate pyramids from screwed-up newspaper, sticks and coal to warm their houses.

The woodyard became my dad's museum when he started moving his collections to a series of drawers under the work bench. He had one for cigarette cards, one for broken toys, and another for pieces of lost and broken jewelry. One day I saw him using a thin rat-tail file wrapped in emery paper to enlarge the ring our Tony had found on the beach at Blackpool. He held it up to a beam of sunlight that was coming in through a gap in the planks.

'Nice ring that, lad, I might let thee have it one day and if this business ever takes off tha can have that an' all when I'm done.'

I looked at the spells in my fingers and muck under my nails and wanted to tell him that I wasn't planning to be a firewood monger, but I thought it might hurt his feelings so I just grinned.

'What's that grinning at now, Cheshire?'

'Nowt.'

'Well here, I've summat to show thi.'

My dad brought out from one of the drawers a drawing he'd done in blunt pencil. The drawing was on the cut-out back of a cornflakes packet, two Clydesdale horses pulling a field gun across the mud. It was good; you could see the strain on the horses.

'Take it to school and tell 'em that thy's drawn it.'
'I can't do that!'
'Why?'
'Because you've drawn it.'
'They won't know t'difference.'
'I will.'
'Well trace the bugger then.'

I didn't know what to expect on this trip. I had three names in my mind. Wilf, Harry and Arthur Ellis. Men who I had seen once or twice in First World War military uniform on photos that Auntie Alice kept in an old handbag. I had a photo that Edward had taken on his iPhone of Wilf's name on the Menin Gate earlier in the year, and now I had seen it with my own eyes as I listened to the local fire brigade band play. I had no idea where Harry and Arthur were buried and the search I had done on the Commonwealth War Graves website had given me no clues. I was on a bus with fifty or so people, all of whom were armed with the cemetery, row number and grave number of their relatives. We were due to stop at more than a dozen cemeteries in Belgium and France. Each of these cemeteries has a directory kept in a box in the wall of its gateway. The chance of me finding one of my ancestors was slim, but I checked every directory at every cemetery we visited and then I started to listen to the stories of my fellow travellers. When the banter on board the bus started to subside and I got used to the 'tourism' industry that had sprung up around the First War battlefields, it became a very moving journey.

We drove down narrow country lanes where farm labourers still pitchfork hay onto stooks. Then, at the opening to a muddy lane, the coach would stop. Our tour guide took to his microphone to announce, 'Sheila, Rosemary and Tom, this is your visit, the rest of you, please allow them to get off first.'

At a cemetery called St Catherine's, I walk alongside a woman from Huddersfield called Joyce. She had come to find the grave of her grandfather, her mother's father. We found the gravestone between us, she placed a small posy of flowers in front of it and a photo of her mother. I took her picture for her on her mobile phone.

'My mother was four years old when her dad was called up. She told me that she could remember a man in gaiters and then a black-edged telegram coming not long after.'

I asked her if she knew how he died.

'My mother told me that he was blown off his horse. My mother died not too long since. Before she died she was sorting out a cupboard at home. She found his photo and put it into a frame and set it on the sideboard. She said, "It's about time I got to know him, I might be meeting him again soon."'

Joyce leaned the framed photo of her grandad up against the stone. 'After my mam died I promised myself that I'd come.'

I left Joyce to her thoughts and wandered round the rest of the cemetery. At the far wall I sat in the sun and looked down the row after row of simple white stones. My friend Tony was poking about in the ploughed field just over the wall. He picked something up and held it up to the light.

'What is it, Tony?'

'Another bullet. I don't think this one found anybody, it's still unspent.'

Tony told me that even more than ninety years after the First War ended the local farmers still find things and in some parts they still fit cages around their ploughs. 'They call it the iron harvest.'

At a cemetery called Tyne Cott there are 47,000 names on the register. Soldiers from Newcastle and the North East fought here. They called it Tyne Cott because the farm labourers' cottages reminded them of the cottages they knew back home on the banks of the River Tyne.

There are a lot of stones here that say on them simply 'A soldier of the First World War'. I start to wonder if any of these could be one of my ancestors. I stop walking to look at some roses, they are the deepest shades of red I have ever seen. A little breeze blows across, moves the roses and the scent comes to my nose. I start to weep and take out my hankie to dab at my eyes. Our tour guide is just over on the next row. He looks across and says, 'Aye… it does that to you sometimes. We all know that one. Come back to the bus when you're ready, there's no rush.'

At the South African memorial at Delville Woods, our tour guide tells us that one of the South African regiments brought a baboon to the war. 'It had its own uniform and could salute and everything. It caught some shrapnel at Delville and lost its leg, so they discharged it wounded. They sent it to Blighty to recuperate and it toured up and down selling kisses and hand shakes to raise funds.'

Later that day we go to eat at a place called The Crocodile round the corner from our hotel. Tony, John and I order three steaks, and John tells the waiter in very slow English, 'If it's 'oss meat, make sure tha teks its saddle off first.' The waiter looks at John, then at Tony and then me. He shrugs and walks away shaking his head. John says, 'I bet he hasn't understood a bloody word I've said, I'm liable to get a knickerbocker glory.'

On our way back to the hotel we bump into two lads from Leicester who have been somewhere else to eat. One of them says to us, 'We went to McDonalds, but none of 'em could speak English, you'd think they'd make a bit more effort when they're serving English food!'

My own grandad was a dispatch rider in the Royal Army Service Corps. I still have his five medals in the original box they came in. After the box was opened, I don't think he looked at them more than half a dozen times. He certainly never wore them. One Remembrance Sunday I said to him, 'Have you ever been to the service at the war memorial?'

He didn't answer. My gran looked across at me. She put her finger to her mouth.

I carried on, 'I just thought that you might like to put your medals on and remember some of your mates.'

He still didn't say anything. He didn't even look up from his *Sunday Mirror*.

My gran said, 'That's enough now.'

I persisted, 'Well, a lot of other people do it.'

My grandad chucked his paper onto the table. 'Let me tell thee this once young man. A lot of them simple buggers who will be standing to attention this morning didn't drink water out of wells in the bloody desert like me. Wells with bloody rotting goats in 'em. They weren't at the Qattara depression when them guns opened up at El Alamein that morning. I can still hear them now. They called it the "devil's garden". Let me tell thee, tha wouldn't want to be in that garden. I want nothing to do with remembering that bloody lot, so don't ask me and don't ask me to wear my medals, you can throw 'em in the bin for all I care.'

He went back to his paper. I listened to him breathing heavy, then he started coughing and spat some black spit into the fire.

My gran said, 'You shouldn't set your grandad off like that, Ian, it doesn't do him any good. I thought for a long time that he wouldn't come home, especially after we lost our Edwin and Fred. And bear in mind we lost all of my mam's brothers in the First War, there's no wonder her dad went funny and started drinking.'

I have thought over the years about my gran's mother, Eliza Annie. She lost her only three brothers within the space of months in the First War. Then within just three months in the Second War she received two telegrams telling her that her only two sons had been killed. In between her father had drunk himself into oblivion.

My gran's brother, Edwin, was a Corporal in The Royal Engineers, 612 Field Squadron. He looks tall and handsome with his military cap almost stuck to the side of his head. On 21 September 1944 the allies liberated the Dutch village of Nederweert in Limburg about twenty miles south east of

Eindhoven. The German army didn't retreat and for two months after the front lines were very close. There were casualties most days on patrols and from minefields. One day Edwin was working to clear mines from a bridge. The bridge blew up.

During the autumn of 1944, when Edwin was trying to diffuse bombs on Dutch bridges, his younger brother Fred was in Antwerp, Belgium. Fred was a gunner in the Garrison Regiment of The Royal Artillery. For months up until Christmas of that year V-2 rockets rained down on Antwerp, leading the press at the time to dub it 'The City of Sudden Death'. One Saturday afternoon just before Christmas, The Rex Cinema in Antwerp showed the Cecil B. DeMille film *The Plainsman* with Gary Cooper and Jean Arthur. The cinema was packed with up to 1,200 people, many of them soldiers. About a quarter of an hour into the film, just as Gary Cooper received news of the massacre of General Custer at The Little Big Horn, the Rex Cinema was hit by a V-2 rocket. The balcony collapsed and the highest number of casualties recorded in a single V-2 bombing of the Second World War occurred. Over 300 soldiers lost their lives. Gunner Frederick Barker, aged 32, was one of the victims. Fred died of his wounds after Christmas. He is buried in a suburb of Antwerp called Schoonselhof.

I was once talking to Richard van Riel, a friend of mine, who was for many years the curator at Pontefract Museum. I don't know how it came up in conversation, but he mentioned his lucky Uncle Karl, an architect of Antwerp. Uncle Karl had also gone to the Rex Cinema that day. He sat watching Gary Cooper with his trilby on his knee. The hat slipped off and rolled between the seats. Karl stooped down to pick it up just as the bomb hit. The seats behind him were blown over the top of him and protected him from falling masonry. Karl waited until all was quiet, crawled from the rubble, dusted himself off and walked down the street to his favourite café bar. He later told Richard that none of his friends could believe that he had escaped unscathed, the only thing he lost was his hat. He recalled Gary Cooper's words just before the explosion, 'I smell danger'.

My Aunt Alice once told me, 'Our poor mam never stopped crying when they told her, she lost her only two lads in the space of three months. That's what war does, lad, it takes all the young men away from you and leaves all the women to grieve, there's nowt gained with bloody war!'

I read a version of 'Ramayana', the great Hindu epic, a retelling by the Patua artist Moyna Chitrakar of Bengal. In her story, Sita, the heroine of the tale, is rescued from imprisonment after a furious battle, by her husband Rama. Sita tells Rama, 'War, in some ways, is merciful to men. It makes them heroes if they are victors. If they are vanquished – they do not live to see their homes taken, their wives widowed. But if you are a woman, you must live through defeat.'

I tried to coax stories out of my grandad now and again. Just occasionally he opened up, but only to tell about something funny that had happened. Once I brought home a chicken madras with three chapattis. I was eating the supper when my grandad rolled in from the club with a gallon of John Smiths in him.

'What's that bloody mulloch tha's eating?'

'Curry and chapattis, do you want some?'

'I bloody don't, I ate enough of that in Egypt. And we ate it like thy does, wi'out a knife and fork.'

Before he went up to bed he told me that he was riding his motorbike through the desert when he saw black shapes in the distance. 'I thought they were bloody vultures! When I got closer I came across some Italian soldiers. I've never seen such a bloody gathering. They'd thrown their guns down and they were dressed like I don't know what.'

This desperate gaggle were starving and tried to surrender to my grandad. In a thick West Yorkshire coalfield accent he asked them, 'Well, old flower, thee tell me what I'm supposed to bloody do with you all.' Then he rode off, leaving them even more bewildered than they were to start with.

I once naively asked him if he had ever shot any Germans. He completely ignored my question and said, 'I knocked a Dutchman out in a fight when we were sailing past West Africa.' The journey out to Egypt on board ship was a long one. It took them round the Cape of Good Hope. A boxing tournament was held between the Allied troops to keep spirits up. My grandad won it by knocking out a heavyweight from Holland. My grandad's proudest moment of the war came in the winning of a fight with a man from his own side. 'I catched him a beauty right on his chin end. I nearly lifted him out of his boots.'

Many years after, in the 1980s, my grandad was woken in bed one night by an argument in the street below his bedroom window. A young drunken couple had started to argue on the way home. The argument got louder and louder. In the end my grandad lifted the bedroom curtain. In the light from a street lamp he saw the man slap his girlfriend across the face. She fell down onto our doorstep and started to cry. My grandad put his dressing gown on and flew downstairs. He opened the front door and picked up the young woman. 'Go and sit on that sofa, love.' Then he walked towards the young man, a big aggressive lad nearly fifty years my grandfather's junior. 'Does tha want to have a go with somebody who can hit thee back?'

'Fuck off, silly old bastard!'

My grandfather spat on his hands and said, 'Come on then old cock, put 'em up.' He went by memory into a south paw stance, not realising that fighting styles in the street had changed since his days.

The young man leapt into the air and kicked my grandfather kung fu style. He then followed up with a knee to the face as my grandad doubled.

What he didn't expect was what happened next. My grandad

straightened up, put his fists either side of his head and laughed. 'Right, young 'un. Tha's had a go, but I'm sorry to have to tell thi that tha's going to have to do a bit better than that.' In the blink of an eye he snaked out a left to the chin and a right to the nose. The lad's legs buckled and he went down like a sack of potatoes. The lad's girlfriend screamed, 'Leave him alone please, he's sorry!'

My grandad pulled the lad to his feet, his nose was badly broken and bleeding. 'Right cock, if thy's sorry, I want to hear it. Tell this young girl that you're sorry!'

'I'm sorry!'

'Good lad. Now get off home and if I hear that thy has touched her again thy will have to have some more.'

A few days later, the young man's father came knocking on my grandad's door. It turned out that the lad he had hit was the son of someone he drank in the club with.

'You've sickened my lad, Ted. He's been laid on the settee for two days.'

My grandad simply said, 'Tell him to learn some manners.'

The man walked away. My grandad came in and said, 'I don't know what all the fuss is about. I didn't catch him half as hard as I clipped that Dutchman.'

I collected cards from packets of Brooke Bond tea. They did a series about famous Britons. General Montgomery was one. I said to my grandad, 'You knew Montgomery didn't you, Grandad?' He laughed and said, 'Did I buggery!'

'I thought he was your general?'

'He was, but I didn't know him!'

'Didn't he ever speak to you?'

'Oooh! Aye. At the start of the battle of El Alamein he came up and said, "Right, Ted old love, pick up thi rifle and come and shoot some Nazis for me."' Then he winked.

Vote the Bastards Out

Some of my earliest television memories are of seeing the misty black-and-white images of Churchill's funeral. For years I thought the mistiness was because, according to my dad, 'we had a worn out tube' on our telly. I've since found out it was a foggy day.

My grandfather is booing the television coverage. 'What are they all crying and upset for? I'm glad the old swine has gone!' My gran nods her agreement.

My grandfather cannot abide Churchill. He says that Churchill hates coal miners, that he was responsible for killing two unarmed colliers in Featherstone in 1893. He wasn't, but you can't tell my grandad that. He also says that Churchill ordered troops to open fire on striking miners at Tonypandy in the Rhondda Valley, after he sent the cavalry in.

My grandfather turns his back on the funeral pictures. 'Turn the bloody television off, Hilda! I don't want to see it! All this bloody nonsense for that thing!' My grandad saved the word 'thing' for the people he really couldn't stand. Churchill was a 'thing'. Later, and said with equal venom, Margaret Thatcher became a 'thing' and also 'a creature'. A man who once stole his pint of beer in the Girnhill Lane Club was 'nowt but a thing', he also got a punch in the face for being a thief as well as a 'thing'.

My gran turns off the television and places a folded cloth over it, as though to completely shut out any trace of an image of Churchill's funeral being accidentally beamed into our front room. She then sits on the chair beneath her budgie's cage and tells her favourite anecdote about the woman she calls a thing.

'Lady Astor was another... she once asked, "Do they let the

coal miner's out of the pit everyday?'" She puts on what she thinks is a posh voice. She is not used to talking without the glottal pauses that her dialect demands, so it sounds doubly funny, the dark humour of the actual words combine with the way she pronounces them, to make a sentence that at first makes us laugh and then makes us think, and you end up feeling sad at the same time as smiling.

I don't know who told her that Lady Astor said that, I'm not sure that Lady Astor did say it, perhaps if she didn't she would have done if she thought of it. It's just one of those likely apocryphal tales that are passed around our area, like the one Mick Appleyard told me, a friend and former union man from Sharlston Pit.

Mick is talking to me about Winston Churchill. 'Churchill and Lady Astor were invited to a shoot on the Nostell Priory Estate. In them days Nostell Pit backed on to the woods. They were walking down the edge of these woods with their shotguns bent over their arms. They saw a gang of black-bright young lads of about fourteen dressed in filthy rags. These lads were scurrying home from the pit to their mams. Lady Astor says to Churchill, "What on earth are they?"' He puts on a posh voice to imitate Astor. 'And Churchill says, "They are coal miners." So Astor says,' posh voice again, '"Oh! My goodness, are we allowed to take a pot at them."'

I ask Mick, 'Is that true?'

Mick says, 'I don't know, lad, but if it isn't true it ought to be!'

I ask Mick, 'If a lot of people in this country worship Churchill as a hero, why do people like you and my grandfather despise him?'

Mick shrugs, 'I can't say as I've ever met anybody who liked Churchill, apart from Tommy Mottram and he was the pit manager.'

I learn a lot of things from Mick Appleyard, he was the union man at my grandfather's pit. A lifelong communist, Mick took holidays in Hungary when it was still behind an unmelted iron curtain. He has an encyclopaedic knowledge of the pits in Yorkshire and at one time would have been able to navigate his way around the county by observing the colliery head gears. He told me that Pope and Pearsons mine at Whitwood was known as 'The Holy Dumpling' on account of the number of Methodists who worked there. He also told me that St John's Pit in Normanton was known as the Irishman's pit because there was a train service straight from the docks at Liverpool to Normanton and that J.J. Charlesworth named the pits he owned in the South Leeds area, 'Fanny', 'Jane' and 'Rose' after his three daughters.

Mick's father, Tom Appleyard, was sacked from Ackton Hall pit after the 1926 strike for being a militant. He found work at the old fashioned Snydale Victoria Colliery where the work was hard and dangerous. 'Do you know, lad, my dad told me that they called that pit "The Bread and Herring" because it was that badly paid you could get five shifts in and still make a claim off the parish relief.'

The union secretary at Snydale was Joe Harper, who later went on to become our MP. Mick told me that after Joe Harper became the MP he rode up to Snydale Colliery in a black, chauffeur driven limousine. 'I'm not sure if it didn't have a flag on it,' says Mick. 'My dad was coming off his shift and Joe greeted him, "I'm pleased to see you, Tom." My dad said, "Well I can't say as I am pleased to see thee, Joe. And from now on, when I see thee in thi big car, I shall call thee Joseph, because thy is now a man with a coat of many colours."'

It's just before the General Election in 2010 and I'm in the taproom of The Shoulder of Mutton, a back street boozer in Castleford. It's teatime and there's three or four of us stood at the bar supping pints of Tetley's bitter. Pete and Martin, two brothers, have been on day shift at the malt kilns, they're still in their muck and have been for a swill at the hand basin in the Gents' lavatory. They are throwing darts with clean hands now. Another Pete, a retired bricklayer, sits in his usual seat by the door, he's reading the obituary column in the *Pontefract and Castleford Express*. On a high stool at the corner of the bar sits Alf. Alf is a former slaughterhouse man and miner who's usually got plenty to say for himself. Today he is tuned into a little hand-held television trying to find out whether a horse he's backed in the late race at Kempton has come in.

An election broadcast on behalf of the Conservative Party comes on the little screen. Alf switches off the telly. I say, 'No, leave it, Alf, let's see what they've got to say.' All heads turn to me and there is a silence. A silence full of unspoken questions, hanging like a dart about to leave a hand on its way to a double.

Alf is the first to let fly, 'What the fucking hell do you want to listen to that shite for?'

'Well, I was always taught to know your enemy,' and I grin. Alf nods, laughs, shakes his head and turns the telly back on. Martin misses his double and mutters 'bollocks' under his breath. His brother announces, 'You want five in bits.' Pete folds up his paper and orders another pint.

The gist of the Tory broadcast is, 'Just because your parents and grandparents have always voted Labour, doesn't mean that you have to do the same.' They show a quick cut edit of various talking heads showing what purport to be working-class people who say they have always voted Labour, but that now 'it is time for a change'.

Alf starts to mutter to himself and then, out of nowhere, announces, 'Well, the bloody, blinding, fucking, thick-skinned, enamel bastards. They're not content with breeding their own, they want us to fucking breed voters for 'em now!' And this time he switches his telly off and puts it into his coat pocket. 'Knackers to the Tories and bollocks to the last race at Kempton and fill this glass for me landlord!'

The first time I ever voted was in a by-election. Joe Harper, who had been our MP since the early 1960s, had died in office. Geoff Lofthouse, another man from my home town and a former coal miner and rugby league player for Featherstone Rovers, was selected by the Labour Party to take his place. When I went to the ballot box for that election in the autumn of 1978, I saw three names: the Tory was called Hugo, the Liberal was Leslie something or other and there was Geoff Lofthouse.

Pontefract was the first town in Britain to have a secret ballot after the passing of the Ballot Act in 1872. At a by-election in August of that year, Hugh Childers became the first man to be elected this way. They sealed the ballot box with a liquorice Pontefract Cake. Almost 106 years to that day I stood with my voting slip and a bookie's pencil in my hand in the booth. There is a saying round our way that has it that they don't count the votes for Labour, they weigh them. Some people say, 'If they put a red coat on a donkey it would win.' I looked at my slip. I put my cross next to Geoff, mainly because I knew that my grandfather would never forgive me if I did any other, but also because at the time I was reading Woody Guthrie's book *Bound for Glory* and listening to his songs. There was one song in particular that I loved, still do, called 'Pretty Boy Floyd'.

Yes, as through this world I've wandered
I've seen lots of funny men
Some will rob you with a six-gun
And some with a fountain pen.

I guessed that Geoff Lofthouse was less likely to rob me with a fountain pen than representatives of the other two parties. At the time I was working in an iron foundry, grinding the flashings from castings at a grinding wheel on the night shift.

The Anti-Nazi League had a meeting at Pontefract Town Hall. The speakers on the podium were Paul Foot, Arthur Scargill and somebody from the Socialist Workers Party, whose name I can't recall now. I went to the meeting because I was aware of a burgeoning Rock Against Racism movement amongst a lot of the punk bands who were my favourites at the time and because I wanted to hear what Arthur Scargill had to say. It was my first ever public meeting and a Pontefract doctor pushed a piece of paper into my hand at the end. It was an invitation to a meeting of the Socialist Workers Party the following Wednesday. The doctor was Jean Lewis, the former wife of the artist Brian Lewis, who became a great friend and mentor in the years after.

I go along to the meeting, it's in a scruffy back room of a pub called The Turks Head. The SWP meeting starts half an hour late. I come to realise later that helping to start the revolution is rarely about being on time. Everybody smokes roll-ups, not everybody has a packet of Rizla, so mine gets handed round. The Whitbread's Trophy keg beer is horrible, there's a lot of whispering going on and I'm not sure what to make of it all. There is a young woman here who tells me that she likes my hair and my lumberjack shirt. She then takes me to one side in the passage and says that she can see the colour of peoples' auras and that my aura is a well-defined mauve. No one has ever told me up to press that I have a well-defined aura, mauve or otherwise. The upshot of the meeting is that the Pontefract branch of the SWP will organise a coach to join in with the first Anti-Nazi League Carnival in Hackney, East London. X-Ray Spex, The Clash and the Tom Robinson Band are to play, so I sign up for a place on the bus. On the way from Trafalgar Square to the Victoria Park in Hackney, a big fat copper from the Metropolitan Police knocks me onto my arse. I bite my tongue and my mouth fills up with blood. In the scheme of things, the knock I take from the copper is not anywhere near on par with the knocks I felt whilst trying to be a rugby league player, but I feel politically christened, especially when the woman who talks about 'auras' screams 'Fascist Pig' at the copper.

At the next meeting of the SWP I wear the same lumberjack shirt after pulling it out from the bottom of my gran's Ali Baba wash basket and take a spare packet of Rizla. This time the talk is of sending delegates to the Marxism conference at North London Polytechnic. I volunteer for that as well. In order to prepare, I buy a selection of buff coloured paperbacks that are printed in China by the Foreign Language Press. The books are recommended to me by a man with a long beard who smells of camphor balls. I buy *Preface and introduction to a contribution to the critique of Political Economy* by Karl Marx, *The State and Revolution* by V.I. Lenin and *The Principles of Communism* by Frederick Engels.

In the Turks Head at Pontefract the man with the beard and odour of camphor balls takes my coins, drops them into an old fashioned pint glass with a handle on it and then goes to the bar for another pint of Whitbread Trophy bitter. He says, 'You might need to read them a couple of times, comrade, before you get the gist.'

I don't think I ever got round to reading them. I carried them about in the pockets of a greasy ex-army jacket for a bit. Many years later I am shown Engels' house in Wuppertal by my friend, Jürgen Bredebusch. He asks me, 'Do you know much about Engels?' I say, 'I've got a couple of his books at home.'

For the week of the Marxism '78 conference I stay at the house of some International Socialists in Crouch End. The house is an old Victorian place on three floors, filled with what these days is called 'shabby chic'. The couple who live there are a teacher and a social worker, who helps to build adventure playgrounds on his Saturdays off. The teacher drinks red wine from Hungary like it's going out of fashion, tells me that I've got 'a cute accent' and feeds me vegetarian lasagne every night. She wears a beret in the house and has a tattoo of Chairman Mao on her shoulder. One night the phone rings in the early hours. I am sleeping on an old Chesterfield sofa in a room adjacent to the corridor. The phone carries on ringing, I decide to answer it, pull on yesterday's underpants and make for the corridor. I am just beaten to the phone by the teacher who stands there shivering and naked. She embarks on a conversation with an American delegate to the conference who has missed her flight from Boston or somewhere. The teacher crosses her legs and scratches at her pubic hair. She is still wearing her beret. I go back to the Chesterfield and switch off the lamp. I'm nicely back to sleep when the big light comes on. It's the teacher. 'I've made some camomile tea.' She sits on a buffet next to the couch and offers me a mug of the tea. She is still naked apart from the beret.

'Which lecture will you attend today?'

'I haven't made up my mind yet.'

'Well you should go to Tony Cliff's talk about the POUM in the Spanish Civil War.'

'Thanks for the recommendation, I'll give it a try.'

We sip our camomile. There is a clock on the wall, a punch clock that looks like it came from a factory. I listen to it ticking.

The teacher says, 'Are you looking at my breasts?'

I say, 'Well it's difficult not to notice them.'

'Well look, comrade, there are oppressed people the world over, there are children starving for want of milk, workers denied even the most basic human rights and comrades in arms willing to lay down their lives in Nicaragua, while you ogle my tits.'

'I'm sorry.'

The teacher stands up, farts loudly and carries her mug of camomile upstairs.

I snuggle down into my sleeping bag and in the distance hear the flush of the lavatory. The phone rings again. I ignore it.

I didn't have much to do with the SWP after that. Not because I didn't like them, it was just that the beer in the Blackmoor

Head was much better than the piss they served in The Turks. And I mixed with a different crowd in there, people of very different age groups who mostly smoked their own tobacco and bought their own ale.

But something that really put the tin hat on my flirtation with the SWP happened when I invited one of the women to my house. I had a lovely little wickerwork basket with a Busy Lizzy plant pot inside it. This woman made a really big fuss over the basket. She kept saying, 'Oooh! It's like, so beautiful, who crafted such a thing.'

I told her that I bought it from a junk shop.

Then she said, 'I have decided that you should give me it as a gift.'

'But I like it too, I don't really want to part with it, because I haven't got many things in this house.'

She got all indignant. 'Well look here, comrade. I believe in the destiny of beautiful things and that wickerwork basket has been waiting for me to own it. Morally it already belongs to me because I like it more than you.'

'How do you make that out?'

'It needs to be appreciated.'

'Well I appreciate it!'

'Not as much as I do.'

'Well, I'm sorry, I don't want to let it go.'

At which point she slumped onto the sofa and in a little girly voice said, 'You are a selfish materialist, a product of capitalism like all the rest.' And then she took out a tissue and pretended to cry.

I gave her a spare copy of The Grateful Dead's *Workingmans' Dead* LP. She didn't even say thank you.

On the Saturday morning we were giving out leaflets for a forthcoming Rock against Racism gig at Pontefract Town Hall. She refused to speak to me.

In the pub later, she let me buy her three pints of Woodpecker cider and then told me that she had made a plant pot holder out of the LP. She asked me to roll her a cigarette and before she had got even halfway down it, she asked for another. I rolled another. She scooped it up and said, 'You could have put a bit more tobacco in it, the problem with you, comrade, is that you don't like sharing.'

Then she put her Afghan coat on and said, 'See you around.'

In 1979 I am still standing at a grinding wheel taking sharp flashings off castings in the iron foundry. Halfway through the afternoon shift it starts to snow heavily. The management put out a message, 'The last bus to Leeds will leave in ten minutes, those who live that way on can go home now or work a double shift through the night if they wish to stay.' Brian Hood complains to the union man that what's good for them at Leeds should be the same for them who live in Castleford. He wants to work a double shift as well. The union man reminds Brian that he only lives in the next street and that the weather won't prevent him getting home. Brian is insisting on 'fair do's' and is permitted to work a double'un, for no other reason than he wants to be the same as 'them from Leeds'. This is the year that Thatcher comes to power and the year that I decide I won't vote for anybody, because whoever you vote for the bastards get in.

My dad never voted for anybody in his life. My mother once wanted to send a postcard to *Opportunity Knocks* to vote for two singers she liked called Millican & Nesbitt, two coal miners who sang 'Vaya con Dios'. My dad dissuaded her, he told her it was a waste of a stamp and, besides, she would only encourage them. At the elections I heard him say that he would like to shove Harold Wilson's pipe up his own arse. I don't know why he said that, I'm not sure he did either. Another time we were doing a quiz and he got mixed up between Enoch Powell and Yuri Gagarin, he announced that 'Enoch Powell was the first man to orbit the earth'. I've often reflected on the irony of a man who avoided marking 'X' on official documents, but that's exactly what he marked on numerous sickness benefit forms and insurance policies which my mother countersigned for him.

Throughout the Thatcher years I ignore voting day. During the poll-tax demonstrations I am taken to court for non-payment. The Magistrates' Court attached to Castleford Police Station is pressed into service for the first time in years to deal with the sheer numbers of people round our way who refuse to pay. It's like a conveyor belt of humanity, put up before the courts by postal code. Before I get called I hear the name and address of every single person who lives in the odd numbers on one particular street in Featherstone. Then after they have been dealt with, I hear every even number from the same street.

The magistrate leans forward and sucks one of the arms on his glasses. 'Have you anything to say for yourself, Mr Clayton?' I have prepared a written speech, but when I feel in my pocket for it I can't find it, so I just make it up as I go along.

'I don't see why I, living in a flat above a hardware shop in Station Lane, should be expected to pay the same tax as Lord St Oswald at Nostell Priory. It is a disgraceful tax and, and, anyhow I'm not paying it!'

The magistrate leans forward, sucks his glasses again and then says, 'Some of the points you make will be better addressed at the ballot box.'

'I don't vote.'

'Well, Mr Clayton, I suggest that you avail yourself of that opportunity at the next election. Next!'

I didn't avail myself and, during the Blair years, I remained just as disenchanted. Then one night I was staying over at Alan Plater's house in London. I was there because a documentary series I had presented was nominated for an ITV regional-television award at a lecture theatre at the Savoy Hotel. The awards were quite flashy, presented by Alistair Stewart, the newsreader, who was having a fag on the doorstep of the Savoy

Place as we went in. When they showed me to my seat smack bang in the middle of a long row of cinema style seats, I knew I hadn't won. I said to my director and friend, Jane Hickson, 'I don't think we'll be going up to collect anything.' She asked me how I knew. 'There's too many pairs of legs to climb over from where we are sitting.' We didn't win.

Back at Alan's house, Shirley, Alan's wife, a woman I take great inspiration from, was floating about in oriental silk. She served lamb and mint sauce for dinner at 10 o'clock at night. We drank champagne. Shirley said, 'It was going to be opened whatever the outcome.' And then Alan reached for one of his best bottles of Highland Park malt. Alan and Shirley have an affinity for the Orkney Islands and stock up with their favourite tipple every time they go. I always know what to get Alan for his birthday. We talk about Frank Randle, a madcap Northern comedian from the 1930s, who both Alan and I share a passion for. We move on to Music Hall, to the fortunes of Hull and Hull KR rugby league clubs, to Hull City and their move from their ancestral home at Boothferrry Park and then we move on to Billie Holiday and Duke Ellington. Alan blows the dust from an old LP and plays a track called 'Harlem Air Shaft', it's one of his favourites. The phone rings, Shirley answers it. Alan turns down the volume on his record player. We listen to Shirley on the cordless telephone. 'Oh! How nice to hear from you... Yes, Yes, Alan is well... and you... oh! Wonderful... Yes, we have guests at the moment, but Alan will be thrilled to talk to you.' Shirley passed the handset to Alan and says, 'Elliot Gould, darling.' Alan lights up two cigarettes at the same time, one for him and one for Shirley. He takes the phone and says, 'Hello, Elliot!' It is a bizarre and surreal moment. I'm one hour after my first ever TV awards ceremony, still dressed in an ill-fitting dinner suit with burgundy coloured bow tie, listening to Duke Ellington, while pulling on a roll-up and Alan Plater is sitting at his dinner table taking a transatlantic call from one of Hollywood's finest. Alan and Elliot Gould became friends after he appeared in the lead role of one of Alan's TV plays, a wonderful piece called *Doggin' Around* about the adventures of a washed-up jazz pianist on one last tour of the seedier joints of northern England.

After the phone call and as Duke Ellington reaches his run out groove, Alan looks for something that he wants to play for me. It is a track by an Australian men's choir called The Spooky Men's Chorale. The track is called 'Vote the Bastards Out', a very repetitive ear worm of a song that builds to a crescendo from the words 'vote... vote... vote... vote the bastards... vote the bastards... vote the bastards out'. The song puts a seed in my mind and by the time I hear the song again some years later when The Spooky Men's Chorale appear at Cambridge Festival, the seed has grown. I make my mind up on a grassy field beside Cherry Hinton Hall in Cambridgeshire that if I can't vote the bastards in, I can do my bit and vote the bastards out.

Thatcher's government changed the constituency boundaries. My home town was moved out of the Pontefract constituency and into Hemsworth, Britain's safest Labour stronghold. Geoff Lofthouse, the man whose name I put my first ever cross by, continued to represent the Pontefract constituency until he was shuffled into the House of Lords just before Blair came in. He became 'Lord Lofthouse of Pontefract'. I think he should have been 'of Featherstone', the town where he was born, but who knows how these things work.

I did a Yorkshire Television series called *My Yorkshire*, which profiled various Yorkshire people and looked at their life. We did an episode with Geoff in the House of Lords. We persuaded him to put on his full regalia including a three-cornered hat for the camera. Geoff looks a bit uncomfortable in his outfit and there's a flunkey faffing about after him, making sure that he looks right. As we pass the wool sack in the chamber, Geoff says, 'I'm very proud y'know, that I am the only man to have been the speaker in both houses.' I say to him, 'Could you have ever imagined when you were growing up in Stewpot Row, that one day you would be saying that to a television crew?' I think Geoff misunderstands my question and says, 'Well, I believe there is a need for some sort of reforming chamber, whether it be an elected one or an appointed one, you have to have something to check and balance.'

Geoff grew up at his gran's house in Stewpot Row after his father dropped dead in a field. His mother was ordered to leave her tied cottage by the landowner, even before the funeral. Geoff became a coal miner, a councillor, a mayor, an MP and, finally, a Lord. He remained a lifelong supporter of Featherstone Rovers and campaigned tirelessly on behalf of coal miners. The inscription on the coat of arms they made for Geoff when he became a Lord says, 'Stick and Lift'. A reference to helping fellow workers down the pit when a heavy load needed shifting.

He was very proud when he showed me around the Speaker's apartments, his office and even the chamber of the House of Lords. They weren't sitting that day and he let me touch the wool sack. At lunchtime he invited me to the House of Lords' dining room. A table had been reserved and a fussing flunkey came fluttering around us. He was just about to launch into a list of the day's special dishes, when Geoff lifted his hand and said, 'Save your breath, brother. We'll have a slice of rabbit pie apiece with mash, roast potatoes and cabbage. And when we have eaten it, this young man will tell you if the gravy you make here is as good as his granny's in Featherstone.'

The waiter looked a bit flummoxed and asked if we'd like to see the wine list. Geoff said no, but we'd have a pot of tea for two.

The waiter came back with a beautiful tea service and china cups and then fetched our dinner. He said, 'Do enjoy your meal and let me know if there's anything else you require.'

Geoff said, 'Do you want a slice of bread for your gravy?'

I said, 'I don't want to spoil my manners.'

Two Tory grandees were sitting on the table next to us and glancing over.

'Don't talk so blooming daft, lad. Yes, we'd like two slices of bread please, no butter.'

The waiter looked flummoxed again.

Geoff said to him, 'Has tha never heard that saying, "Dip your bread in while the gravy's warm"?'

The gravy was alright, but not as good as my gran's.

Geoff died just before Christmas in 2012. He didn't do too bad for a Featherstone lad who started down the pit at 14. I missed Geoff's funeral, I always regret that.

I often wondered what I'd do when I heard of Margaret Thatcher's death. A lot of my friends had spent years planning street parties. On the day she died I was running a creative writing workshop at the Castleford Learning Centre. The Castleford Learning Centre had started life during the big strike as a miners' wives support group. Its members organised food parcels, talks and a shoulder to lean on for fearless women during that time. If I had planned to be anywhere on that day, I couldn't have picked a better place. After the workshop I called into the pub where I raised a glass. When I got home I wrote a poem.

My few lines on the death of Lady Thatcher, with apologies to a better poet, Frank O'Hara ('The Day Lady Died').

It's 14.55 in Castleford, a Monday
one week after Easter bank holiday, yes
it is 2013 and I want to go for a quick pint
because I need to catch the Ross' bus
back home, it's my turn to make the dinner
and I'm making shepherd's pie.

I walk up Carlton Street, cold sun peeping
from behind the Crystal Bowl bingo hall.
I call in at the Santander bank and
I can't find the cheque I want to deposit
so I check every one of my pockets
and the lady behind the glass says
'Are you putting in or taking out?'

And in the Junction pub I order that pint
It's pulled from a wooden barrel and it's a pale ale
then I go to the front door for a roll-up
and smoke and watch the traffic
and my mobile makes a noise to say I have a message
and the message says 'the witch is dead'.
I'm grinning now and thinking
and leaning on a railing that separates me from the traffic
and it seems like all the cars have stopped
and the passers by have started to breath again.

On the day of Thatcher's funeral I watched some people
burning an effigy strapped to an old sofa over in Goldthorpe. I
raised a glass to them as well.

Candid Camera

I don't know what 'Staffy' Jack Fletcher would have made of me visiting Buckingham Palace to do an interview with Prince Andrew. I think I know what my grandad would have said. My gran, who was in her eighties at the time said, 'I'm only glad your grandad isn't here to know about it, he'd have gone up the bloody wall!' My gran had recently taken to wearing all-red clothes, with matching shoes and handbag, ever since the Labour Party had got back in power under Blair. She despised Blair, said, 'His eyes are too close together and he only pretends to look at folk when he's talking,' but she was thrilled that fourteen years of Thatcherism had come to an end.

In 1998 the Arts Council celebrated 'The Year of Photography and the Electronic Image' and in conjunction Yorkshire Television commissioned six half-hour programmes which I was chosen to present. Each programme was to include an interview with a famous person who was interested in photography. This included members of the anarchist pop group Chumbawamba, who had recently had a number one with the song 'Tubthumping'. They celebrated at the Brit Awards by chucking a bucketful of iced water over John Prescott. Then there was Lord Denis Healey, who insisted on being put up at The Hilton in Leeds and doing his interview at East Riddlesden Hall, a seventeenth century manor house near Keighley. I think his title is Baron Healey of Riddlesden. He took photographs of me as I interviewed him, I don't know why, but some weeks after he sent me one of the photos. I was supposed to interview another Lord, David Putnam, at the Victoria and Albert Museum, but it didn't happen, because on the day of the interview he phoned to say that he had come down with gastric flu. I did go to a little house in Clapham though to interview Rebecca Stephens, the first British woman to climb Mount Everest. She had a beautiful collection of photos that she had taken on her expeditions.

When Mike Best, my boss at YTV, called me into his office to tell me that I was to interview Prince Andrew, my grandfather came straight into my mind. He despised royalty, he said that they were bloodsuckers and that they caused wars. I know that he would have stopped talking to me. There were men who had been his friends once, who had scabbed during strikes, who he refused to talk to ever again. And for over a year after he discovered that I'd smoked cannabis he ignored me. He only gave in because one Sunday lunchtime my gran begged him to relent. My gran had been poorly and I had made the dinner while he was at the club playing dominoes. He came home three sheets to the wind and ate his dinner like a wolf. He scraped his plate with his knife and said, 'Bloody lovely that, lass.' When my gran told him that I had made the dinner, he said, 'If I'd known that I would have scraped it onto the back of the fire.' I'd be about 22 at the time, I stood up and said, 'You're a bloody hypocrite.' He was well into his sixties, but he stood up, knocked his chair over, spat on his hands and took a south-paw stance. 'There's plenty of room outside if you want to have a go.' I was shaking and frightened. Even in his sixties he cut a formidable figure, he was still big and strong and, though I thought he was well out of order, I backed down.

'Bloody good job!' he slurred, 'Because this one's Pontefract Infirmary,' he pointed to his right fist, 'and this 'un is Pinderfields Hospital!' Then he laughed.

My gran said, 'Pack it in now the pair of you and shake hands.' I offered my hand. He looked at me and then took my hand. He couldn't resist squeezing it. You knew where you stood with my grandad, just as long as you didn't expect him to ever back down.

My dad remained terrified of my grandad and flinched

whenever he was near him if my grandad so much as twitched. One afternoon my dad offered to throw a ton of coal in for my gran after she said he could keep a couple of sacks for himself. He was throwing the coal in the drizzling rain, not aiming very well in his half-soaked way and making a mess of the yard. My grandad came home from the day shift, walked down the yard and said, 'Ay up simple bugger, watch where tha's throwing it.' My dad, wet through, bedraggled and now offended said, 'Look! Get in thi kitchen, get the bloody dinner and mind thi own business for a change.'

My grandad strode over to him. 'Whoaah, hold thi bloody horses and anyhow, who's telled thee tha can get my bloody coal in?' He then pushed my dad who fell backwards onto the heap of coal. My dad jumped up, picked up the shovel and held it over his shoulder like a baseball player poised to strike. 'Watch who tha's pushing!'

Grandad put his snap bag onto the yard wall, was out of his coat in a flash and said, 'Why? What's thy going to do?' My dad stared at him for a few seconds and then carried on shoveling. My grandad picked up his coat and bag and came in for his dinner. My gran said 'Eeeh! Eddie, I wish you'd leave the poor simple bugger alone.' I came out with a yard brush and helped my dad tidy up. Under his breath my dad muttered, 'He thinks he's bloody Primo Carnera.'

So, there I was, in a glass-sided office at Yorkshire TV's Calendar studios on Kirkstall Road in Leeds. I'd been a presenter there for a couple of years and now I was to present a flagship programme, interview a senior member of the Royal Family and the first thing I think about it is, 'What would my grandad say?' Ten years before I had sat by his bedside at Pontefract Infirmary and held his big hand in the hour before he passed away, his lungs filled with dust. I cried and cried that night for my awkward, cantankerous, aggressive, hero. Now I'm in an office being glad he's not here to see what I'm about to do.

I was a bit naive about it all. I thought at first that they would be bringing Prince Andrew up to the studios at Leeds. They told me, 'No, you're off to London to do it.' So, I thought they'd be hiring a studio there. Wrong again. 'You're off to Buckingham Palace,' they said. So then I thought that there must be some sort of media area at the Palace that they use. I was wrong about that as well.

When we get to the Palace we are greeted by a man whose name I can't remember, so I'll call him Rupert. He looks like he has been a guardsman, he's about six-foot-four, I can't even see over his shoulder. Rupert tells us to follow him and takes us up in a lift. We walk down a corridor and he knocks on a big oaken door, then lets us into a room. He then excuses himself and says he'll be back in a moment. The four of us stand there, turning round and looking. Jane, our producer, is dressed in a tailored trouser suit and has a clipboard under her arm. Ralph, our sound recordist and union rep, brushes his hair with his fingers. Jim, our Glaswegian cameraman, is standing in a pair of shoes he's borrowed off Ralph, because for some reason he's packed a pair of trainers by mistake and they don't go with his suit. We all look at one another and giggle like nervous school kids on a day trip to a castle.

I say to Jane, 'Do I look alright?' Jane tells me later that she had been under strict instructions from Mike Best not to let me wear my usual lumberjack check shirt and boots to this job. Now, she just smiles. I have forced myself into a suit that Scary Mary from YTV's wardrobe department has given me. I think it had once been worn by a detective in David Jason's *A Touch of Frost* series.

I must have looked a bit like my dad did when a woman from down the street gave him a John Collier suit that had belonged to her late husband. It was a peculiar green colour and far too big for him. Every time he wore it my gran said, 'Well doesn't he look a closet! If we aren't bloody blessed!'

We must have been a bit dishevelled because Jim had insisted we have another couple of pints in the hotel bar at one o'clock that morning and I had spilt some egg on my lapel when I attempted a full English breakfast at six o'clock. A Lithuanian waitress had tried to wipe it off with a paper serviette dipped in water.

We wait for Rupert to come back with Prince Andrew. Jane looks at some photographs on top of a piece of furniture of Andrew and Sarah Ferguson with their children when they are babies. Jim and Ralph start to sort out the gear. I walk over to the window, look down The Mall and pretend to wave at my subjects. This is the balcony which the 'Fathers for Justice' campaigners once jumped onto dressed as Batman and Robin. I turn and say, 'Come on everybody, come and wave to the people.'

Rupert comes back in again and gives a little cough. I jump. He walks over to me and says, 'Mr Clayton, a little word if I may.' I say, 'Right oh!' He smiles down diagonally at me like a cloaked school prefect had once done. I can't remember exactly what Rupert said now, but it was something like, 'On first meeting His Royal Highness, may I suggest you use the address "Your Royal Highness" and after that simply as "Sir".' I blinked and I'm sure I went as red as a Tetley beer mat as I looked across at Jane. Rupert excused himself again and this time left the big oak door to the connecting room slightly ajar. Jane looked back at me and said something under her breath that I didn't catch. I said to her, 'I can't call somebody Highness, my grandfather will be spinning around North Featherstone cemetery for ever more.' I looked at Jim and Ralph; they both shrugged their shoulders and put the palms of their hands out, like they were carrying a piece of cloth.

I don't know whether they heard me, but within a moment Rupert and Andrew were in the room. Andrew comes straight over to me, sticks his hand out and says, 'Hi, I'm Andrew, very pleased to meet you.'

I take his hand, he squeezes my fingers together. I say, 'Hello, I'm Ian.'

'Right, let's bloody get on with it then, I've got a busy day.'

We sit in chairs opposite one another, knees almost touching. Andrew laughs when he realises that my feet won't reach the floor. He has a portfolio of photographs next to him, Rupert sits to my left, making notes.

'You have described yourself as a keen amateur photographer, what was the catalyst that sparked your interest?'

'Hey?'

I started again, 'You have described yourself as a...'

'Yes, I heard that, I thought you wanted to talk about me being the Patron of the Year of Photography.'

'I do. So what first sparked your interest in photography?'

'Well I err, I suppose, I found really that I err, had an eye for it. I'd taken the, um, odd photograph and then I had a friend called Gene, who was a master printer and he helped me get started.'

'You must have gone on a steep learning curve, because you say you started taking photographs in the early eighties and by 1985 you had published your own book.'

'Err, yes, well, I took it rather more seriously then, than perhaps necessarily I do now and shortly afterwards Gene moved to America, so I didn't have the same impetus after that.'

'How do you go about your photography then, do you go on expeditions or do you stuff a camera in your pocket and take it with you wherever you go?'

'Well it's a bit of both really. I do go on photography assignments, but yes I do put a camera in my pocket sometimes and I encourage my daughters to do the same. My children each have a camera that the Duchess of York bought for them.'

'I can't imagine that you go to Boots to have your films developed.'

Before he can answer, a military band strike up outside. They play the old Cliff Richard song 'Congratulations', some people had come to the Palace today to receive medals. Ralph asks if we might wait until the music subsides a bit, as we won't be able to edit the film around the music.

'Yes, I rather thought that myself!' He then asks his assistant to make a phone call and tell them to cut the music. I start coughing and nearly choke. Andrew tells Rupert to fetch me some water from the next room. He obliges and comes back with a half-full bottle of Malvern Still with a tiny bit of bread floating about in it. In the meantime, Andrew has taken the phone, but slams it down when he realises it's engaged.

'Well, look here,' he says, 'unfortunately when you come to the Palace, you will have to occasionally put up with the fact that there is a guard change.'

I get myself all nervous now. I'd come in all cocky with a very clear plan of what I wanted to ask. I had been over a dozen or so questions time and again in my mind on the way down the M1 the day before, but started to get confused about what I wanted to ask next.

Prince Andrew leaned forward and examined the emblem on my skew-whiff tie. 'What's the emblem?'

'I play rugby league for a club called Featherstone Miners Welfare, that's our club tie.'

'Oh! I see.' Then he starts to laugh and says, 'Never bloody heard of them!' He laughs some more, louder, and looks at Rupert. Rupert carries on taking notes.

I compose myself and say, 'Shall we look at some of the photographs of yours you want to show us?'

We look at a selection of black and white prints that he has taken, they are a mixed bag; there's a ghostly image of a young woman in a thin dress standing petrified on a dungeon staircase at Windsor Castle, it looks like it was taken with a plate camera. There's a long-shot of Balmoral with the Queen, a herd of corgis and a helicopter in the foreground.

'Yes, we parked the cab on the lawn and the Queen happened to be exercising the dogs.'

My favourite was of what I think is a ptarmigan flying low over a moor being pursued by a goose.

'Now,' I said, 'What about this one of polo at Balmoral?' As soon as I said it, I could have bit my tongue off. Andrew looked at me and started laughing his head off.

'You're wrong on both counts. It's not polo, it's croquet and it's not Balmoral, it's the Castle of Mey, Queen Elizabeth the Queen Mother's Castle.'

I felt as daft as a brush. Andrew carried on laughing and looked at Rupert, hoping that he'd join in as well. Rupert kept his head down, taking his notes, but I think he sniggered.

Andrew then came over all mysterious. 'The interesting thing about that photograph is that at least four of those men playing croquet were on very special operations. But I'm not allowed to tell you what, because if I did, I would then have to eat you... if you know what I mean.'

When we finished, Jane asked if we might have a photograph of the two of us together. Rupert took it.

We were driving out of the Palace gates when Jane's mobile phone rang. It was Mike Best, he was phoning to check that everything had gone smoothly. When Jane put her phone back into her handbag she looked at me and laughed. She said, 'He wanted to know if you had been detained for treason.'

The day after I was sitting in the make-up room at YTV. Jeanette was putting some foundation on my cheeks before I went on the live magazine show *Tonight* to talk about a film I'd made with a pig farmer near Malton. In the chair next to me having her lips done was Britt Ekland. She was on the same show promoting something or other. Jeanette said, 'Can I introduce you, Miss Ekland. This is one of our presenters, Ian Clayton. He was at Buckingham Palace yesterday to interview the Duke of York.' Britt Ekland pouted in the mirror, swivelled in her chair and held out her hand. 'Oh! Really, darling. Well I could tell you one or two stories about him.'

I smiled at her. 'Aye, lass, I bet you could.'

Not long after I was with my old mate Terry Cryer, the brilliant jazz photographer. I told him about my adventure. He said, 'Ian, always remember what I have always told you, when you're in a spot like that, the aristocracy and the royalty are very similar to the old fashioned working classes, they sleep with their dogs and piss in the sink!'

I went to see my gran at the weekend. I mentioned that I'd been to do my job at the Palace.

'Don't tell above a dozen,' she said, and added, 'Did you bring me any rock back?'

I think I'm still one of the few television presenters who has interviewed a senior member of the Royal Family in their own living room. I shudder when I think about it.

I worked in television on and off from 1988 until 2010. My favourite TV work was a series I did for Yorkshire Television called *My Yorkshire*. It was a simple idea. We would sit down for a day with someone from our region and talk to them about their life and then film them on another day at a place of their choosing in the Yorkshire landscape. In a lot of ways it was just building on something I had been doing for YTV for years. All of the little films I did, and I believe I did more than 400, were about people or places.

Once I went to an old stone mansion at Boothtown near Halifax. This mansion once belonged to Percy Shaw, the inventor of cats' eyes. It was the house of a great eccentric. In the kitchen there was a centrepiece of stepped shelving in the middle of the room. Percy didn't like storage cupboards or pantries and liked to have all of his provisions on show. There was space for tinned food, packet food, flour, eggs, sardines, soup and custard powder, and more space beneath for bleach, Brillo pads and Daz.

His main room was like the concert room at a working men's club. There was a billiard table and toilets on either side of the wall. One marked 'Ladies' the other 'Gents'.

I first came across the story of Percy Shaw when I watched his famous interview with Alan Whicker in the 1960s. Percy told Whicker that he liked to have four televisions all on at the same time. One was tuned to ITV, one to BBC1 and another to BBC2, the fourth one was a back-up. He said he didn't like to get up out of his chair to switch the telly over. He kept crates of brown ale next to each settee and an easy chair for when his mates came round, and wouldn't have carpets down because he liked to flick his cigar ash onto the floor. In this respect, Percy Shaw was like my dad. I once came into our front room one Saturday afternoon. My dad was laid on the settee. He was watching wrestling on the telly. Jackie Pallo was asking Les Kellett to submit. He had a half-smoked Players No. 6 in the corner of his mouth, his eyes half-closed to stop the smoke going in them. He flicked his cigarette onto a little pyramid of ash at the side of the little table on which stood his pint of tea. I told him that my mam had said he had to stop flicking his ash onto the carpets.

'Well let me tell thee summat young 'un and tha can tell thi mam this from me as well,' he announced, lifting himself onto his elbow, 'That ash is very good for the carpet, it keeps the moths down. Now stick that in thi pipe and smoke it!' He then said, 'Now, pull that curtain across for me will tha, t'sun's shining on t'television.'

Percy Shaw's house had no curtains. He famously told Whicker that, 'Windows are for looking out of, not peering into.'

The *My Yorkshire* series ran in episodes of half an hour with a commercial break in between. We focused on one person in each half of the programme, which I hope captured slices of real life. We always tried to feature people that you don't normally see on television, we featured a lot of musicians and artistic people too. I guess we were trying to meet people who could interpret where they were from. And a lot of them wanted to talk about their debt to their parents.

The Sheffield musician Richard Hawley, who has since become a close friend, told me that his dad had been a big influence on him. His dad had played with the old bluesmen who visited Britain in the sixties, people like Sonny Boy Williamson and John Lee Hooker. One day, he'd been off school with tonsillitis and had been mooching round the house. He found his dad's guitar beneath a sofa and opened the case. When his dad came home from the steelworks he wanted to know what Richard was doing with his guitar. Richard said that he'd like to learn to play it and at that moment his own musical journey began.

I asked Richard where he got his ideas for songs from.

'Sheffield', he said, a bit non-plussed. 'My songs come from the same place that I come from.'

Sometime after, I saw Richard in concert at the Crucible Theatre on the last homecoming leg of his European tour. He had a man playing musical saw. In the dressing room after, I asked him what gave him the idea to have a musical saw player. 'Mi grandad played one.'

Another Yorkshire musician we featured was the darling of the folk world, Kate Rusby. We sat on her mam's settee and she sang the old Iris DeMent song 'Our Town'. After, we went up to some autumn woods and kicked up the leaves while Kate recalled her childhood. She suddenly stopped on a hillside and pointed across a valley. 'Look at that church over there, Ian.' I followed her pointing finger. 'That's where mi mam used to sing in the church choir.'

The Archbishop of York took us to Flamborough Head, because he wanted to relive memories of childhood holidays there just after the war. His father had an old Austin car that was noisy and slow. They travelled for hours over the steep hills of the Yorkshire Wolds, not speaking because they couldn't be heard over the noise of the engine. His mother sat in the back and every time she wanted to wee, she took out a white hankie and waved it out of the window at his father who was concentrating in the driver's seat.

My Yorkshire I suppose helped me to find a lot of things that I had been looking for. How personal history connects you to where you are from. How following a route to the lodestone takes you to where you want to be or how listening to the voices of your ancestors helps you to decide what routes to take. Perhaps the one that made me think most about all of this stuff was the film we made with Steve Huison, the Leeds-born actor who starred in *The Full Monty* and played Eddie Windass in *Coronation Street*. He took me to an area on the edge of Leeds city centre where he had been brought up. We stood on a wasteland and surveyed piles of bricks that had been left by some JCBs. He talked about his dad who had taken him to Communist Party meetings when he was knee-high. Then he mentioned his fondness for the hustle, bustle, noise and colour of Leeds' indoor market. He seemed sad when he said, 'It's one of the few things from my childhood that hasn't altered too much, all the rest of it seems to have been knocked down.' It's true to say that Leeds' industrial and commercial appetite has eaten up what were once thriving neighbourhoods near the city centre. We looked down at the broken concrete.

'You know, Ian, where we're standing now was once my school. This is where the corridor to the cloakroom was.' He hovers his hand in mid-air, 'And there was a radiator I dried my anorak on just here.'

Later he tells me that he had been back a few times to survey the dereliction. 'The last time I came I saw pigeons tumbling through the sky. They were trying to find their way home. But where they once roosted had gone. There was just the sky left for them.'

I spent four days in the company of Arthur Scargill when I presented a half-hour documentary that celebrated his 70th birthday while looking back over his life. Arthur revealed that an enormous part of his drive was for the love of his parents, for their sacrifices and the support they had given him. On the last day of filming we travelled to the Yorkshire Dales, to a very remote place where there was a tumbling down old building called 'Scargill Castle'. Arthur touched the ancient stones and claimed them on behalf of his Norwegian Viking ancestors, then laughed. It was a lovely end to our filming and when Jane the director called 'a wrap', we all headed for a nearby pub.

The pub was a very posh gastro-bar with a huge blackboard on which was chalked a list of local delicacies. There was rabbit pie, duck in orange sauce, local pheasant and black pudding on a bed of mashed swede. The waitress, resplendent in pressed black apron tied in a bow at the back, came to take our order.

'Can I take your drinks first? We have a selection of six locally brewed real ales on cask, I recommend the Golden Pippin, it's in superb condition today.' The cameraman, Alan, and sound recordist, Terry, and I ordered pints of that. Jane had a dry white wine and then the waitress looked at Arthur.

Arthur said, 'A glass of water for me please.'

'Would that be still or carbonated, sir?'

'Tap!' said Arthur at high volume.

The waitress then took our meal orders. Alan and me had the rabbit pie, Jane had a salad of goats cheese and wild rocket, and Terry had black pudding. Arthur didn't even look at the blackboard. 'Cheese sandwich for me please, sliced not grated and no pickle.'

The waitress paused with her pencil hovering over the notebook. She studied Arthur. 'Right, sir. Would you like that on granary, wholewheat or a breadcake?'

She had only nicely finished her list, when Arthur announced, 'White sliced!'

We tucked into our rabbit pies and washed it down with a lovely golden beer or two. Arthur sipped his water and munched his cheese sandwich, he left a bit of crust on his plate. As we came out of the pub he walked alongside me back to the car. 'You know, Ian, the politicians and bosses were always inviting me to places. I never went.'

Another hero of mine I got to work with on a number of occasions was Barry Hines. I made two TV films with him. When I first read *A Kestrel for a Knave*, which was later made into the film *Kes,* I thought it had been written for me. The words leapt out of the pages and lifted me up, made me hover, if you like, on a breeze above my home town. There's a scene in that book where Billy Casper jumps over a fence while delivering some morning newspapers. He lands in the wet grass, then a pile of dog shit. He wipes his hand on the grass, then smells at his fingers and runs on. When I read that, I said to myself, 'I do that'. *Kes* was the first story I ever read that had me nodding my head in recognition. At the end of almost every page I found myself saying, 'I've done that', or 'I know that feeling'. His house was full of arguments like mine was and the only people who ever had any conversations with him were sympathetic school teachers. I adore that story and its imagery swirls in my mind to this day. The famous poster of Billy sticking up two fingers adorns my kitchen wall alongside the tagline, 'They beat him, they deprived him, they ridiculed him, they broke his heart, but they couldn't break his spirit'.

In one of the films I did with Barry Hines I went to the pictures with him, so that he could review the film. We went to a cinema in Sheffield to see *Shakespeare in Love*. As we were going in he said, 'I don't know why the bloody hell you have brought me to see this, I don't like this stuff, people putting on different outfits so they can pretend to be someone else!' I was a bit disappointed. I'm not sure that I knew what he meant, but I was excited to be at the pictures with him. I sat there munching popcorn in the back row, hardly noticing what was going on in the film because I was sitting alongside a man who I believe to be the greatest British writer of the late 20th century. I've thought from time to time why he said what he did about 'dressing up to be someone else'.

Summer
Taking Tea To China

'Learning is when you understand something
you have known all your life, but in a new way.'
Doris Lessing

Must Needs Be Fair

I can't say as I ever heard my dad say this, but I think he thought that you were born to be what you become and that education doesn't change too much. I never did get my dad's attitude to education. He seemed to think that not going to school had 'never done me any harm'. It's not that he didn't appreciate original thought, in fact he prided himself on knowing things that he didn't think anybody else had come up with. It's that he thought that somehow if you learned something from someone else it wasn't real. My dad thought that noticing things was better than somebody telling you them. He used the word 'student' as a kind of insult, that meant if he saw anybody on the news protesting about something he'd say 'must be a bloody student'. Anybody who had long hair was a student and if someone said a word that he didn't know, well of course they must have been a student and they were trying to fool him. Our Andrew told me that when he told my dad that Heather had gone to university, he said my dad replied, 'Well she will do, she's a bloody student!'

I don't really know what my dad thought about my own learning, he never asked me anything about that. I don't know how he thought I had learned things either. He did grudgingly tell people occasionally that 'Our Ian is intelligent' and he more than once said to me, 'You want to slow down a bit studying, it's not good for your mind and you'll end up with headaches.' He didn't accept that there was such a thing as learning in the academic sense, he seemed to put everything down to 'the road you were born'. In my dad's world you either had the sense you were born with or you were simple to start off with. The one thing I do have to thank my dad for though, is the fact that he never tried to make me be like him. He laughed at me for doing too much 'book reading' and called me 'Educated Archie' if I answered a question right on a TV quiz programme, but at the same time thought that's just how I was. In the 1970s I read Kahlil Gibran's book *The Prophet*. It was the sort of book we were all into at the time. There's a line in there that goes: 'Your children are not your children. They are the sons and daughters of life's longing for itself.' I guess that my dad would have said that if he had thought of it first.

My friend Jo Westerman asked me if I would run some creative-writing workshops at the University of Leeds Staff Centre. All sorts of people came, there were professors of ethics, visiting Americans who worked in IT, an Egyptologist and a Somalian woman who mopped the corridors. One day a Chinese woman came in breathless after running across the campus and up three flights of stairs. At first I thought she was a visiting student, then discovered she was Dr Hui Xiao, an economist on a year's visit to Leeds. She was also a quite brilliant writer who came to the workshop with a blank piece of paper and left a few hours later with a moving story she had written about her wish to visit her Japanese grandfather's grave. I recognised a fellow traveller and opened up to her about losing my daughter Billie. There was a moment in the middle of the workshop when we both wiped a tear.

Writing workshops are often emotional, you end up visiting memories that you don't remember every day and you say things to strangers that you don't always say to those closest to you. Talking to a woman from thousands of miles away, from a culture I knew next to nothing about, was a liberating experience for me.

Dr Hui Xiao stayed in my mind in the days and weeks after the workshop. We were supposed to meet again for a short course in creative writing later in the summer. The course didn't happen, we couldn't recruit enough people to make it worthwhile for the Staff Centre. I e-mailed Hui Xiao to say that I was sorry that I wouldn't see her again before she returned home to China, but if she had a morning to spare perhaps I could show her a favourite village of mine and we'd have a pub lunch.

I met Hui at Castleford railway station and took her to see the new walking bridge over the River Aire. I recited an old local poem as we looked at the water tumbling over the weir near Allinson's flour mill.

Castleford lasses, must needs be fair
For they wash in the Calder and rinse in the Aire

She smiled, the sort of polite smile that says, 'I don't know what the hell he's talking about.'

Hui's spoken and written English are impeccable. She hails from Changchun in the north-eastern province of Jilin, where she lectures at the university. Changchun is a huge city known for its railways and car manufacturing. The region is what we once knew as Manchuria, it's about as close to Vladivostok in Russia as it is to Beijing. The Japanese occupied this part of China during the 1930s. Hui's father married a local Chinese woman and Hui was raised in one of the world's most beautiful landscapes, the Changbai mountains near the North Korean border.

We stand on the bridge at Castleford and watch the water flow fast beneath our feet. My fear of water below wooden boards no longer comes over me, but the river is particularly fast today, it must have been raining heavily in the Pennine Hills, north and west of Leeds. Hui asks, 'Can you cope with the psychological affect of being so close to the fast river?'

I realise that here is a woman who knows maybe three things about me. First is that I'm a lad from a coal-mining village, second is that I write books, and third is that I am the father of a daughter who drowned in a fast-flowing river.

I tell her, 'I like to face my fear and besides, I like to look at this river. We shouldn't turn our backs on rivers. Rivers are our history.' I then tell her the tale of how the cowboy Buffalo Bill once came to Castleford with his wild-west show and watered his horses in this river. It's all a bit bizarre.

We walk across the fields from the bridge. The barley is waiting to be harvested and is dotted with wild poppies. We walk four miles and more to a village called Ledsham and a pub called The Chequers. We have a steak sandwich apiece and I introduce Hui to a local real ale from a micro brewery called Brown Cow. I like to bring guests to this pub. It's a very English one with a lovely garden and it's next to a bonny church called All Saints. After lunch I show Hui the church. We came to this village for Auntie Alice's ninety-first birthday, the same year Billie died. Billie liked churches and wanted to see this one. She wrote in the visitor's book 'Lovely quiet place, Billie Holiday Clayton.' I find the visitor's book and leaf through it to find Billie's name. I show it to Hui. She reads the message and then runs the nail of her index finger over the handwriting.

'She did beautiful writing.'

'She did.'

It upsets me to do it, but I still love to look at Billie's handwriting. I have an alphabetic list of names of our friends and their telephone numbers on the back of our kitchen door. I like to look at it, not to find phone numbers, but to look at the lovely, neat way she made each individual letter, even her commas and question marks were made with care.

'If you come to China, I will show you the art of Chinese calligraphy. Would you like to visit China?'

Hui tells me that she would like to put my name forward to her senior professors at North East Normal University in Changchun with a view to me being a visiting lecturer.

'But I'm not an academic!'

'I know, but you know how to run writing workshops.'

We take a taxi back to Castleford railway station and I stand in the drizzle to wave to Hui through the train window.

A few days later she was on another train, this time to London for a flight back to Changchun via Beijing. In her luggage, Hui carried some copies of my books: one I'd edited about the work of St. George's Crypt, a homeless charity in Leeds; one about my love of music and where music takes us; and another about losing Billie. I kept in touch with Hui by e-mail after that. She put her idea up to her superiors. I tried to imagine what senior Chinese literature academics would make of my stories of growing up in a West Yorkshire pit village. By the autumn I received an invite from Professor Yuchen Yang, Associate Head of Foreign Languages School at North East Normal University. She asked me to travel to Changchun the following summer to give lectures and run workshops with undergraduate students in the Business English Department and in the Foreign Languages School. I wrote back to Professor Yang and told her that I had no letters behind my name, but that I thought I could run a decent storytelling workshop and that I might be able to help with idiomatic English and conversation. She told me that she had received a glowing recommendation from Dr Hui Xiao about my teaching ability and that she thought the students would benefit from a 'different' approach. We ping-ponged e-mails back and forwards and then, as Christmas approached, I wrote to say that I wasn't sure that I would make it to China after all.

Blood and Apples

Heather and I celebrated 33 years of not being married together in the September not long after my birthday. Throughout the summer Heather had complained about headaches, sweating a lot and told me that one minute she wanted to laugh and the next she wanted to cry. 'I don't know if I'm coming or going some days,' she said. I told her to join the club and suggested that it was our age. She told me to stick my theories on ageing where the sun doesn't shine. 'If you want to be an old man before your time, that's up to you, but don't include me, I've still got plenty I want to do, I'm not ready for the knackers yard or the armchair yet.'

The symbol of the armchair gets to me. I think of my father's chair by the fireplace with its curtain draped over it to keep the muck off. But also about the chair my grandad lived in after he retired from the pit. On that retirement day he came home with his overcoat flapping like washing on a line, his flat cap skew-whiff and told my gran, 'I'm done, Hilda.' He sat down in the armchair, poked the fire, picked up his *Daily Mirror* and switched the televised snooker on. He filled his pipe and tamped the 'bacca down, struck a Swan Vestas and that, for the next six years until he died, was about all he did, day in, day out. He stopped going to the club, rarely took fresh air and coughed and coughed. He only seemed to want to argue and then started having his fits and looking under the furniture. For six years he told me to get a haircut, press my trousers and asked me how much a pint cost.

Heather's headaches got worse and she decided she was going through the change. She was persuaded to go to the doctor's and she told him the same, he agreed with her and offered supplements. Heather decided she would handle 'the change' in her own way and started drinking a lot of unsweetened soya milk, pomegranate juice and eating beetroot and mixed nuts.

In 33 years of adventures together, Heather and I have argued, made up and argued some more. When we lost Billie we decided that all we needed was love. Heather has a red beret and pinned to it is a tin heart-shaped badge with the words 'All you need is love' stamped on it. She started to wear her beret every day. We tried our best not to blame the stress and grief for our bickering and kept reminding each other 'Love is all you need'. Then we argued about everything, from the runniness of a boiled egg, unhoovered carpets, leaking window frames and me farting whilst laying on the sofa.

One day I mentioned to Heather that whatever arguments my gran and grandad had been having, they were all forgotten on the doorstep at five o'clock in the morning when she waved my grandad off to the pit. She always kissed him on the lips at the doorstep.

'Well I'm not your bloody granny and you're not your grandad!'

I was invited to the Royal Festival Hall in London for the weekend. Jude Kelly had organised 'The Festival of Death' and wanted me to talk about coping after losing Billie. On the morning I set off I went to kiss Heather on the doorstep. She turned her face and I ended up planting a kiss somewhere near her right ear. I said, 'What's up?'

She didn't turn to face me, just said, 'I'm not sure love is enough anymore.' I carried my weekend case to the taxi that was to take me to the station. I came back for my phone charger and found Heather crying in the kitchen, she was holding her head. 'Shall I cancel the job?'

'No, leave me be, get off, you'll miss your train!'

'Let's talk.'

'I don't feel like talking.'

'Well shall I go then?'

She didn't answer.

I went and all the way down to London I thought about us and tried to make sense out of something I couldn't fathom. Richie Havens' version of the 10cc song 'I'm Not In Love' kept going round and round my head. I never knew what that song was really about until I heard his version.

When we were younger, Heather's parents and my grandparents used to ask us, 'Isn't it about time you two got married?' We always laughed and sang that Joni Mitchell line 'we don't need no piece of paper from the City Hall, keeping us tied and true'. The reality now is that Heather and me have been together longer than both our sets of parents put together.

When we met we were joining in with Jimmy Pursey when he sang, 'If the kids are united, they will never be defeated.' We have sung along to Everything But The Girl doing 'I Don't Want to Talk About It' and to Aztec Camera's 'Oblivious'. During the miners' strikes we played a record by Test Department and the South Wales Striking Miners choir. In the early nineties, when Heather went to university as a mature student, I sang Sinéad O'Connor's 'Nothing Compares 2 U' to her. By the turn of the millennium we danced around the living room to Spiller's hit 'Groovejet' – 'If this ain't love, why does it feel so good'. We made our children laugh. More recently Richard Hawley's Sheffield made romantic ballads have moved us. At Billie's funeral, Van Morrison's 'Sometimes We Cry' made us hold hands and cry.

When we last reorganised our record collection, Heather wanted her own sections. She's gone all PJ Harvey, Leonard Cohen and Cat Stevens. Every Christmas she brings out her Loreena McKennitt CDs and we eat our turkey to new age takes on 'God Rest Ye Merry Gentlemen'. I've got lost in the nether regions of ancient folk music, what Heather calls, 'beard and finger in the ear old men's stuff!'

At the back end of November we were invited to the sixtieth

birthday of our mate Jürgen Bredebusch in Wuppertal, Germany. Jürgen and his brother Volker have been close friends for thirty years, they call us 'HeatherandIan'. Heather spent most of the time at Leeds airport listening to Leonard Cohen on her iPod. She was quiet on the aeroplane and as we came through arrivals at Düsseldorf she clutched the side of her head and told me it was boiling.

'Boiling! How can your head boil?'

'Well, it's all fizzing and popping inside.'

I went for a bottle of water and told her to sit down on a seat. When I got back she said that whatever it was had gone and that she felt alright now.

We stayed in Germany for four days over a weekend. Heather looked pale and, rather than being the life and soul of the party we're all used to, she seemed distant and uninterested. On the Friday after we got back she was sick before her dinner. She made another appointment with the doctor and he referred her for a CAT scan at Pontefract Infirmary. On the Tuesday morning over breakfast we joked about what they might find. At one o'clock that afternoon, Heather phones me and says, 'It's quite serious, Ian, they have found a brain tumour.'

I say, 'Right.' Then I don't know what to say next.

Heather says, 'It's a big one and they need to see to it straightaway.'

She sounds ever so calm and matter of fact. 'Right... Get a taxi home and we'll sit round the kitchen table and talk it over.' I feel hopeless and helpless.

'Do you want to talk to the lady doctor?'

'I don't know... yes.'

The doctor takes the phone, 'Did Heather tell you that we have found something?'

'Yes, shall I come to the hospital?'

She goes stern and says, 'Well, I think if my wife had just told me this I would come to the hospital immediately.'

'No, I don't mean shall I come, I mean can I come?'

I start to think about Pontefract Infirmary on the day our twins were born. Edward and Billie were taken to incubators and Heather went to sleep. I sat on a steel-backed chair in a corridor. The midwife came to me and said, 'Are you still here?' I told her that I was waiting. 'What are you waiting for, you're no good to nobody here, get off home and get some rest, you're going to need it.' I sloped off to catch the 147 bus.

The doctor's voice on the phone brings me out of my reverie. 'We're keeping her on the ward until we can find a bed at Leeds General.'

'Right. Well I've got my lad coming home from school soon, I've told him that his mam has gone for a check-up on her eyes, what shall I tell him now?'

'I'll hand you back to Heather.'

Heather says, 'They want to do brain surgery as soon as they can, this tumour is as big as an apple.'

'I'll come as soon as Edward gets home.'

'Bring me a nightie and a toothbrush. I know now why I kept having headaches.'

I tell Heather that I love her.

'I know.'

When Edward gets home he drops his bag and goes straight up to his room to check his Facebook. I stand at his bedroom door and say, 'Are you alright?'

'Why, what's up?'

'There's nowt up!'

'Where's mi mam?'

'Well, you know she went for a check-up on her eyes this morning.'

Edward's eyes widened and he closed the lid on his laptop. He waited for me to carry on.

'They've found something on the back of one of her eyes and they need to do a little operation.'

190

'Oh, that's alright then, I thought you were going to tell me something serious.'

'We'll go and see her after our dinner, shall I make a shepherd's pie?'

Heather is sitting up reading a book by Haruki Murakami called *Norwegian Wood* when we get to the hospital. She puts her bookmark in and gives Edward and me a hug. Edward says, 'Haven't you got a telly?'

Heather smiles and touches the side of her head. 'I'm waiting for an ambulance to take me to Leeds General.'

Edward wants to know how long she will be kept in. 'Will you be home the day after tomorrow?'

'I don't think so, Edward.'

'What about the day after that?'

'I don't know, we'll have to see.'

'What are they going to do to you?'

'I'm having an operation.'

I tell Heather that I brought her nightie and a toothbrush and some magazines. Edward starts to fiddle with the hospital radio. For ten minutes he doesn't look up. A nurse comes in and offers Heather a menu. Edward and I sit watching Heather push some steamed fish and peas around her plate.

On the bus on the way home, Edward says, 'She'll be alright won't she, because she's tough.'

'Yes, she's the toughest woman I know. Once when she had flu she said she had a bit of a cold and carried on.'

Edward went straight to his room when we got in. He didn't say goodnight. At midnight when I went up, I knocked lightly and peeped round the door. I guessed he was sleeping, so I closed the bedroom door lightly.

'Leave my door open, Dad.'

'Oh, alright, lad. Goodnight, son.'

He didn't say goodnight back, he just said, 'Alright.'

I didn't sleep much. I started to sweat and Billie's funeral came to me. Heather and me standing at the graveside looking at a swallow skimming over the heads of the mourners. Then I saw Billie in the school field at All Saints School, she was throwing a javelin and dancing with delight when she threw it further than the boys in her class.

I had a head full of swirling images; Heather's paintings gave way to photographs of her that I treasure, one where she walks alone on a beach in Devon, another of her at a party in London with a Mohican haircut and yet another of her sunbathing on a beach in Brittany. I started to dream about meeting her when she was about two years old, we were sitting on a step of a house she was born in, in Halfpenny Lane in Pontefract, she was stroking a rabbit. This didn't happen in real life, but it was so real in my dream that I could have touched that rabbit.

My eye was always caught by Heather's clothes. She has a way of combining stuff that she rummages for in jumble sales with clothes that's she's taken in, altered or dyed that makes her look different. She rarely goes out looking the same way twice, in the same way that Billie Holiday never sang the same song the same way. When we first met in 1978, it was all do-it-yourself punk chic; slogan T-shirts, zips, pins and tartan leggings. The strange thing was, Heather always returned to the look her young Auntie Val liked; cheesecloth, ethnic skirts, beads and long blouses that smelt of patchouli oil. With Heather you never knew what year you were in. It was like going to see Wishbone Ash on the way back from The Clash. Once in Prague I bought her some lovely dangly art nouveau earrings off a young woman sat on a bridge. She wore them with a Belstaff motorcycle jacket and Doc Martens cherry reds. It was a strange mixture, but Heather carried it off like it was normal. The one constant companion in Heather's wardrobe has been a red beret, which she wears with everything; it provoked our old pensioner mate Arnold to christen her 'Resistance'. When we discussed the scar Heather might be left with after her operation, her mate

Jan said, 'Well she'll be wearing her beret anyhow, so it won't matter.'

Heather has variously been Audrey Hepburn, Janis Joplin and Siouxsie Sioux. There was just one thing I commented negatively on and I wish I'd never opened my mouth. It was the pink mohair jumper, a big pink mohair jumper and I couldn't stand it. I didn't – or daren't – say it, but it reminded me of Spam. One night we were getting ready to go out and Heather put the pink jumper on. I must have been looking for too long. She said, 'What are you looking me up and down for?' I said that I thought it didn't go too well with the trousers. 'How would you know about clothes? You dress like your grandad! You wouldn't know style until it'd gone out of fashion! I'll dress how I like!' I must have been the wrong road out. 'Well! If people can dress how they like, I'll wear something that I want to wear and you can stick your pink jumper up your arse!'

Outside on the pavement there was a small builders' skip full of old plaster and bricks, amongst the muck was a ripped yellow waterproof coat. It was lathered with cement and grease. I retrieved it, put it on and fastened it with a piece of old washing line round my waist. I came into the front room and admired myself in the dresser mirror.

'Don't be stupid!'

'Who's being stupid? You said people can dress as they like without interference.'

'If you're doing this to make me change this pink jumper you have another think coming. I was going to put something else on just to please you, but I'm not now.'

We went to the pub. Heather in her big pink jumper and me in my yellow waterproof held together with a washing line. Bert said, 'What the fuck have you two come as?' Big Frank said he thought we looked 'stylish' and that we were making an anti-fashion stance. This from a man who was wearing a suit that someone had probably been demobbed in. By nine o'clock

I was sweating so much under the PVC I had to give in and take it off. Bert said, 'I don't know what's worse, that yellow coat or that fucking jumper you've got on.' Heather just went, 'See!'

It was the first time and only time I have challenged Heather about clothes. It was also the only time I tried to be more stubborn than her.

Heather's taste in music is about as eclectic as her dressing up. We argue a lot about what music we should listen to and we hide each other's CDs on pretence of 'filing in a sensible order'. I don't share Heather's passion for Clifford T. Ward, nor Leonard Cohen, but I do delight in watching her listen to that stuff. And I take a lot of amusement in watching her sing along to it. At school, when she joined the choir she was told after a few rehearsals to 'just mime' if she wanted to stay in the choir. Heather has an extravagant understanding of what key a song is in as well as a tenuous grasp on the actual words of a song. For ages when singing along to Donovan's song 'Remember The Alamo' she sang, 'Remember the animals'. Once, when I pointed out that she was inventing new lyrics, she said, 'Well it would have been a better song if it was about animals instead of fighting.'

I love all these things about Heather; her dress sense, her stubbornness, her musical tastes make her different. I like different.

We were supposed to go to Paris for Heather's 50th birthday. Some work came up for me and, instead of turning it down like I ought to have done, I took it and postponed the trip. It was one of those decisions you never hear the last of. When she was 51, I thought I'd surprise her and organise the Paris trip again.

We travelled by Eurostar. On the train under the tunnel she said, 'I suppose it's alright to celebrate your 51st birthday in Paris, most people would come for their 50th.' We laughed. It rained most of the time we were there and our umbrellas blew inside out twice. Heather had her heart set on a visit to the

Louvre, but the queues were too long. We stood in the middle of the square and argued whilst holding inside-out umbrellas. I suggested that a visit to the Musée d'Orsay would be a good compromise. Heather has her sarcastic head on and said, 'Why? Have they moved the bloody Mona Lisa across the river?' We walked over to the d'Orsay and queued there for above an hour, the rain still falling. I went to a kiosk and bought us a coffee and a pastry apiece. Heather said, 'If you think you're going to get round me with a cardboard cup of warm coffee and a stale bun, you've another think coming.' It stopped raining just as we entered the gallery, it started again as we came out.

'I told you, we should have come last year.'

Now, it was my turn for sarcasm, 'Why, do you think nobody wanted to see the Mona Lisa last year?'

'Well I bet it wasn't raining!'

'It always chuffing rains in Paris in the springtime! That's what it does. It rains! Then people who are in love come here, hold hands, get piss wet through and buy umbrellas from North African urchins at silly bloody prices!'

A raindrop rolled down Heather's nose. I smudged it onto the back of my finger. Heather smiled, 'We're like them two in that Woody Allen film *Midnight in Paris*.'

'How do you mean?'

'Well, we've come here and neither of us seems to know what the other one wants from it.'

'You tell me what you want to do, I'm happy to go along with it.'

'See!'

'What does that mean?'

'You don't know what you want to do, so you're making me decide.'

'Right then, follow me.'

I took Heather down to Saint-Germain-des-Prés. I showed her the Aux Trois Mailletz, the cellar nightclub where all the jazzers played in the forties and fifties. 'T. Bone Walker played there you know.' Heather's eyes glazed over. 'Show me something interesting.' We walked around the corner towards the river. I put my hands over Heather's eyes and said, 'Just let me steer you, you'll have a nice surprise.'

'What now! Are you going to show me where Miles Davis once had his dinner?'

'Open you eyes.'

I had brought Heather to the front of Shakespeare and Company bookshop. She turned and smiled again, a great big smile this time. 'Now you've got the hang of it.' She must have spent three hours in that bookshop. I heard her shout 'Whooa!' at the door to every little room, nook and cranny. She was like Juliette Gréco searching for a muse. I sat on a wall outside and watched her come out with bags full of books. Her face was a picture.

Heather's voice came into my head. It was something she said as I left the hospital at Pontefract earlier, 'I'll be alright now that they've found out what it is.' I got up at four and took the dog for a walk down the fields. He wondered what we were doing in the dark. Later that morning Heather had a five-hour brain surgery to remove her tumour. They wheeled her on to the ward at three in the afternoon, I was waiting, sitting on a plastic chair at the bottom of the bed. She said that she was pleased to see me and she dozed off. She opened her eyes after about ten minutes and said, 'It's a bit sore. Do I look alright?' I told her that she looked fine. While she had been sleeping I had counted the steel staples in her head. I think I counted sixty.

For about two months before the diagnosis, Heather had been painting swirling patterns and small squiggles on her canvases that she bought six at a time from Home Bargains. When I asked her what she was painting she told me, 'Things I can see.' I had been thinking that she meant things she saw in her mind's eye.

'I can't see the squiggly lines anymore.'

On the Saturday I arrive at the hospital at two in the afternoon with a pair of slippers that once belonged to my gran. Heather can't stop in bed, after just three days she is wanting to walk about. She is sporting two huge black eyes and carrying a bag filled with blood that is draining from the top of her head down a pipe. When she sits in the chair she rests the bag on her stomach. She calls it 'The crimson Louis Vuitton'. The staples glint in the sunlight coming through the window. In the two beds opposite are two elderly ladies surrounded by their families and in the next bed to her is a woman with tattoos who used to be an Hells Angel.

Heather's sister arrives and says, 'I'm surprised you didn't go private... do you like my new top? I got it in the sale at Miss Selfridge!'

Heather smiles, licks her finger and turns a page in her magazine.

We eat some grapes.

Heather's sister says, 'I had six tequila slammers last night. My head's still spinning.' Heather laughs loud and the visitors opposite look across and don't quite tut tut, but they look as though they want to. More pages turn, more grapes are eaten. The room smells like the inside of a warm plastic bucket. I drift to a wooden bench in my childhood. I'm eating crisps for the sake of it, crisps I neither asked for nor wanted. I lick salt and vinegar flavouring from my fingertips and wonder what it's like in the darkness and smoke of the taproom. When it's time for visiting to finish, I kiss Heather's swollen eyes and tell her I'll see her tomorrow. Her sister straightens the flowers and Heather puts the headphones attached to her iPod into her ears. She looks like a serene and wounded princess.

'What are you listening to?'

She says, 'Hey?' without taking the phones out.

This startles the other visitors again.

'I wondered what you were listening to?'

'It's that album by Isobel Campbell and Mark Lanegan, *Ballad of the Broken Seas*!' she says at the top of her voice and again everybody in the room looks round at her. The Hells Angel woman beckons me over, 'She's a character, isn't she?'

I smile, squirt some hand gel onto my hands and tell Heather that I'll phone her later.

'Bring me some more knickers!'

After six days Edward wants to know why he hasn't been invited to see his mam. I tell him that I thought he didn't like hospitals. 'Well I'd like to see her, what will I see?'

'Your mam.'

'What does she look like?'

'Your mam!'

On the way to the hospital I tell Edward that his mam's head is a bit swollen and that she's got quite a big scar. When he walks through the door of the ward he takes one look at her and then looks around at me. 'Is there something you haven't been telling me?' Then he steels himself and goes over to give his mam a hug.

'I think you might be in here for a bit yet.'

'No, I'm going to ask if I can come home tomorrow, you and your dad can look after me, I want to be right for Christmas and I haven't done any shopping yet.'

Edward smiles now.

The doctor says she sees no reason why Heather can't recuperate at home if there is someone there to help her and if she is willing to be visited by occupational therapists. We gathered Heather's washing and books and two bagsful of tablets and walked to the hospital exit. By coincidence we shared the lift with the young surgeon who had removed Heather's tumour. He smiled, 'Going home?' Heather smiled back, 'Yep! I hope he's cleaned round.'

Ten days after an operation to remove a tumour as big as an apple from the side of her head, Heather is home and a week later she wants to visit the German Christmas market. It's a frosty morning and the pavements are covered in ice. When I tell Heather that I don't think it's a very good idea to go shopping today she finds her most sensible shoes.

'Look! You can't wrap me in cotton wool. I want to go shopping today and I'm going shopping whether you come or not and that's final.'

We go shopping.

She holds my arm as we skate and slide around the German Christmas market.

When the occupational therapist visits she wants to do some tests. She has a kind of card game and shuffles the deck.

'Now, Heather, I'm going to turn these cards and if you think the card I show is the same colour as the previous one I'd like you to say "yes". If it's a different colour, just say "no".' She turns the cards, Heather says, 'Eight of spades.' The therapist looks at me and turns another card. Heathers says, 'Four of diamonds!' The therapist says, 'No, I'd like you to say "yes" if it's the same colour.' She turns another card, Heather says, 'Red!' I start to laugh. The therapist puts her cards down. I say, 'I'm sorry, it's just that Heather was never any good at following rules and logic before she was poorly, so I think we might have even less chance now.' The therapist only came twice and made a couple of phone calls and was then satisfied that Heather was fine, eccentric, but fine.

After Christmas I wrote to the Chinese university to tell them I wouldn't be able to take up their offer. When I told Heather she said, 'Don't be so bloody stupid, get back on that e-mail and change your mind again. I'm as right as rain now, in fact I'm going back to work myself after my birthday.' Heather's birthday came at the end of April and she went for a spa treatment at Harrogate Turkish baths and a night in a posh hotel. Heather discarded the woollen hat she had been wearing to cover her scar, satisfied herself that her head was no longer bumpy by checking herself in the mirror at the back of the kitchen sink. At the restaurant in the hotel she said, 'Pick me a bottle of good wine and don't look at the price.'

Between New Year and her birthday, Heather painted a lot of pictures, the squiggles disappeared and were replaced with blood and apples. In May I prepared for a trip to China.

The thought of what I would actually do in China terrified me. I discovered that the North East Normal University in Changchun was far from normal, but a very prestigious one that educated some of China's most brilliant young minds. I got an e-mail from Dr Yuchen Yang a few weeks before I was due to go that laid out the teaching schedule. Part of the schedule involved giving a series of talks about Shakespeare's impact on English drama. I nearly fainted when I saw it. I came into our front room. Heather was watching *Borgen*.

'I'm not going!'

'Where?'

'China!'

'What are you talking about?'

'They're asking me to talk about stuff that I don't know hardly anything about.'

'Well, write back and tell them that you'll talk only about stuff you do know about.'

'Because they want Shakespeare not bloody rugby league, allotments and growing up in a pit village.'

'You're talking out of your arse now. You know about how to tell stories and write them down, don't you? Tell them you'll do that.'

'What if my dad dies while I'm away.'

'You're just making excuses now... get on with it!'

I phoned my friend Rachel van Riel for advice. She told me that I had much more to offer than a few thoughts on Shakespeare. 'Just send a polite note back and tell them that

Shakespeare's is not your area of speciality, they'll understand that, they're academics, they all specialise and they don't step out of their areas of expertise, so they wouldn't expect you to.'

I wrote back and told the people at Changchun that I didn't feel comfortable enough giving four two-hour talks on Shakespeare, but that I would reference him in some talks that I intended to give on the social-realist literature of northern England in the 1950s and 60s. They seemed happy enough with this. Now all I needed to do was put both belt and braces on my thoughts about that particular school of storytelling.

A few years before, I had made friends through Facebook with Gary McMahon, aka Dr Riff-Raff, a Manchester academic who had written on Kurt Vonnegut and more pertinently on the kitchen-sink films. I arranged to meet Gary in Eccles. Changing trains at Stalybridge on the way, I found I had half an hour to kill so I went to buy him a bunch of flowers from Aldi. On my next train I was joined at Manchester Victoria by two young Asian women. They sat opposite me. I moved the bunch of flowers off the table and held them. One of the women said, 'What beautiful flowers, someone waiting is very lucky!'

Dr Riff-Raff was waiting at the platform for me when I got off the train. We shook hands, our first meeting outside of cyberspace. I gave him the flowers. He pointed down the platform and said, 'Follow me.' As we walked towards the platform ramp I looked up and saw the two women going by as the train set off. I waved. I wondered what stories they would tell about the man on the train with flowers.

Dr Riff-Raff couldn't find a vase, so he put his flowers into an old thermos flask and set them on the draining board next to his kitchen sink. He didn't have any tea so when I said I would drink water he offered me a soluble orange vitamin C tablet to put in it. We sat at his laptop that was on the table overlooking the back yard of his terraced house.

'Did you bring some books with you?'

I had, I brought well-thumbed copies of *A Kestrel For a Knave*, *Saturday Night and Sunday Morning*, *A Kind of Loving*, *Room at the Top* and *This Sporting Life*.

We started with *Kes* and its opening lines.

'There were no curtains up. The window was a hard-edged block the colour of the night sky. Inside the bedroom the darkness was of a gritty texture. The wardrobe and bed were blurred shapes in the darkness. Silence.'

Dr Riff-Raff asked me what I thought Barry Hines was saying here.

'Well, I think he's describing a very typical early morning scene in the cold back bedroom of a Northern working-class household.'

'Yes, but look at the words. They tell us a lot about nothingness. There's an absence of things. Even the few possessions here, the wardrobe and bed, are blurred, out of focus, as though they hardly belong. There aren't any curtains, even the poorest of people have curtains, but this family haven't even got them. And "Silence" is a refrain, even an absence of sound adds to the nothingness.'

'I get you.'

'And grittiness is there, "Grit" is a word analysts use in describing Northern realism, here "gritty" means hard, unforgiving, not soft textures.'

'Or do you think he might have been playing with the theatrical phrase "Curtains up", here there are "No curtains up" meaning this story is not a make-believe play, but reality.'

'Fucking hell! I hadn't thought of that. But you're right. Now that's Barry Hines ticked off, let's have a look at the other stuff.'

It's what Barry had been saying at the screening of *Shakespeare in Love*. 'People putting on different outfits so they can pretend to be someone else!'

We spent five hours in Dr Riff-Raff's freezing cold front room analysing Sillitoe, Barstow and David Storey.

'I think you're going to be fine, Ian. Throw a bit of D.H. Lawrence in and some stuff about your own work on the oral story-telling tradition and you're on to a winner. But just remember scholars need to feel that the work they do on curating and deciphering literature is important, so give a nod to that as well.'

When I got home I started work on what became a 20,000 word paper on my own literary influences and the importance of writing workshops that create a new body of work for analysis. I attached the paper to my next e-mail to the professors at Changchun. I don't know if anybody read my paper, but they told me by return that they were very happy with what I was proposing.

Dr Riff-Raff gave me the confidence to believe I could do it. I called for a couple of pints when I got off the train from Manchester. Heather had a shepherd's pie in the oven when I walked through the kitchen door.

'How did it go?'

Between mouthfuls of mashed potato and mince I told her that I was happier now.

'So you're off to China then?'

'Yes.'

'See!'

'See what!'

'I told you, you were nattering for nowt.'

Open Up Your Door

My dad was given six weeks or so at the beginning of the year. Throughout the spring he fought a fierce battle with his cancer. I phoned our Andrew up every now and again and he told me that Dad was still laughing in the face of it and still saying, 'I think I can get on t'top side of this if I can get out and about.' In May when I phoned, Andrew said he was down to about six stone and that he had terrible bed sores.

As spring turned into the start of summer he was still a swinging gate, hanging by threads. I started to wonder when he would die. I was due to go to China at the end of May. A part of me was wishing he would go before then, but another part was hoping that he would fight on. I knew, we all knew, that he was only going one road and he wouldn't get right, but from what our Andrew said and from what I had seen, he seemed to be still relishing his battle.

Before I set off for China I phoned Andrew again. I asked if I could speak to my dad. Andrew said, 'You can, but you might not make out what he's saying, because he's taking a lot of medication now and he doesn't seem to know who he is anymore.' My dad shouted down the phone, 'I'm still bloody here tha knows, I haven't disappeared yet!'

'Are you comfortable?'

'Am I bollocks. I'm dying, lad.'

'Is Andrew looking after you?'

'No, he's like my arse. But he does his best.'

'I'll come to see you again when I get back.'

'Right-o, I'll wait a bit longer then afore I go then.'

'Have you thought about a nursing home?'

204

'Hey?'

'I said have you thought about a nursing home?'

'I heard what tha fucking said.'

'Well, what do you think?'

'Never think, lad, 'cos you know what thought did don't you?'

'No, nobody ever told me what thought did.'

'Well he didn't end up in a fucking nursing home and this one won't either. And you can tell them Sid Clayton told you that for nowt.'

I heard my dad hand the phone back to Andrew. He said, 'All that fucking education and he knows nothing.'

On the back of the seat in front of me there's a screen that shows the flight path of the China Airways flight from London to Beijing. On it there's a little aeroplane and this little aeroplane has been my companion on and off for the last few sleepless hours. In the middle of the night I have tried to watch the James Bond film *Skyfall* and Abraham Lincoln played by Daniel Day-Lewis. I can't concentrate, so I keep coming back to the little aeroplane. I have watched it over Helsinki and Tartu, then St. Petersburg and now I'm 68 kilometres short of Kyzyl and Ulaanbaatar lies beyond. I'm having a chuckle about something that happened in Heathrow airport. The baggage check-in clerk told me that my bag was too heavy. I could either pay for the excess or try to redistribute some of the weight into my carry-on luggage. I unzipped my big case and started to take heavier items out; some books I brought as teaching aids, some spare shoes and a jacket that I put on even though I'm boiling and it's nearly 26 degrees. The lad behind the desk smirks and says, 'Why are you taking a packet of Yorkshire Tea?' He looks down at the stuff still in my check-in case.

The penny drops. 'Aye, I see your logic. Why would I be taking tea to China? Well, I don't know to be fair, I just take tea with me everywhere I go, I suppose I won't need it in China, eh? Do you want it?'

'I drink coffee.'

'Well I'll take it then. You never know when it might come in.'

At Beijing airport the temperature is 38 degrees. Inside my jacket I'm lathered with sweat. I'm tired, I haven't slept for nearly thirty hours, it's two o'clock in the afternoon, but my body thinks it's breakfast time.

I'm in a huge modern building with about six floors in downtown Changchun. The building is called KTV and you can hire a private suite here for your friends to sing karaoke. It feels like a casino, there are marble-top tables, chandeliers, exotic fruits and faux leather buttoned sofas.

On the table in front of me are bowls of nuts and popcorn, bottles of beer, pots of tea, a selection of microphones and some tambourines. On the wall opposite is a huge flat-screen television built into a gilt frame, the sort of ornate frame you might find around a portrait of a bygone alderman in a town hall.

I'm here with a gang of professors and teachers and it's my turn to sing. I'm about to do a duet with a professor of economic theory. We're going to sing 'Edelweiss' together. The professor has a soprano as high as the hills where lonely goat herders ply their trade and I struggle to find my way into the song. As we get to the bit where 'blossoms of snow bloom and grow' we blend and it doesn't sound half bad, and, by the end of the song she looks 'happy to meet me' and I'm 'blessing her homeland forever'.

The gang cheer and shake tambourines.

As my grandad used to say, 'I've done some bloody stuff in my time but...'

For the last two hours we have been treated to a playlist the like of which has never been heard, even on the most bizarre iPod shuffle you could think of. Peking opera followed Creedence Clearwater Revival followed Frank Sinatra followed Inner Mongolian folk song. Birds have flown over Tibetan meadows, we've been caught in a trap where we can't go back because we love our baby too much, and we've spread the news that we're leaving today. In between, Mariah Carey in the shape of a young English teacher called Li made a guest appearance and we rounded off all living in a yellow submarine. At the door three beautiful girls in long silk dresses wave us off into the siling down rain.

In the car on the way back to my apartment at the university I wonder if all of this really happened. We queue in traffic by a flyover and beneath the flyover some couples are ballroom dancing. I start to laugh to myself. Hui, who has hosted our evening's entertainment, asks me why I am laughing. I tell her that it has been an overwhelming day and that China has this wonderful habit of throwing me completely out. 'China disorientates me!' I say. Hui smiles and nods.

Earlier in the day she took me to Jilin University to meet her mentor, the very eminent Professor Yang, an economic theorist and calligrapher. Professor Yang is a little bird of a man, like a wren hopping about in a garden. I don't know how old he is, but it doesn't matter. He asks me to tell him something about myself. I don't know what to say. For some reason he reminds me of Lady Clegg, the widow of the great educator, Sir Alec. So I tell him about meeting her.

'I once met the widow of the man who educated many of the working-class boys in my region. She and her husband believed that everybody could be creative, even the poor and unwashed sons of coal miners if only given the opportunity.'

Professor Yang nodded sagely and said, 'I started as a son of a peasant in the countryside.' He then talked about his interest in the thinkings of Keynes and Marx and with relish about Confucius and Tao, which seemed to be his real passions. Then with a flourish he jumped out of his swivel chair and declared that he would make something for me. He took up his calligraphy brush and rolled out a piece of paper about ten feet long and wrote something based on the Analects of Confucius. We called at an art shop in the market and had it framed.

After karaoke and Confucius, I can't sleep. I lie on my sofa and watch the English-speaking news channel on CCTV. There is a beautiful weather lady called Bo-Yee Poon, she speaks in a very strong American-accented English. She talks about the winds of the 'Ty-Bettan-Pla-Tow,' the rainfall in 'Moss-Kow' and before she signs off says 'Y'awl take care now and enjoy the rest of your day'. I start to think of my journey so far.

I'd been greeted at Beijing airport by Ming, a close friend of Hui, who lives there with her husband Qian, a hospital doctor. In the evening Qian and Ming took me to eat at a restaurant called Kitchen No.44. Qian said, 'A speciality of this place is black goat with water chestnut.' I washed it down with a bottle of Tsingtao beer.

My hotel room is stiflingly hot. My body clock is all over the shop and I can't sleep. My dad comes into my mind. He's lying on his bed waiting to die. He replays cowboy pictures that he's seen in flea pit cinemas. He's Les Kellett the wrestler reckoning to be punch-drunk and staggering around the ring in striped swimming trunks. Then he's Nat King Cole and he's singing 'Smoke Gets in Your Eyes'. When I close my eyes I see him with oiled-up hands mending a bicycle chain. My mother is there too, she's washing some clothes in the kitchen sink. She makes a lather with a lump of green Fairy soap and rubs the clothes together with the heels of her hands. My dad drops his chain onto a sheet of newspaper that he's put down. He goes towards my mother and is about to put his arms around her from behind. She catches sight of him in the mirror over the sink, or perhaps she senses what he's about to do. She spins round, throws up her arms in the air and suds spatter onto my dad.

'Nay, lass' my dad says, 'I'm only trying to cuddle you, love.'

'Well keep your filthy bloody hands away from me, I'm not in the mood and don't *love* me.'

Early the next morning Ming knocks at the door of my hotel room. 'We will take the underground train to Tiananmen Square.' And we do. We come up the stairs from the subway into a burning hot day. I buy a bottle of mineral water from a lady on a bicycle wearing a face mask.

'Do people wear these masks because of pollution?'

Ming says, 'Some of them might do, but mostly it is to stop the spread of germs if they have a cold.'

We are approached by three girls from Marin County, the posh part of San Francisco. They speak perfect Chinese, but talk to me in English.

'We go to an Immersion school, all of our lessons are conducted in Chinese. We are conducting a survey about tourism in Beijing, would you like to take part?'

Less than a week ago I was in Pontefract market place and I was stopped by a young man who wanted me to give money to the Red Cross and a woman who was against the culling of badgers. You could put me in a desert and I would get stopped by someone with a clipboard who is doing a survey.

'Can I ask where you are from?'

'I'm from a town called Featherstone, in the north of England.'

'Is that Scotland? My folks were from Scotland and Norway.'

'I can tell you knowledge of Chinese is better than your geography.'

The young Californian pulls her lip and goes off to speak to Ming in Chinese. And I go to take some photographs of a portrait of Chairman Mao and some marching soldiers near the Great Hall of the People.

At lunchtime, I sit in the shade under a tree next to some children, they are all wearing red neckerchiefs. It's Children's Day and the red neckerchief is a symbol of that. They are eating corn on the cob and drinking lychee juice. They all finish their corn and juice at the same time, uncross their legs, stand up together and form a crocodile behind their teachers to move on. Ming has bought tickets to see the Forbidden City and we pass through the Gate of Heavenly Peace. The Forbidden City was off limits for ordinary people for five hundred years, today it is swarming with folk. We are carried forward on a tide of visitors eager to see how the Emperors lived. There are more than 900 buildings in the Forbidden City: there's a Palace of Kindliness, a Hall of Mental Cultivation and a Tower of Enhanced Righteousness, there's even a building for the Imperial Telephone. There was also for a short while a Starbucks but that seems to have disappeared. Somewhere between the Gate of Heavenly Purity and The Gate of Great Ancestors I trip over a cobble and fall flat on my backside whilst walking backwards to take a photo. It doesn't seem right to fall on your arse near to a gate called Heavenly Purity so I jump up as quick as I can and trot over to take some more pictures near the Well of the Concubine.

In the afternoon, Ming and I meet up with some of their friends and drive for a couple of hours to The Great Wall. I meet James, a twelve-year-old piano and sax playing maths genius. He wants me to analyse the works of Conan Doyle as we climb the wall. He then starts humming works of classical music to me. I recognise 'The Trout'.

'Is that Schubert?'

'Yes it is, do you know that the arpeggios on the piano represent the fast-flowing river where the trout swims?'

'No, I didn't know that James, but I do now.'

We climb the wall for nearly an hour and when we reach the top, I say to James, 'Can you see Blackpool Tower from here?'

'Sorry, I don't understand.'

'I'm just kidding.'

'Ahh! An English joke, I like jokes.'

I'm doubled up now, completely out of breath and I've started to get dizzy. I know that at any moment James is going to ask me to tell him some English jokes. I tell him to look up to the sky and wave.

'Why?'

'Well, you never know, a passing astronaut might be looking down and waving back.'

'Ahh! but this is not true. It is a popular myth that the Great Wall of China can be seen from craft orbiting the earth.'

We walk down now, to a village halfway down the mountain. Two Cypress trees intertwine to form a gateway to the village. One is called The Dragon, the other The Phoenix. Next to here is a yardful of hens and in the yard are some tables and people cooking on open stoves. It doesn't look too hygienic, but the food is delicious. I eat dry beans, tofu and chestnuts. Bottles of beer are brought to the table and as night falls and the stars start to twinkle we bat away flying insects and start to sing. A table full of doctors and their wives, a man from Yorkshire and a twelve-year-old boy who could talk for China in the foothills below the Great Wall and we're singing Eric Clapton's 'Tears in Heaven', John Denver's 'Annie's Song' and a rousing finale of 'Take Me Home, Country Roads'.

On the way back to the cars, James asks me if we might keep in touch by e-mail. His mother thanks me for keeping him entertained and tells me that he is normally a very quiet boy. At the car park, an old woman with a wicker basket full of tourist tat wants to sell me something. I buy a copy of Chairman Mao's little red book. James asks me if I will read it.

'I have it already.'

'Mao was a great poet.'

'Yes and so could you be.'

James trots off to the back seat of his dad's car, belts himself in, smiles and waves through the window.

My journey up to the north east and the city of Changchun started at Beijing railway station. Ming came to wave me off, she gave me a bottle of Tibetan mineral water for the journey, some cakes and yoghurt. On the platform she asked me out of the blue if I had seen the film *The Iron Lady*.

'No, I'm afraid I will never watch that film.'

'What is your opinion of Margaret Thatcher?'

'I cannot think of one good word to say about her.'

'Yes, I saw on Chinese news that many people in the north of Britain do not like her.'

'Aye, that's right.'

Then she thought for a bit and said, 'But I am very fond of Meryl Streep!'

I smiled, bid her 'au revoir' and jumped on to the train. 'Ladies and Gentlemen,' said a voice over the speakers, 'this is the train master speaking, I wish you have a nice trip.'

I am on my way to Changchun. One of the people who will help me there is Danny, a teacher who specialises in the romantic poets. One day Danny told me, 'If you look at a map of China it is in the shape of a cockerel, then look for the eye of the cockerel and that is where you find Changchun.'

Even in my wildest dreams I have never landed in the eye of a cockerel.

*

There are some thick curtains up at the window, but through some gaps the street lights peep through. I can just about cope with this when I put my head down to sleep. What I can't do with is the sound of pneumatic drills on the main road nearby. It's midnight and the road menders are still working on the road between the university campus and the entrance to the zoo across the way.

I sandwich my head between two pillows, one under and one on top of my head. Then silence. I get up and peer through the curtains to see if they have already stopped. I can't see anybody for poplar trees that sway in the night air. I get back into bed. I toss and turn, then sit up and put the light and my glasses on. I pick up my notebook and go over what I'm going to do in the morning.

I am in an apartment on the campus of Changchun University.

When a lot of men reach middle-age they buy a Harley-Davidson motorbike and some leathers or else join a gym and squirt shower gel onto receding hair after a session on the dumbbells. I have come on my own to China.

On the bedside table next to me is a red telephone with a curly wire that keeps falling out of the receiver, a half-drunk bottle of Tibetan Mountain mineral water, a packet of roll-up tobacco and two books; Bill Bryson's *Shakespeare: The World as a Stage* and Barry Hines' *A Kestrel for a Knave*. The telephone rings.

The only two people in the world who know my number are my son Edward and my partner Heather. Before I pick up the phone I shove the curly wire into the receiver to make sure it doesn't fall out. I pick up and say, 'Hello, love.' A man's voice on the other end says, 'Oooh! I didn't know you cared!' This is Ned Thacker, my friend and former colleague from when I worked at Yorkshire Television. Ned directed a lot of the early programmes I presented. In fact, it was Ned who introduced me to work on Yorkshire telly.

'How did you know where to find me?'

'I've just phoned Heather. She was having her tea and she gave me this number.'

'Do you know what time it is?'

'Teatime.'

'Well it's after midnight here! Go on!'

'I've been talking to JP Bean, the Sheffield author. We were discussing Barry Hines. You know he's in a nursing home?'

'I do.'

'Well, he might not know you now. I don't think he knows anybody anymore. Except the other week he had some sort of seizure and after that he started to remember some things. JP Bean met his partner Eleanor the other day and they were talking about who might write his biography. Your name was mentioned. Would you be interested in going to see him when you get back?'

'He's my hero!'

'I know, that's why we thought it might be a good idea!'

'I'd love to if I could.'

'I'll send you Eleanor's phone number. I'm not stopping on because I don't know how much it's costing me.'

China has done funny things to me. There have been times over the past few days when I haven't known whether I was coming or going. I haven't been sleeping very well, road menders on the night shift, indigestion, and nattering about what I'm saying in the lecture rooms have seen to that. Now I don't know whether I'm dreaming or awake. I look at my watch and pick up Barry's book. I read the famous opening lines 'There were no curtains up. The window was a hard-edged block the colour of the night sky.'

I sleep for about two hours. I'm woken by a voice on my mobile phone, 'It's six o'clock, time to get up.' By seven in the morning it's already near 30 degrees and it's raining again. In Changchun the winters drop down to -24 degrees and in summer it goes to 34 plus. They don't have much autumn and the students here long for spring, though it doesn't last too long. Winter turns to summer quickly and just as quickly back to winter.

At the door of the lecture room I'm greeted by a young woman in horn-rimmed glasses and pinafore type dress.

'Dear Professor, I have been waiting to meet you, I have read twenty-three of Shakespeare's thirty-eight plays and almost all of the sonnets and I'm looking forward to discussing them with you.'

Aye, aye, here we go.

'Well, we won't be doing that this time. I want to know where you are from and what it's like to be there.' The student looks startled, pushes her glasses back onto the bridge of her nose and says, 'Oh, I see!'

There are roughly twenty-five students in the lecture room from all over China. They are mostly women except for three lads in T-shirts who are fiddling with their smartphones. On the T-shirt of one of these lads is the slogan 'Rock Against Racism, Victoria Park, London'. I tell this lad that I was at that gig back in 1978 and ask him how he comes to be wearing a T-shirt for an event that took place thirty-five years ago. He shrugs, 'I don't know, I just collect T-shirts from London.'

'Okay. Does anybody like stories?'

Twenty-five pairs of eyes look at me. Nobody says anything. I try again, 'Does anybody like stories?' The woman who has read a lot of Shakespeare says, 'Do you mean in the critical and analytical sense?'

'No, I mean do you like to read or listen to stories.' The lad in the Rock Against Racism T-shirt says, 'We have all read *Beowulf.*' A young woman on the front row says, 'I am currently trying to understand Daphne du Maurier's book *Rebecca.*'

'Okay, that's a start, what about something more recent. Does anybody know a story about the last few days?'

All the eyes go down. Somewhere on the back row a tone rings out to say someone has a text message.

'Right then. The other day I got lost in Beijing...' and I tell them a story of a walk I made from my hotel room into the city. 'I couldn't read any of the writing I saw and I couldn't understand what anybody was saying. It was dark and starting to rain. I got lost and a beggar with no legs and only one arm pointed the way for me with a combination of hand gestures and grunting sounds. On the way back everyone I passed was either texting, or sheltering under a brolly. Nobody looked at me, if they had done, they would have seen a man happy to be lost in the rain in the back streets of Beijing, finding a way home. I think some people live in one place while others travel, yet the ones who travel further often need the help of those who live in the small world. Anyhow, I'm here now and I brought that story with me.'

I'm greeted with a mixture of puzzlement and that look

people give when they are waiting for more. When I worked on the telly we used to smile and nod when we wanted our interviewee to expand upon what they were saying. Some of the students smile and nod. I bow my head slightly and say, 'The end.' More smiles, more nodding and then a little ripple of applause. The Shakespeare woman puts her hand up and says, 'Dear Teacher, your story is somewhat reminiscent of the story of the Peng Bird and the little sparrows as told by Zhuangzi.' Her fellow students look at her and nod approval. She is slightly embarrassed and shuffles in her seat.

'Tell me the story of the Peng Bird and the sparrows.'

She blushes.

'I'd like to hear it.'

The students giggle and nod again, then they look to their classmate. I ask her to come to the front and tell the story, she does slowly and shyly, twisting her fingers into her pinafore.

She speaks in a quiet voice.

'Can you hear at the back? You'll have to speak loud like me.'

'Zhuangzi told the story of the little sparrows' small happiness.' The students giggle again.

'Come on mates, give her some respect.'

On the word respect the students stop giggling straightaway and sit up straight-backed.

'The great Peng Bird can soar at a height of 9,000 miles. Below in a tree some sparrows laughed at him, "Look at that crazy bird, he wastes his energy flying so high, not like us, if we want to sing, we just sit on a branch and sing and if we want to eat a worm we flutter down to the grass and take one. We couldn't be more carefree." The teacher came and scolded the sparrows. "You need to realise that there are differences between the realm of the sparrow and the Peng Bird. We shouldn't laugh at the little sparrow in his small world, neither should we envy the Peng Bird in all his grandeur."'

The student finishes her story and doesn't know what to do

next. She looks at me, then at her mates and then at the floor. Her fingers fast in the folds of her pinafore. 'Thank you, I like the story, please take your seat. Now, everybody, tell me, when I was in the back streets of Beijing, was I a sparrow or a Peng Bird?' The words Peng Bird murmur and echo around the room.

'Well I think I'm a sparrow. It's just that I left my little world and lost my way a bit. Let me tell you a bit where I'm from. All my male ancestors were coal miners and when I grew up I was happy to grow in the streets where I was born. Every now and again I peeped round the corner at the top of my street and imagined what adventures I might have one day, but mostly I was happy to be where I was from. All of my grandfather's stories took place on the walk between his house and where he worked or between his back door and his favourite pub and my grandmother's tales happened in her kitchen or the yard outside. They both told brilliant stories about where they were from, the food they liked to eat, the clothes they wore, the sounds they heard and things they picked up. My grandad told me, "Whenever you see a big stone, always pick it up to look what's underneath." From them I learned that the best stories can start anywhere and that we all have stories to tell. Now, I want you to tell me some stories about where you are from. Don't tell me the name of the place, just use your five senses and allow me to smell what you smell, touch what you touch and then I'll know.'

There is half an hour of scratched heads and the scrape of pen on paper, a rapid pressing of digits on smartphone keypads in an attempt to locate the right word and then I say, 'Right, let's hear what you have come to, who wants to be brave and go first?' They all look at the Shakespeare lady. I point a finger at one of the women on the middle row and say, 'Would you like to share your story?'

She stands up and blushes. 'I feel the sand between my toes and hear the screeching birds swirling above. The waves are rolling in and I can smell the salt breeze. We sit on a blanket and eat pineapples and ice cream.' She sits down abruptly, lets her hair fall over her face and closes her notebook.

'Beautiful!'

She looks up and sweeps her hair back with her hand, holds it on top of her head.

'You're from a long way away aren't you?'

She smiles. 'It took me three days to come here by train, it is the first time I have been away from home.'

'Okay, now tell me the name of the place.'

'I am from Hainan, it is China's most southerly province, an island in the South China Sea.'

'You must have been frightened to make this journey.'

'No. Not frightened, just excited.' She lets her hair fall again and smiles now.

I look at another woman in the second row, 'Would you like to tell us what you have written?'

'I hear the whistle of a train in the night. The wind is like ice and it goes into my bones. Coal is everywhere. The dust on our skin and the smell in our noses.'

I laugh and say, 'That sounds like where I am from.'

She says, 'From my window I can see to Russia.'

We go around the room, suddenly everyone is eager to read. We hear about red-tiled roofs on low houses, the morning cockerel, grandmother's cooking, kites flying over the cultural square and parcels of sticky rice called *zongzi*. I mention that I'd like to try these sticky rice parcels and a few days later at the next lecture one of the youngest students brings me a Tupperware boxful of these traditional snacks. 'My mother has made these for dear Teacher,' the young woman says.

'Can I eat one now?'

All the students laugh at me and then nod.

I unwrap the bamboo leaves on this food parcel and eat the sticky rice inside. It's flavoured with dates.

'Delicious!'

The students laugh again.

'Tell your mam she's a good cook.'

The young student smiles and her mates on either side nudge her.

'Do they keep?'

Some puzzled looks greet me.

'I mean to say, do I need to eat them all today or can I save one or two for my breakfast?'

There are looks on all the faces that say, 'Who is this crazy man?'

'Now, comrades. You might think I have an unusual approach, but as we sometimes say in England, "There is method in my madness." I know that you have all analysed Shakespeare and that's good. But that is English from a long time ago. And I know that you have all spent years revising the grammar of my language, but you might get a shock if you ever come to England when you find that we don't really know it as well as you do.'

Grace, the Shakespeare student, gives me a look. I tell them that Britain is an island but its language is not set in stone. It floats on the water. That yesterday's stories are waiting to be written on clean sheets. 'English is organic, constantly shifting and changing and growing again. It's up to us to find the new stories and these stories live where we are from.' Grace nods. I wink at her. She doesn't quite wink back, but she gets what I'm on about.

I teach on Mondays, Tuesdays and Fridays. On Tuesdays Hui has an afternoon free so offers to show me around. There's a vast area of park and woodland that she calls 'The Moon Lake' park. One Tuesday afternoon we go there to walk. I have an upset stomach, I've been told to only drink bottled water, but occasionally the heat gets to me and I have a swig from the tap. I'm also missing my home and family and feeling a bit sorry for myself.

Today it is Dragon Boat Festival day which commemorates

the death by drowning in a river of an ancient leader called Qu Yuan, a thinker and a poet. This is the day on which families make the sticky rice parcels wrapped in bamboo leaves. Originally these parcels were made by villagers who lived near the river in which their leader died. They wanted to feed the fishes so that they wouldn't eat their leader's body before the dragon boats could find him.

Hui and I walk up to a tower that offers panoramic views of the city of Changchun. I lean on a rail and take it all in. Hui senses that I am feeling sad.

'What are you thinking about, Ian?'

'Oh! Just some stuff!'

'What stuff?'

'I'm thinking about my dad and Heather and Edward and about Billie.'

'Okay. Let me show you something.'

We walk back down the steps from the tower and by the edge of a lake to a Buddhist temple. The temple is simple and beautiful. We buy some incense sticks and ask one of the monks where we can light them. He pours some oil into a little tin bucket and sets fire to it. I have twelve incense sticks and there are four altars, one at each side of the courtyard. I light the sticks and Hui shows me to the first altar. She shows me what to do, places a stick upright in the pile of ashes left by burned out sticks, then bows, takes a step or two back and closes her eyes. She mouths something under her breath and gestures for me to do the same. I visit each altar and repeat the mantra. I picture Billie on the placing of the first stick, Heather and Edward on the second and third, my dad on the fourth. My picture of Billie is of her in a red duffle coat on her way to school, Heather and Edward are sitting on the sofa watching *Coronation Street*, but no matter how I try, I can't get a clear image of my dad.

The monks here seem to be self-sufficient, there is a huge, lovely garden, well-tended where they grow beans, tomatoes, potatoes and cabbages. They sell bracelets crafted from wooden beads and ornaments. We stand in the garden in the rain. Hui says, 'When the moon is full, I like to come here and imagine that people who I miss are looking up too and we both are looking at the same moon.'

On the way back to the campus she puts a CD into the player. It is Nick Drake. I have brought presents of typically English music, Fairport Convention is one, Nick Drake another. In a traffic jam near a roadwork Nick Drake sings 'One of These Things First'.

I could have been a signpost
Could have been a clock
As simple as a kettle
Steady as a rock

I sing along to the lyrics and look for the moon.

On the Sunday, Danny Chen calls and asks if I would like to take lunch with him in the teachers' dining room. I like it here, the waitresses wear red polo shirts and yellow marigold gloves when they mop the floor and smile at me every time I walk in. They say, 'Nee-Hao' and I say 'Nee-Hao' back to them. I have been taught some words phonetically and 'Hello' is the only word I can think to say at first. Over the weeks I learn that please is *ching,* rice is *mee-fan,* bread is *miam-bau,* beer is *pijou,* beef is *neo-roe* and thank you is *shie-shie.* You can go a long way with please, rice, bread, beer, beef and thank you.

The waitresses have grown accustomed to me over the weeks. As soon as I sit down and take off the cowboy hat I wear to keep the sun off my head, they bring a menu book full of pictures to make it easier for me to order, an ashtray, a pair of chopsticks and a glass full of hot water. They then stand smiling and wait until I look at the pictures and point to something that I'd like to eat. They take the top copy of my order to the kitchen and a carbon copy to a big counter. Behind the counter sits a lady in horn-rimmed glasses beneath a lit-up picture of Chairman Mao fastened to a cupboard door with three drawing pins and a piece of tape. Danny asks me what I would like to eat. I tell him that I have been eating more or less the same things each day because I don't know what else to have and nobody here can speak English to me.

'Okay, what have you had so far?'

'Beef stew, bread and rice.'

'Well, let's try something different. What about duck, do you like duck?'

'I do like duck.'

'Okay, let's see what they have.' Danny leafs through the picture book menu. 'Ahh! Here is a speciality of the house.' He shows me a picture of six ducks' heads that look like they have been roasted. Their beaks are still attached and point towards the middle of the plate.

'This should be very good, would you like to try it?'

'I'm not sure, I've never eaten a duck's face before.'

The waitress waits and smiles. 'I'll tell you what Danny, I'll have beef stew and bread. I like that.'

After our dinner Danny asks me if I would like to visit his mother and father. They live in an apartment on the campus and look after his seven-month-old baby when he is working. The welcome Danny's mother and father give is warm and kindly. Dad makes a pot of green tea and goes out to the street market to buy watermelon. Mam proudly shows me a picture of a waterfall she made for her son while he was away in America for 12 months studying. It is an exquisite tapestry that took six hours a day for a whole year to complete. Danny's mother says something in Chinese to him and he translates, 'My mother says that she missed me so much and was so anxious about me in America, that she thought about me with every stitch.' I don't know what to say, so I ask Danny to tell his mother that I think she looks too young to be a grandmother. She turns her face away when he tells her and goes off to fetch the baby. I want to ask if I might hold the baby, but I don't know if this is the right etiquette. One thing I have learned here in China is that manners can be very formal. I think through my repertoire of nursery rhymes and recite 'Hickory Dickory Dock' to the baby, then follow it with 'Baa Baa Black Sheep' and 'How Much is That Doggy in the Window'.

The following Tuesday, Hui takes me to a market. I buy some silk for Heather and some iPod headphones for Edward. Hui then asks if I would like to see the food market and when I say yes, she says, 'You don't have to, because you might see something that you don't like.'

We walk past a row of Korean butchers. On wooden chopping boards at the front of their stalls are pieces of dog. On one of the boards there is a dog's head and neck, the teeth are still in its mouth.

Later in the afternoon, Hui drives me to the countryside. Thunderstorms gather and the rain falls in huge drops. We park in a village surrounded by sweetcorn fields.

'I'm not sure that I should show you this. It's dirty, old, rural China, not modern or clean.'

When we get out of the car the air smells of cow shit.

'Do you see what I mean?'

'Don't worry, Hui, I'd sooner smell the exhaust of a cow than that of a car, any day.'

She laughs.

'The people here still have no bathroom and the toilet is outside.'

'Well that's nothing, Hui. I didn't have my first bath in a bathroom until I was sixteen. And my grandfather was still using our outside toilet up to 1985 when he moved to the council flat.'

I didn't tell her that my grandad was afraid to use the indoor bathroom when we had guests in case he farted too loudly.

Hui says, 'I like you to see the different parts of China.'

I tease her and say, 'Okay, when do I get to go to a Party meeting?'

In a country lane on the way back we see a young man hitching a lift in the pouring rain. We are in the middle of pastureland with the odd red-tiled low house dotted around, at least ten miles away from the skyscraper and cranes in the city beyond. The young man wears a neatly pressed shirt and suit and carries a briefcase. We give him a lift. From the back seat he tells us he has been negotiating a deal with a farmer to take his company's cattle feed. We drop him off near his office on the outskirts of the city.

I say, 'That was a bit odd.'

Hui didn't think so at all. 'Many young people can't yet afford a car so they hitchhike even in their best suit or walk home in the rain. I admire that work ethic so I always give a lift to them.'

On the roadside as we start to reach the city, some older men and women in old army camouflage jackets are wielding brushes and shovels.

'Does everyone in China work?'

Hui thinks for a little bit and says, 'Yes, apart from lazy people.'

China makes me feel like I'm a long way from home one minute and at other times I think I understand. It is a bewildering, confusing, frustrating place, but I see things here that suit me. I like the manners, the kindliness, just the way.

Some evenings Hui takes me to the Cultural Square. Artists, poets, musicians and kite fliers come here to express themselves. I love it here. One warm evening I was down here as a slight breeze ruffled the people's flag that was being held by one of the men in an amateur choir. I stood transfixed by one of the women, she stood straight-backed, singing at the top of her voice with her head tilted to the night sky. Above us kites were flying, in her hand this lady held her shopping bag. The choir sang an old peasant song, 'You plant the seed, I'll do the watering, together we will grow.' When the song finished a man recited one of Chairman Mao's poems about The Long March.

Tonight a band are playing to a crowd of perhaps three hundred people. There is a keyboard player, a jazzer with a soprano sax, a drummer, singer, acoustic guitarist and a traditionally dressed man on the two-string Chinese fiddle. They sing a beautiful song from the Silk Road and Hui translates. A boy asks his girl to lift her veil so that he might see her 'lips that are like cherries and cheeks like pears'.

One of the musicians notices me, the only Western face in the crowd. He comes over, 'You are English?'

'Yes!'

'Ahh! From Liverpool?'

'No, from Featherstone.'

'Do you know Beatles songs?'

'I know "Hey Jude".'

In the blink of an eye I'm coaxed into the middle and introduced as a guest singer from England. The crowd cheer. I don't know if McCartney could ever have envisaged a version of 'Hey Jude' that started with an overture on the Chinese two-stringed fiddle and soprano saxophone, but this one did. To my own surprise, I remember all the words and even have the confidence to pull them back when they try to get to the 'la la la' bit too quickly. It is just magical. The rain having cleared, the evening is balmy, there is a sea of smiling faces all encouraging us and clapping in time to the beat and now, here we go, all together now.

'La, la, la, la, la, la la, la, la, la, la, Hey Jude!'

I walk back through the crowd to Hui. The band are already into their next number, a 'red song' in praise of Chairman Mao.

On the other side of the square, a man wielding two scruffy calligraphy brushes with long handles is painting Chinese characters onto the floor with water. The lettering is gorgeous, he does it back to front, last character first. Hui translates, 'We look up to the moon and down to find our home,' by the time she finishes the translation the water lettering has evaporated.

I can't tell what anybody is saying and I can't read hardly anything either. The CCTV television channel gives me Chinese news in English and the odd phone call from home gives me a connection to what I know, but I do feel lonely, not in a sense that I'm alone, because my friends here are as good as gold at helping to make my time here a great adventure. I'm lonely because I don't understand half of what my senses are telling me.

I start to find a way. Almost every student here wears a T-shirt with an English slogan on it. Yesterday I saw a plump girl with a shirt that said 'Be Kate Moss' on the front and 'Yeah Right!' on the back. I've seen others that say 'Big Girl Now', 'All you need is love', 'Not easy, just Sunday Morning' and 'Just do it'.

I bump into a Ghanaian student called Elvis in the lift and invite him to drink tea. He tells me that he too has had a difficult time trying to make sense of China. He seems more lost than I am.

'I left my father in Africa. He was seriously ill. I was torn between the need to look after him and continuing my education. Two months after I came here, my father died.'

I can see a sadness in his eyes and a wondering of what on earth he has let himself in for.

I befriend some more African students. At the weekend they buy crates of Harbin beer and go to sit at the side of the lily pond near an ice-cream van. They rig up a sound system and a mixture of reggae, Gangsta-Rap and Congolese Soukous music blasts out across the campus. I christen this place 'African corner' and now and again I go to sit there and take it all in.

The jangling guitar sounds of Congolese Soukous music drift into the night air and over the lily pond. A dozen or so African students start to dance and I join them. There is a string of twinkling lights above the ice-cream shed, some of the Africans are wearing long traditional African shirts in a variety of colours and the patterns start to swirl together.

For the first few weeks in China I have felt like a broken kaleidoscope, all the pieces are there, all the colours, the focus puller works but the patterns don't come. On this night in a university campus in north east China, in the company of people from all over Africa, dancing by a lily pond to music coming from a system hooked up to a generator at the back of an ice-cream shed, it all starts to make sense.

I'm still not sure where the heck I am in my head, what I'm doing here and what it's all about, but I'm happy, I'm part of something, whatever it is, and I'm dancing.

My kaleidoscope that is made up of fragments of my childhood, the onset of middle age, an attempt to reconcile with my dad, a journey of self-discovery and thoughts about my family is starting to mend. I need to connect to something in China that will help me understand why I have fallen for this place in all of its surreal, mystifying glory. I want to find a space somewhere in the middle of all this where I feel at home.

One morning I stand on a corner of the campus between the School of Physics and The Lake of Quietude, I'm watching some lads playing basketball and some girls sitting under a tree showing each other things on their smartphones. An American professor who I met briefly on the second day I came here walks by and asks, 'How's it going?' I tell him that the lectures have been a wonderful experience, that I think the people here are very welcoming and open to ideas from abroad. He says, 'Yeah! I came here a few years ago, I married a Canadian teacher over here.'

'Where are you from originally?'

'Chattanooga, but please don't say choo choo to me.'

'Okay. Bessie Smith! She came from Chattanooga.'

'Hey! Get you man.'

He then asks me what I'm doing when I'm not working.

'Oh! I just wander about. I like to see the markets and the back streets, but I find it all a bit bewildering.'

He thinks for a moment and says, 'Yep! Your world can go very small here, but you can always find interesting things in the back streets.'

Hui wants to take me to a coffee house she used to go to. When we get there it is closed down. We walk down back streets and find a place called Freedom Café and part the plastic streamer curtain that hangs over the open door. A polite woman welcomes us in and shows us through to a little room at the back with three tables and about eight chairs in it. The walls are lined with book cases and pictures, it feels like an English greasy spoon from the sixties, but there is a real atmosphere of calmness and tranquillity here. We order a pot of 'pu're' tea and the woman prepares it with great care, washing the tea first and warming the pot. She speaks no English, so Hui translates. The lady runs the café with her younger sister. Before they came the café had a bit of a reputation as a place that attracted heavy drinkers and rowdies. The lady and her sister were gently turning it into a calm oasis for bookish students and arty people, a place for wiling away time with good coffee and proper tea, a place for gentle conversations and the exchanging of ideas and creativity.

The hour we spent in that café planted a seed in me. I didn't know what the seed was, but I knew that the little space in China I had been looking for had appeared. I told the lady I would return. I actually went back, just a few hours later. I had left my cowboy hat on a chair back and realised when the sun started to burn my head. When I arrived, the lady's sister was waiting with my hat in her hand, she presented it to me with a flourish. I put it on and then lifted it again and said, 'Why thank you Ma-am!' She had no idea what the heck I was talking about of course, but gave me that smile that goes beyond the understanding of words. I'm eager now to go back to this little café and one lazy

Sunday afternoon I do. I want to take the sisters something. Something that says how thrilled I am to have found my own bit of China. I sit on a patch of grass near my apartment and take out my notebook. Two blue magpies flit between the grass and a nearby tree. I press the button on my biro and start to write:

> For my friends in the Freedom Café
> I travel without a map.
> My way takes me to the streets
> where the wind blows yesterday's newspapers.
> This is where I find the music of today,
> the kind of people I like
> and the freedom we all desire.

I carefully tear out the sheet I have been writing on and I clap my book shut. The two blue magpies fly up. I make my way to the back streets.

There are no other customers in the Freedom Café. The two sisters are standing behind the counter and greet me with a warm handshake. The older sisters says 'pu're' to me and I say 'pu're' back. I sit on a high stool at the counter and roll a cigarette, the younger sister indicates my tobacco pouch. I hand it to her, she smells the tobacco inside. I reach in my bag for my poem and place it on the counter. It occurs to me that they will not be able to read what I have put. I offer it anyhow. They both greet the gift with a puzzlement and speak to each other in their native tongue.

The older sister picks up the keyboard and places it in front of me and turns the computer screen towards where I'm sitting. On the screen I can see a translation package. I type in, 'I am a writer. I wrote a little poem for you.' Older sister types in Pinyin Chinese, 'Would you like to read it to us and then use this to translate?'

I read my poem in English then type it in and hit the 'enter' button. The sisters lean over the screen, read the translation and seem thrilled. Older sister types again, 'We will frame it and put it on the wall.' We spend two hours playing keyboard translation ping-pong, communicating through fingers. In that time I establish that older sister is also a writer, who now runs the café and occasionally plays the stock market, and the younger sister, who seems incredibly shy, is a painter and some of the works on the wall are hers. They tell me that the café door remains open all day every day and that they hope to fill the place with new ideas and artistic opportunity. They repeat the phrase 'opening the door' a lot. When they tell me that they want to programme playlists in order to create an ambience I type in, 'A friend of mine wrote a song called "Open Up Your Door". His name is Richard Hawley and he lives in the same part of England as me.' Older sister types, 'Richard Hawley' into the search engine then downloads 'Open Up Your Door'. Within seconds it is playing on the café's speakers. Two Korean men in suits come in and order coffee. Hawley is on repeat play by now and one of the Korean men comes up and in excellent English asks, 'Who is this singer? We like it very much.'

'He's called Richard Hawley, the song is called "Open Up Your Door".'

'Ahh! Okay.'

In the blink of an eye the Korean man had downloaded the track onto his smartphone.

A few days after I get back from China, I have half an hour on the phone with Richard. I tell him about the little café in Changchun and what happened with his song. He laughed and laughed and said, 'Well, fuck me!'

When I walk back the half mile or so to the university, there is a breeze and the seeds from the Yang Shu, the Chinese birch tree, are blowing all over. By the time I get back to my apartment block I am covered in a white snow of birch pollen. When I tell Hui later about what had happened she says, 'You

230

have planted many inspirational seeds here in China and now China is planting its seed on you!'

I visit the sisters in the Freedom Café for a third and a fourth time and take more musical ideas. Martin Carthy's version of 'Scarborough Fair', Sandy Denny's 'Who Knows Where the Time Goes' and Iain Matthews' version of 'Woodstock'. I tell the sisters that 'Who Know Where the Time Goes' was played at Billie's funeral and that Iain Matthews came to play 'Woodstock' at one of Billie's memorial concerts. They tell me that they know about our loss of Billie, because they have researched me on the Internet. They type in the translator 'We are sorry, she was a beautiful girl'. They then tell me that they have adopted Richard Hawley's 'Open Up Your Door' as the café's theme song. I smile at the thought that this son of a Sheffield steelworker, this hard-drinking, rockabilly rebel should be the mascot of a delicate little flower of a place, an oasis in a back street in Changchun, China.

The sisters give me a heart-shaped package of tea before I leave, all wrapped in coloured ribbon and tell me I am welcome anytime. I have goodbyes to say as well to an elderly lady in the laundry who has ironed my shirts for six weeks. In all that time we have exchanged no words, only gesticulation and me miming the action of ironing, pointing to my watch and then coming back at the appointed time with some coat hangers. This time she pats me on the shoulder when I mime being an aeroplane and say 'London' and then 'bye-bye', she says 'baa-baa'.

My final goodbyes to the teachers here who have helped me are said at a restaurant above a department store on the night before I fly home. We eat dumplings and chickens' feet and drink the potent Chinese wine.

And my last goodbyes of all are said to the six waitresses in the staff dining room who have brought me food every day and know nothing about who I am, where I'm from and what I am doing here. I take Hui up with me to the third floor where the dining hall is. I ask her to tell them a few words about me. When she does, they all start to laugh.

'Why are the laughing, Hui?'

'They thought you were a cowboy!'

Autumn
Scattering the Ashes

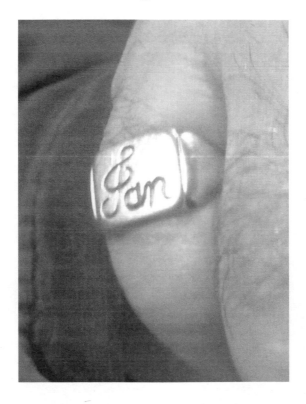

'The treasure of life is missed by those who hold on
and gained by those who let go.'
Laozi

No Going Back

Just after I get back from China, I go with our Tony again to visit my dad. The evening before we set off I say to Edward, 'Do you want to come to see him? I know he's never bothered with you, but he is your official grandad.'

Edward thinks for a bit and then says, 'What sort of shape is he in?'

'Rough. He's dying, but he can still talk alright.'

'I'm not sure I need to see him.'

'Okay. Sleep on it and tell me what you want to do in the morning.'

Edward decides not to come and watches his box set of the comedy series *Early Doors* instead.

This time my dad is fast in bed. He can't walk anymore. He has a special hospital bed now with an air-filled mattress to stop bed sores. I don't know how they have managed to get the bed into his little council flat bedroom, it takes up nearly all the space. Me and our Tony shuffle around the bed sideways and share a seat on a blanket box. Our Andrew says that he'll make a pot of tea and goes off to the kitchen.

As soon as he's gone, our dad says, 'He's pinching my pension.'

I look at our Tony, he shrugs.

'Don't say that. He's trying his best to look after you.'

'I'm telling you he's pinching.'

'How do you know?'

Our dad reaches under the bedclothes and pulls out a wallet from the front of his underpants.

'There should be more in here than there is.'

Our Andrew comes back in with four mugs of tea in two

235

hands. He places the mugs on a moveable tray that wheels over our dad's bed. He spills tea out of two of the mugs.

'You bloody half-soaked bugger, you're going to scald me.'

'I'm sorry, it'll wipe up.' Andrew uses a flannel from the bedside cabinet.

'Well, you simple git, I use that to wipe my face on a morning.'

'I'll swill it under the tap.'

He goes off with the tea stained flannel and comes back with it twisted like a spliced rope, places it gently on the cabinet and then as an afterthought dabs at our dad's mouth with it. 'I've wrung it out, don't worry!'

'It's your bloody neck that wants wringing.' Then he laughs.

Two minutes after telling us that Andrew is pinching his money our dad says, 'I don't know what I'd do without that lad, he's been like an angel to me. He knows how to get every benefit that's going.'

Our dad has been very poorly for nearly a year now. In all that time Andrew has been his helper and companion. They bicker and squabble like two birds left in a nest and then settle down and tell each other stories before they go to sleep. On a morning the routine starts again. My dad clenches his cig between worn out lips and Andrew lights it for him with a cheap Bic lighter, then hides the lighter in his pocket.

In front of him our dad has his tray. On the tray is a packet of Turner roll-up tobacco that he gets cheap off pirates, a packet of Bull Brand papers, a bottle of liquid morphine and a copy of the *Daily Star*.

Dad moves the bottle of morphine slightly and taps it on the lid. 'That's a drop of grand stuff you know, I wish I'd known about that years ago.'

Our Tony says, 'You want to be careful with that stuff, you can get addicted to it.'

'What's thy on about? Calling your father a drug addict!'

'You'll end up seeing stuff.'

'Aye, I know. I saw John Wayne last night in the bottom of my tea cup. He was in *Red River*, have you seen that one?'

Our Andrew, our Tony and I look at one another.

'Lovely picture it was, it's where he drives all them cattle up to Missouri and has a fight with Montgomery Clift at the end and it's his own son.'

'What? And you saw this in your cup?'

'No! I nipped across to the ABC in my underpants and bought a ticket for the upper circle.'

Our Andrew moves the medicine bottle to the edge of the tray.

'I thought he was going for his gun then. Did you see that? John Wayne did with Montgomery Clift.'

He sighs and starts to straighten his bedding. 'I'm going to watch *Rio Bravo* tonight. That's where Dean Martin and Ricky Nelson sing "My Rifle, My Pony and Me" and Walter Brennan plays his harmonica and says, "That's real purty".'

He repeats himself 'That's real purty' under his breath and then says, 'John Wayne doesn't sing though, he's the sheriff, you wouldn't get John Wayne singing or doing sissy stuff like that. Not John Wayne.'

Our dad is like teak. He is in constant pain and discomfort, but he won't give in to it. Every time he hurts, he laughs; he'd laugh if his arse was on fire. He has refused chemotherapy, hospital appointments and a care home. He wants to die with his boots on. Our Andrew has organised visits from care workers. Our dad has upset nearly every one who has come. Recently a young woman came and said, 'Hello, Sidney, would you like to take your trousers off so that I can wash your bottom.' Sid said, 'Aye, if you drop yours first love.' She hasn't been since. The next time, they sent a more mature lady, she said, 'Right, Mr Clayton, I think we'll have you in the bath today!' Our dad asked her what day it was. When she told him it was Tuesday he said, 'I won't bother then, I have my bath on Friday, always have done, whether I need one or not.'

I look at Tony and Andrew, I wonder what they are thinking. I start to remember a conversation I once had with Vernon Nelson, a mate who I meet up with at Cambridge Folk Festival. He once said to me, 'Do you know, Ian, my old man was only five-foot-two. He was a miner from the Durham Coalfields, one of 14 kids, as hard as iron. He wondered what the fuck was happening when I grew my hair and started hitchhiking everywhere. This was in the sixties, man, and he thought the fucking world was ending when I took myself off to Cornwall to build boats. We made it back though before he died, he started talking.'

My old man wants to listen to his record player, but when Andrew plugs it in, only the radio works. 'Turn it off! I want Bing Crosby, not bloody bing bang bloody wallop.' When it comes to the time to take our leave, Tony and I head sideways again round the bottom of the bed and go to shake Dad's hand. He says, 'Does anybody fancy an arm wrestle before you go?' He laughs again. 'Get your hair cut and I'll meet you when the sun goes down!' It's a phrase he used a lot when we were young. Our dad claimed that hippies were putting barbers on the dole and that there were enough people out of work to start with. Our Andrew sees us to the door. On the threshold I ask him if he has been taking money out of Dad's benefits.

'Have I heck! He gets confused about how much he's got. He wants enough to pay for his own funeral and says he'll be embarrassed if you have to put to it.'

'Well just be careful and keep reminding him not to worry. It's going to be hard for you both in the coming weeks. Are you preparing yourself?'

Andrew nods. Our father shouts from the bedroom, 'Who's got my bloody wallet?' We troop back in. The wallet is on the floor at the side of the bed. I pick it up and hand it to him. He flicks through a wad of ten pound notes and, satisfied, puts it under the bedclothes. 'It's like bloody Fagin's gang in here.' The Dickensian reference makes me smile.

'What's tha bloody grinning at? Tha's like a Cheshire cat!'

'You're funny!'

'Aye well, you've got to laugh else you'd bloody cry.'

An image of my dad on his allotment comes straight to my mind. He is looking after Mandy, his goat. The goat is very poorly and can't get to its feet. My dad says it will die before the night is out. He has mixed Indian Brandee with warm water and he tries to get the goat to drink if from an old tablespoon. The goat closes its big eyes. My dad covers it up with an old overcoat. He picks up the Tilley lamp that he has lit the goat's shed with and turns to look at me. I can see tears shining in his eyes.

'Are you crying, Dad?'

'No, lad, it's just t'fumes off this lamp. Never cry, lad, never cry!'

'Right, we're off then. Edward is playing his piano at a concert tonight and I want to make him some dinner before he goes.'

'You didn't bring him with you, did you? Doesn't he want to see me?'

'Well he doesn't really know you, does he?'

'That's my fault, isn't it?'

'It's nobody's fault. It's just how things are.'

'If I had my time to come again, it'd be different.'

'Would it?'

Sid shuts his eyes and thinks for a bit. 'You can't go backwards though can you?'

'No.'

'You never told me owt about China. How did you get on?'

'I was there for six weeks. It was alright.'

'That's alright then.'

He thinks some more and then says:

Hichikorychiumpompairymanaunnawessunchinchinpink.'

'What's that?'

'Chinese alphabet. Didn't they learn you anything?'

'No it's not!'

'Well it was when I was a lad, I learned it off a window cleaner.'

'Give over!'

'I'm telling you! They called him Mr Wu.' Then he laughs again and starts coughing. 'Andrew, roll me another cig will you.'

Andrew tuts under his breath and takes a ready-made roll-up out of his tin. Sid doesn't light it, but puts it behind his ear. 'I'll save that for Ron… Later Ron!'

He winks and then says, 'Go on then bugger off and don't forget, Umpa! Umpa! Stick it up your jumper!'

On Visiting My Hero

I'm standing waiting at Swinton railway station in South Yorkshire. Eleanor, Barry Hines' wife, is coming to pick me up to take me to see Barry in the nursing home. I'm going over what I'm going to say to him, wondering whether he will know me anymore, wondering what he will look like now. Eleanor is cheerful, brisk, reassuring. She's been through some hard times over the last few years. 'Everybody will tell you, "It's not him anymore" when somebody goes like this, but I say it is. Of course it's still Barry. You'll see.'

We sign the visitor's book and enter quickly, Eleanor pulls the door to, before any of the women that she calls 'The Escape Committee' can get out. There are two women here who carry baby dolls about in shopping bags who insist that they're being held under false pretences and they need to get home. In the distance I hear an elderly lady singing an old music-hall song in a croaking voice.

Barry is sitting in a high-backed orange-coloured chair. He is dozing. On the wall at the back of him are some replica film posters, one is for a Diana Dors picture called *Blonde Sinner*, there's an Audrey Hepburn one and an album cover on the Music for Pleasure label, Buddy Holly's *Rave On*. Nostalgia in nursing homes isn't about 'Roll Out the Barrel' anymore, it's catching us up.

Eleanor kisses Barry on the lips, he opens his eyes and stares. 'Ian has come to see you.' Barry doesn't look at me. He glares at the daytime television that is on full blast and growls. I move my chair so that I'm in his eye line. I take his hand and say, 'Can you remember when we went to see *Shakespeare in Love*?' Barry

Hines, who wrote the best book about Northern working class life I have ever read, closes his eyes and says something under his breath. Eleanor says, 'He's trying to remember.' I'm not sure, I think he's trying to go back to sleep.

I don't know why this should be, but seeing my hero Barry Hines in the home upset me more than seeing my dad bed bound and swigging liquid morphine. When my dad cried as he said 'I only wanted the best for you' it didn't make me want to cry. On the train on the way home from visiting Barry, I shed a tear at the thought of him being fed forkfuls of mashed potato and gravy. When I phoned Eleanor to say I wanted to see him again, she said she would pick me up and drive me over.

One Sunday morning she arrived for a coffee. I showed her a photograph that I display at the top of our staircase. The photo is of Barry, Eleanor and me drinking wine at a book launch at Barnsley Town Hall. I love that picture and the stories it reminds me of. The launch was to celebrate the publication of a book called *On a clear day you can see Barnsley Town Hall*. It was a book I edited of stories about the environment. We collected the stories in the former pit village of Grimethorpe, which some years after became famous for the setting for the film *Brassed Off*. One day Barry joined me for a morning. We walked around the old village, which by that time was on the point of being knocked down. Our guide was a bloke in a greasy flat cap who lived on Margate Street. The streets in the old village were all named after seaside places. As we came to the bottom of the street we had to jump over a beck. The bloke in the flat cap said, 'Watch where you're going lads, you can't see t'water for carpets.' Barry laughed and laughed. He loved the rhythms of the South Yorkshire dialect and the juxtaposition of seemingly incongruous terms. He thought it was the funniest line he'd heard.

On this Sunday morning as Eleanor and I drive across this same South Yorkshire countryside, she reminds me that Barry liked to quote that line whenever my name came up. 'You'll have to tell him that story again, Ian. I'm sure he'll appreciate it.'

We're driving down a road that was paid for by European money designed to bring prosperity back to this area after all the pits were shut; 'Coalfield Regeneration' they call it. The road bypasses the former pit villages it's supposed to help regenerate, so I don't know how it does its job. There's a section called the 'Dearne Valley Parkway' that passes near to Cortonwood Pit – whose proposed closure sparked off the year long miners' strike – and on to Orgreave where some of the bloodiest battles of the strike were fought out at the coking plant. I once came here with Arthur Scargill and he leaned on a chain-link fence. 'Just look at it, Ian,' he said, 'for months and months during that strike the government told us that this site must be kept open at all costs. And now look at it. It's a wilderness where nobody works and there's nothing to see apart from wasteland.'

Grass has started to grow here again on some of the recontoured muck stacks and slag heaps. There's a nature reserve where bird watchers sit with binoculars. As we drive past I see a kestrel hanging in the breeze. I say to Eleanor, 'An old lady in a pit village near me who was nearly 100 after the strike told me that she'd seen it go from green to black and back to green again.' Eleanor smiles. I look out of the side window. The kestrel has something in its focus. Some tiny thing far below. It swoops down, then flies up again and wheels off.

'Barry has started to see little people,' she says. 'The other day he was directing them, like a schoolteacher taking his pupils across a busy road.'

'My grandad was like that. Every now and again he'd have what we called "a fit" and he'd start looking under the armchair for something. Then he would crawl to the kitchen and look under the fridge and washing machine.'

Eleanor tells me that she thinks Barry might have a form of Parkinson's disease called 'Lewy body'. One of the symptoms is seeing people who aren't really there. The writer Mervyn Peake suffered from it.

We sign in at the door. Barry is dozing in his chair. Eleanor kisses him and straightaway he tries to rise up and says 'Course!' then shuts his eyes again. The term 'course' said in that way is South Yorkshire dialect for 'of course it is' or 'yes, I can guarantee that'. Children here say it as a sign of affirmation in the schoolyard. As in 'Are we playing football after tea?'… 'Course!' Eleanor tells me that Barry is reverting more and more to the dialect of his childhood.

The care assistant brings a plateful of dinner and Eleanor feeds Barry. He eats and chews slowly, as though he's struggling to swallow. It takes a long time to get just a quarter of the way across the plate. When Eleanor needs the toilet, she hands me the fork. I shovel a bit of potato, mashed suede and well stewed meat onto the fork. I hold it in front of Barry's mouth. He looks at me and says 'Course!' again, this time in a whisper and then opens his mouth. I place the forkful in like feeding a bird in a nest. When he has had enough Eleanor finishes the dinner off herself using the same fork.

I start to tell Barry that since the last time I came I had watched his TV drama *The Price of Coal*. I talk about the very funny scene where Jackie Shinn who plays the pit manager is showing off the recontoured muck stack on which he has planted grass seed in time for a visit by Prince Charles. Shinn announces to a gathering of Coal Board officials that if they look carefully they will see that the grass is growing already. They all bend down with their arses towards the camera to put their eyes in line with the muck stack. Before I get to the end of the tale Barry has closed his eyes again. When I laugh at the thought of the scene, Barry jumps and says something, but I can't tell what is it, a jumble of syllables in a South Yorkshire voice, like a song below the racket of machinery.

'Tell him about when you went to Grimethorpe, Ian.'

I start to tell the tale of 'not being able to see the water for carpets'. There is a flicker across Barry's face. The care assistant comes by and says, 'He's taking it all in, I'm sure he knows what you are talking about.' Eleanor leans over to kiss him again.

'He still likes to kiss.'

The care assistant says, 'That's because he loves you.'

Barry looks across at me and says, this time in a very clear voice, 'Fucking hell!'

We all laugh and Barry laughs as well. When it's time to go, I go to put my arms around Barry and he kisses me on the cheek. I feel my face going red.

'Shall I come again, Barry?'

He looks at Eleanor, then at me and says, again clearly, 'That'd be nice.'

Eleanor drops me off at Elsecar station so that I can catch the train home. The ticket collector comes. I'm wiping tears from my eyes on my hankie. He says in a South Yorkshire dialect just like Barry's, 'What's up old cock? Are you alreight?' I ask for a single to Castleford and say, 'Course!'

Siren Song

I'm at the Ferens Art Gallery at Hull, killing time while waiting for a ferry to Rotterdam. I stand in front of a painting, it's a dramatic work by the Victorian classicist Herbert James Draper. It tells the story of Ulysses and his journey from Troy. His ship sails past some rocks where sirens are singing, tempting the sailors to their doom. Ulysses lashes himself to the mast and orders his men to plug up their ears and keep rowing. The painting is a sensuous one and you can almost hear the sirens singing. Ulysses wanted to hear the sirens' song even though he knew the song would drive him mad.

After Billie drowned, I thought I would go mad. For months, I woke from sweating dreams believing I was in the water. After our canoe tipped over I didn't see Billie again until I had to stand by her in the hospital theatre and agree that the doctors should stop trying to revive her. Somewhere between the canoe going over and the air lift to hospital by helicopter from the river bank I lost my daughter. In my dreams I try to change the story and how it ends. I try to dream her back again, as though somehow I can turn back the hands on a clock and start all over. My dreams always end with me looking into the river. I never see her. Sometimes I wake and I dream that my arms have come off, other times the river is a mirror and in the mirror there are birds flying above. At first Billie was always waiting for me. Now she is a mermaid and she has swum to a grotto under the water that is filled with coloured stones and lights and there are seals singing lullabies, but I can never join in.

I dream about Billie still, the nightmares have gone and they are lovely dreams most of the time. I don't know that I have come to terms with being the father of a daughter who was just nine when she died in a river. I don't even know that there is such a thing as coming to terms with something like that.

When I look at my grandfather's shaving mirror I talk to Billie. I talk to her in the mirror more than I do when I stand beside her gravestone. I tell her how her twin brother Edward has grown, about what he has learned to play on the piano and how he's getting on at his education. I tell her about her mam and about the lovely paintings she makes, that she inspires.

I had the great honour of being invited to give the annual David Jones Memorial Lecture. It was an honour first of all just to be asked; these lectures are normally given by politicians or opinion makers; Dennis Skinner and Paul Foot have been before me. It was also an honour to speak from the very platform where Arthur Scargill once stood to give great rallying cries on behalf of the most powerful union this country has known. The lectures take place in the inner sanctum at the NUM headquarters at Barnsley, it's a beautiful place full of the echoes of rousing voices and adorned with silk banners.

David Jones was a hard-working young collier at Ackton Hall Pit who died on the picket line in 1984, fighting for a cause, the basic right of every man to have a job and bring home pay to his family.

I spent weeks writing my speech, crossing out, editing, adding bits that came to me. I finally finished it the night before; a speech about coming from a coal-mining family, believing in my heritage and standing up for right being right. I was pleased with what I wrote and hoped that the political references would go down well. I was onto a winner anyway, the audience would be a mixture of left-wing people and the families of miners. I almost felt like a politician.

On the morning of the lecture I arrived about an hour early and started to natter. I felt sick and gipped over a lavatory bowl twice. I used to get like that before a big rugby match, trying to breathe steadily and tapping my studs on the tiles of the dressing-room floor.

Ten minutes to go now and I am escorted to the chamber and shown where I will be sitting. Just before I mount the steps I am introduced to a very dapper elderly gentleman. 'Ian, this is David Jones' father.' I gulp and offer my hand. David Jones' dad touches my outstretched hand and moves it to one side. He then embraces me and kisses me on the cheek. He holds on to my shoulders, there is a tear in his eye. I feel that I am welling up as well. Then he says, 'I know that you know how it feels to lose a child young man. It's the wrong way round, but what you are going to do today is good for you. We must never forget. Don't you forget.'

I walk up the steps and take my place in a line of blokes in well-worn suits and union ties. I am called on by the chairman to deliver my talk. There is a warm round of applause. I take out my typed notes and then something comes over me. I look at David Jones' dad in the seats, he is smiling and nodding.

I hold up my speech and say, 'I've spent above a month writing this, but something important has just happened to me, so I have decided to talk about something else. I hope you won't mind if I leave my political points to one side, while I talk about how I have tried to cope with the death of my daughter.'

I told them about the Zen master Sengai, who once wrote 'Grandfather dies, father dies, son dies', a simple message about the natural order of things and therefore a natural way to grieve. Then I asked the question, 'What happens when the son dies before the father or the daughter dies leaving the parents to grieve?' We have no answers for this, so we make our own. Every year Davy Jones is remembered in a lecture at the NUM headquarters and, every spring, Billie Holiday Clayton is remembered by giving away violins at a memorial concert at the school her twin brother Edward goes to. Simple acts of decency help those that are left behind.

I dedicated my talk to David Jones' dad. People in the hall stood up and gave me a five-minute standing ovation. I swelled up like the balloon I once let go over the bull field wall at the back of my gran's house.

I had a cup of tea and a potted meat sandwich after with David's dad. He'd been sitting near Arthur Scargill, I had kept looking at them throughout my talk. I wanted to do well for them both.

He said, 'I have been to every one of these lectures and I will come to every one as long as I live. I'll always remember this as the one that explains what I've been through. I know now why I try to keep my lad's name living.'

He made me cry.

Finding Art

After I watched Georges Méliès film *Le Voyage dans la lune*, it kept coming into my dreams. I was standing by the graveside of Méliès himself. The dream ended when I started to chase a pair of cinema tickets around the graveyard.

On Heather's 51st birthday trip to Paris, as we sailed down the Seine on a water bus, out of the blue Heather said, 'Let's go to the Père Lachaise cemetery, I'd like to see Oscar Wilde's grave.' We got off the boat somewhere at the back of Notre Dame and took the Metro to Père Lachaise.

At the cemetery gate we bought a little map of the graveyard from a news kiosk and plotted our route to Oscar Wilde's tomb. On the way up to it, I had an urge to turn off between some tombstones. Heather said, 'Where are you going now?' I didn't know, but then I did. I found the grave of Georges Méliès. I don't know whether it was like it was in my dream, but something very strange happened. In front of the headstone, underneath a little rock, someone had left some cinema tickets. I lifted the rock and the tickets blew away on the breeze. I caught them and put them back under the rock. It was like a film about a dream, putting the now to a memory, like knitting a cardigan for a ghost. 'Plaiting fog' my gran would have called it.

I used to sit at my grandmother's knee to hold her wool. When her eyes dimmed I found the eye in her needles. This way I learned how to tell stories.

When she finished her making and mending, my gran said, 'Sam them threads up for me lad.' She didn't know it, but she was using an ancient Anglo-Saxon verb 'samnian', a cousin of the old German term 'sammeln'. My gran had a lot of the old language. She called a pavement 'a ramper' or 'a causy'. A song thrush was 'a mavis' and a sparrow was 'a cuddy'. I collected these words like I gathered her threads. Sometimes I think I have spent my life gathering threads.

In the local shop, Mrs Johnson the shopkeeper kept a stool to one side of the counter. This stool was for my gran to sit on when she came to buy bits and bobs, but mainly so that she could sit comfortably to tell her stories. My gran could make the buying of a few slices of boiled ham last for an hour. She told stories about things that had happened, the day before, that morning, or a long time ago. She even told stories about what was going to happen.

Not long before she died, I asked my gran to write some of her stories down. She said, 'Who the bloody hell would want to know about my life!' I told her that she had been telling people about her life for more than eighty years. 'That's different. I don't mind telling stuff to folk that I know, but I don't want folk I don't know knowing.'

She did write a few pages in an old Silvine notebook. When I asked her where the rest was she said, 'It's unravelled somewhere and it all wants gathering in.' My gran collected stories, like she collected buttons in a tin. She didn't do much with them, just got them out and let people see them now and again.

I'm walking with my dog down an old path across the fields near a place called Parkfield Farm. This was once a dairy farm called Copleys who bottled milk in a barn from their own herd. The dairy herd has long gone and the farm is no longer a farm, just the fields and the path are still here. In the distance next to the old muck stacks, where Glass Houghton pit and brickworks once stood, is the Xscape indoor ski slope and Junction 32 shopping centre. The M62 cuts across these fields taking lines of traffic to Hull one way and Manchester the other. High pylons in the fields carry lines of electricity from Ferrybridge Power Station, whose cooling towers steam about three miles away to the east. It's a peculiar place, because amidst all the noise of the traffic on the motorway and the crackle of the electricity lines when it's misty, you can still hear skylarks. Hares sprint across on a morning and partridges make that farting noise as they fly up out of the hedge bottoms when my dog disturbs them. I watch swallows at the beginning of every summer as they skim into the old barns with beaksful of mud to nest-build as they have done forever. Probably since the old barns were built from stone that was recycled when they knocked Pontefract Castle down after the English Civil War.

This morning I come across the olive coloured egg of a partridge rolling gently in the breeze along the path. I pick the egg up. It is intact. How it comes to be on the path I don't know. I take out my hankie and wrap the egg and put it into my jacket pocket. When I get home I drop the egg into a washing up bowl full of water; it sinks. I take out a needle from our sewing box and prick two holes, one at the point and one on at the fat end of the egg. I stir the insides a bit with the needle and then blow the contents down the sink. I admire the egg shell and then place it in some cotton wool in an old mortar next to bottles of olive oil and jars of herbs on one of the kitchen worktops. The blown partridge egg stays in the mortar for months after and, from time to time, when I'm reaching for a grinder of black pepper I stop to look at it.

I'm a bugger for picking stuff up that I find interesting, I collect things that I pick up or find. I don't know why I do this. Sometimes I think it's because the wind blew these things my way for me to look after. It could be a piece of metal or a stone, an interesting shard of glass or wood. I just like picking stuff up to bring home.

I think birds' eggs is where it all started. I'd be about seven years old. There was this old dying tree, bare of leaves, that looked like a skeleton. None of our gang had climbed the tree to the top. One day I decided I would. And I did. And when I got to the top I noticed a nest in a hole. I reached in and felt some warm eggs. They were a beautiful pale blue, the eggs of a starling. I took one, put it into my mouth and climbed back down. About four feet from the bottom I jumped. The egg hit my teeth and broke in my mouth. I spat out the bloody red foetus of a baby starling. Paul Hickman said to me, 'It's a deepy! Tha didn't want that anyroad. Next time tha gets one, hold it up to t'light, if tha sees a shadow, tha'll know not to take it.'

'Deepy' was the colloquial term we used round our way for eggs that were fertile as opposed to just 'yolky'.

There was a lad down the road from us who had a huge collection of eggs that he kept in Oxo tins; the old-fashioned ones that had tin dividers. He was the envy of everybody, because he had managed to get hard-to find eggs like black redstarts, grasshopper warblers and ring ouzel. Then we found out that his uncle had pinched most of them from a museum.

I kept my eggs in an old cake tin half-filled with self-raising flour. I made small indentations in the flour with my thumb and placed the eggs in the hollows. On the pantry shelf was my egg tin, with birds' eggs sitting on flour and my gran's tin with flour sitting on spare money.

We were down a lane near Ackworth. I found a wren's nest with four eggs in. I took one and held it in the cup of my hand in a beck. The egg sank, I knew now that it was 'yolky' and not a 'deepy', eggs with chicks in float. As I stood back up, a jay flashed across the front of some trees. I'd never seen a jay before. I thought it was one of the most exciting things I'd seen. We looked for its nest and found it at the top of a big old blackthorn bush. I climbed and cut myself to bits on the sharp spikes. The nest had just one egg in it. I was about to take the egg when something came over me. 'If I take this egg, another lad like me might not have the chance to see a jay in full flight.' I pulled my hand back from the nest and climbed back down. I told my mates that the bird must not have laid yet. I never went bird-nesting after that.

On my thirteenth birthday I was given a quid by my Aunt Laura. There was a record stall in the indoor market at Pontefract. Half-fare to Pontefract then was two pence, a single from Mrs Jay's record stall was forty-eight pence. On the Saturday morning I went by bus to Pontefract. I bought 'Telegram Sam' by T.Rex and their latest record, 'Metal Guru'. I already had 'Get It On' and 'Jeepster'. I tossed the remaining two pence piece to see whether I should walk the two miles home or take the Number 69 bus that said 'Dewsbury' on the front. I bought a packet of cheese and onion crisps and ate them as I walked home.

They say every record you own has a story to tell. I must have more than 10,000 stories to tell, because I have saved just about every record I have ever owned. And the more obscure the record is the more I want to know about it, cherish it and keep it. Sometimes I don't even listen to it, a very strange admission I know, but it's just that I don't want the chase to end. Like a kitten with a ball of wool, I want to keep following it until I get there and then when I do I'm not interested in much more than pawing at it. I know that one day I will listen to it, I just don't mind waiting until that right day comes.

The Japanese-born British novelist Kazuo Ishiguro once said, 'There is this kind of treasure chest you have sitting in front of you, and if you were American or perhaps Irish you might have opened it by now, but because you live here it probably hasn't occurred to you to do so yet.' He was talking about delving into the folk tradition and went on, 'I would urge you to open that thing up and delve inside it, because I believe you'll find there a sublime vision of the British Isles as it has been lived over the last few centuries; and it's the kind of vision that you can't readily get from the works of say, Dickens or Shakespeare or Elgar or Sir Christopher Wren. If you don't open that treasure box I think you are going to miss a certain dimension, a whole dimension of cultural life in this country.'

I think that is what I mean when I talk about trying to

embrace the *other*. And it's in the *trying* that I get most of the enjoyment. I don't want everything now. I like the finding out, the searching and, yes, the finding, but that process to me is continuing, just because I find something doesn't mean I've got it. The rescuing and saving part is just as interesting. I'm just as curious in not knowing now as I am in knowing then. And what we don't know now, we can know then.

One of the holy grails for record collectors in recent years has been a label called Holy Ground that was set up in the 1960s at Wakefield just a few miles from where I live. Holy Ground specialised in hippyish experiments in folk, blues and psychedelia and they recorded stuff in a back bedroom. Bill Nelson, who went on to form Be Bop Deluxe, made early recordings for the label, which had been set up by some college friends who drank in a pub called Moody's. The first album was called *No 9 Bread Street*, the address of Moody's pub.

At the beginning of 1972, in the middle of a miners' strike, a young alternative comedian called 'John' went to Holy Ground to record a benefit single for the striking miners. It's a bizarre song called 'The Miners' Song', a spoken lyric over a funky proto-disco beat. My copy of this record is signed, strangely on its 'B' side by the then miners' leader, Joe Gormley, in blue ballpoint pen. Why the heck I would want this record in my collection I don't know, except there is a story to it.

'John' it turns out was the one-time beau of a woman I know called Maureen Prest. Maureen was the personal assistant to James Corrigan, the Northern entertainments entrepreneur who set up Batley Variety Club and attracted stars like Shirley Bassey and Louis Armstrong to an otherwise unassuming and gritty little textile town in the West Riding. 'John' was a minor player in showbusiness. He had once recorded with musicians who became 10cc. He had a minor chart hit with a record called 'The Man from Nazareth' which made it into John Peel's 'worst records ever on *Top of the Pops*' programme. He was really an early 'alternative' comedian who indulged in risqué jokes about the Vietnam War and sex. Bernard Manning once put him on at the Embassy Club in Manchester and introduced him with the words, 'Now you might not like this next act, I don't know what the fucking hell to make of him.' John came on and opened with 'Ladies and gentlemen, if I said the word "bomb" to you, you might not be too offended, but if I used the word "titty" oh well then, I might offend. But I put it to you, you would rather have a titty in your hand than a bomb, wouldn't you?' Not many people laughed. I don't know where John's career went from there, except that one day I got a phone call from Maureen Prest.

'I know you're interested in coal miners and music, Ian, I've got a little gift for you, next time I see you.'

And in this way, forty years after it was recorded at the Holy Ground studios and raised very little for the miners, because the BBC refused to play it, 'The Miners' Song' came to me. I treasure that record; not because it's good music, not because the lyrics speak to me, not even because it's rare; and it is undoubtedly rare now. I don't even want it because I'm a record collector. There's something else and that something else is in the story of the artefact.

My gran collected buttons, not because she liked buttons, but because she thought 'They might come in one day if I make something that suits them'. Then she collected buttons because she'd always collected buttons. And after that she collected buttons because she couldn't bear the thought of parting with buttons that she had had for years. And finally the buttons became a story. She once held up an almost opaque blue button to the light from the front room window. 'Do you know, I cut that off your mother's first coat in 1939, just before your grandad went off to war. I was going to put it into his pocket so that he could take it with him and have something to bring him luck. I can't remember if I did or not now, but it's ended up back in this tin.'

'It might have been to El Alamein then?'

'Aye, it might have been.'

I love this point where the almost meaningless artefact crashes into some previously hidden part of history. I don't know what it all means, but it's the only way I can explain why I try to gather threads. It's why my gran said 'Sam it up', echoing an ancestor over a thousand years earlier. It's why I pick up a rolling partridge egg on a farmer's track, the reason I chase chipped old 78 records over continents. And as I get older my collections grow dustier, harder to find in my house, let alone my head, and the cobwebs start to tell a tale. Sometimes I'm still that little boy at my grandma's knee holding on to her wool. I think I am an archaeologist who doesn't know where to dig, so I dig everything in the hope that I'll find something. The strange thing is I'm not even bothered if I don't find anything, I enjoy the looking. Stranger still, I'm not even bothered if I do find something. I'm only interested in what I discover when I can make a story from it. The art of collecting anything is not in the having, it's in the finding and in the finding lies the art.

When I find something, I'm not really bothered about what it is, I just want to know what it says. I don't care if it's expensive, cheap, in vogue, old hat, tat, battered or new, I like to know what its story is. Then I save it. I never know whether to put it on a shelf, in a shed or use it, I just save it. Then when I've got too many or it's caked in dust, I blow on it, shake it and decide again; shelf, shed or use. I don't like to throw away and rarely do. My hand has hovered over my wheelie bin many a time and then I bring whatever it is back from the yard and put it in a drawer, under a chair or in a corner on top of something. I'm running out of corners, chairs and drawers. Just lately, I've started to shed.

Twenty years ago a dustbin man gave me a cardboard bound album of 78rpm classical records that he found outside somebody's back door. He said, 'You're the only bloke I know who can play these, so you can have 'em.'

I said, 'I'm not sure that I want them.'

He looked sloughened, 'It's a shame to let them go to the tip, they're all in lovely nick.'

'Where did you get them?'

'From an old lass's house. She died last month. She was a lovely piano player. She allus wore pearls, spoke right posh and drank tea off a cup and saucer. I think at one time she'd been somebody.'

'Who was she?'

'I don't know. Happen a teacher, she sounded like one and she used to help them in Africa.'

The binman handed the records to me like a parcel in a game of 'when the music stops', gently at first, then whipped his hands away when he knew I had hold. As he walked down the yard, he looked round, like people do when they wave you off at a railway station. I clutched the records closer, as though to say, 'I won't drop them.'

I put the records under an old cabinet gramophone player; The Illingworth, one of the few cabinet record players made in Yorkshire in the 1930s. I can't remember ever playing them. They stayed under the cabinet until one day when I found moths had eaten the wool on the carpet and it had to be replaced. The records got shunted about the house until eventually I found them near the back door. Heather said to me, 'All that stuff in that pile wants looking at. And if it's no good it wants chucking in the bin.'

I pick up the records album in one hand and with my other hand lift the lid on the wheelie bin. Then I close the lid and rest the album on top of it. I start to turn each record, they come away from the album's spine. It is raining and the drops land on the label of each record. I wipe off the drops with the back of my hand and start to read. First is 'Prelude in C Minor Op. 28' and 'Mazurka in A Minor Op. 68' played by John Hunt on the

Neo-Bechstein piano. Then 'Mozart's Serenade 'Eine Kleine Nachtmusik K. 525, 1st Movement Allegro' played by London Philharmonic Orchestra conducted by Sir Thomas Beecham.

I like all the words. I brush a finger over the 'His Masters Voice' logo. I want to lift the lid on the bin again, but I can't. There's something I need to do. I take the records back in the house and place them on our piano stool. I imagine a little old lady sitting there in pearls. I go off to the kitchen and make myself a cup of tea. I root through the cupboard under the work surface and find a saucer. I carry the tea cup and saucer back into the room where we keep our piano, push the records to one side of the stool and sit beside them. I sip at the hot tea and then make the tea drinker's sigh.

I want to play one of these records and I can't decide which. I tip the album on it's side and choose the one that slides out of its cover the most. This is Bach's 'Toccata and Fugue in D minor Part 1', Leopold Stokowski and The Philharmonic Orchestra. I wind up the player, click off the brake, blow on the record, place it on the platter and move the arm across with a new needle on it. It is much louder than I expected. I look around the room as though to see if anyone is listening, sip my tea and shut my eyes. The grinding noise on the run-out groove brings me to my feet. I lift the arm and place the record back in its sleeve. I carry the album to the wheelie bin and place it on top of some carrier bags full of potato peelings and egg shells. Then I lift it out again and flick through it one last time. As I do this, a faded piece of notepaper falls out. On the paper is says, 'Wensleydale Cheese, Fairy Soap, Steradent, Andrews Liver Salts and Doctor'. The handwriting is beautiful, sloping slightly forward, written with a fountain pen. On the back of this paper is a fragment of an address in London, a chemist in Old Bond Street. I realise that this is a receipt for a bottle of eau de cologne from the famous maker, Johann Maria Farina. I drop the records and the receipt back into the bin. I raise a thumb in salute to a little old lady who wore pearls and the perfume of Johann Maria Farina when she sat at the piano. Then I drop the lid and wheel my bin down to the causeway's edge. When I get back to my gate I look round like folk do after they have waved you off. I blow a kiss.

Viv Nicholson started to visit the taproom at The Shoulder of Mutton now and again. She lived just round the corner in a modest terraced house, the fortune she won on the pools that she promised to 'spend spend spend' had long since been spent. Viv had become a Jehovah's Witness and, as far as anyone knew, had stopped drinking and partying to live a quiet and reflective life. We would occasionally see her through the pub window, trotting by with bags of shopping in both hands and some of the blokes who knew her waved to her.

When the smoking ban in pubs kicked in, I found myself standing by the front door with my roll-up. I liked to talk to Viv when she went by. She always looked good, expensive outfits, good shoes, a snake-skin purse in her hand and hair done beautifully. She took to coming in for a glass of white wine.

One Christmas a rough-looking bloke with a Staffordshire bull terrier on a thick chain came in, looking worse for wear. He stood at the bar next to Viv, ordered a bottle of Pils and told his dog to 'Sit'. Somehow Viv contrived to stand on the dog's paw and set it off growling and barking. The bloke pulled hard on its chain and kicked it in the ribs. Viv said, 'Just you stop that now or I'll give you a kick in the ribs.'

'Fuck off and mind your own business you silly old cow.'

Big mistake. Viv spun round and punched the bloke straight on the end of the chin. According to Tetley Dave she hit him so hard she nearly lifted him out of his shoes and hung him on the coat rack. The bloke didn't bother to finish his beer. He skulked out of the door with his dog behind him. Viv spat on her hands and rubbed them together. 'Right! Landlord, I think we'll have drinks all round.' Viv's generosity was legendary. Dave's eyes lit up and he pulled pints and filled glasses for everybody in the taproom.

'That'll be thirty-seven pound thirty please Viv, we'll call it thirty-seven for cash!'

Viv opened her snakeskin purse and pulled out a credit card. 'Take it out of that, landlord.'

'I don't do credit cards in here.'

'Well, you'll have to pour the beer back into the pumps then, but I'm not telling them!'

Dave's face was a picture.

I last saw Viv in the pub late one Saturday afternoon. Everybody had gone home for their tea and there was just Dave and me sitting in front of the wood burning stove chewing the fat. It was cold out and a wintry mix of rain and sleet was coming down. Viv came in through the back door, wet through and bedraggled. She didn't look very well. Dave said, 'Come and sit with us and get warm, I'll bring you a glass of summat.' Viv said, 'No, I don't want to stop. I want to go home, lend me a bottle of wine will you.'

Dave said that he didn't have any bottles of wine, only the wine that comes inside bags in cardboard boxes.

'Well, I need a bottle now!' She looked like she did.

Dave offered to swill out an empty Newcastle Brown bottle. Viv nodded. Dave put the bottle under the tap, swilled it round, filled it with wine, then took an old metal cap out of the plastic holder attached to the bar. He slapped the cap on with the flat of his hand. Viv took the bottle, said thank you almost under her breath and walked out. We watched her go by through the window. Dave announced, 'That's not like her. And I can't see me getting paid for that wine either.'

We saw neither hide nor hair of Viv after that. I asked a lot of people about her, but nobody seemed to know where she was. One afternoon I saw her in town holding hands with a Chinese woman. She looked frail and had lost the dash out of her step.

When I said 'Hello, Viv' and went to kiss her cheek, she didn't seem to know me. She just said, 'Don't talk to this lady, she's Chinese, she won't know what your are saying.' The lady who was helping Viv smiled.

I found out that Viv was in a nursing home. One Saturday morning in a second-hand shop, I found a Smiths record 'Heaven Knows I'm Miserable Now' which features Viv on the front cover. It's a classic shot of her, not long after she won the pools. Some newspaper photographer had taken her back to the pot-holed back streets in the rain. She has her hands in the pockets of a white three-quarter length coat, feet in pointed suede boots and bleached blonde hair piled high on her head. She looks like somebody out of a French Nouvelle Vague film, cut-out and pasted onto the rainy terraces of Castleford. I took the record when I visited Viv. She said, half-jokingly, 'Is that me?' When I said, 'Yes' she said, 'I'm not her now though, am I?' I wasn't there long before her son came to take her to the cinema. Before I left she picked up a black biro and asked me to spell my name. She wrote on the record cover 'To Ian, Viv Nicholson, Spend, Spend, Spend.'

When Jack Millar, the great writer on all things Billie Holiday, passed away he left me some ultra-rare items in his will. One was a white label sample 78 on the Decca label, 'Painting the Town Red' by Teddy Wilson with vocal refrain from Billie Holiday. When they talk, as they used to in Ray's Jazz shop in Shaftesbury Avenue, about 'hen's teeth' rarity, they are probably referring to records like this. This white label is hen's teeth, rocking horse shit and those who can sell coal to Newcastle all rolled into one ten-inch piece of black plastic. For ten years or more I didn't even take it out of its sleeve, I just held it now and again and kept it on a shelf next to some art books.

I belong to a record listening club called 'Classic Album Tuesdays', we meet in a converted garage at the back of a mate's house on alternate Tuesdays. It's like a book club, only, instead of reading and discussing, we listen and then talk about what we heard. We started off with *Sergeant Pepper*, *Pet Sounds* and *Bringing It All Back Home*, but then over the months each individual started to introduce us to their own taste and semi-polite arguments started.

We don't play anything other than vinyl at the CAT club. This means blowing the dust off collections that have spent the last decade or two in storage, trawling around cardboard boxes full of stuff at record fairs and jumble sales and bidding on eBay. Occasionally someone who is throwing stuff out thinks of us. In this way we come by a collection that had been put together by a well-known GP called Dr David Kidd. Dr Kidd had been a clarinettist in the army and had entertained troops as a POW in Berlin during the second war. When he died his collection gathered dust in storage until it found its way to us. There was blues, folk, jazz, classical and one of the best collections of what has become known as World Music that could have been assembled in the 50s and 60s; Dr Kidd had collected early Topic label stuff and many pieces from the East European Supraphon label. In this way lovely ten-inch records in colourful colours that go from Romanian folk dances to Hungarian gypsy tunes to Czechoslovakian ethnic songs found their way to our house. There were a couple of ultra-rare Topic records, including a *Songs from the Aegean* on flute and harp. For David Suff, who now curates that label's archive, these were records of the 'hen's teeth' variety. Through the foresight and collecting passions of Dr Kidd, we have been able to fill a few gaps that were missing in the Topic archive.

On an occasion when it was my turn to pick a record for The CAT Club, I decided to present some old jazz 78s and play them on a 1928 HMV horn player. I took the Teddy Wilson promo that Jack Millar had left to me. For the first time that night I took it out of its sleeve and then played it. I don't know what came over me, it just felt the right time to do it. I knew the song of course, it's been reissued on CD loads of times by Columbia, but there was something that evening that was like listening to a ghost. Somewhere between the dusty grooves of that record there's something magical and captured and I don't want to let it out too much, so when I put it back in its sleeve, it's stayed there since.

Sometimes you don't know why you want to go somewhere. You just feel the pull. Then when you get there you find out why you wanted to come. It's like Van Gogh wanting to spread the word. For years he tramped the street of coal-mining towns in Belgium because he wanted to be an evangelist. He thought it was his calling, but he was rubbish at it. Then, without any background in painting and no experience, he decided one day to become an artist. He saw some orchards in blossom, ready-made art, and he extracted it. He made more than 2000 drawings and paintings and wrote nearly a thousand letters in less than ten years. Then, one day, he thought he was a failure and shot himself in the chest. Van Gogh adopted a lot of the characteristics of Japanese painting. Perhaps instead of shooting himself he ought to have gone to Japan.

I went to Amsterdam once to learn about Van Gogh and Rembrandt. I found out these things about Van Gogh and that Rembrandt had a gang of lads collecting the skins of dead dogs. He used dog skins to print with. Dogs sweat through their tongues, they don't have pores on their skin, so it puts ink to paper in a smooth way.

The best things I learned in Amsterdam came to me by happy accident. I came out of Rembrandt's front door and the rain was siling down, that slanted rain that surrounds you. I ran to a little corner shop and the shopkeeper must have seen the weather forecast. He had a rack of umbrellas by the front door. They were horrible things with cannabis leaves printed on beige background. I bought one. When I pulled the eight euro sticker off, it said three euros underneath. I walked under my umbrella to a little bar on the edge of Dam Square. It was full to overflowing and the seats outside were wet through. I crossed over the square into the red-light district. My umbrella blew inside out and all the spokes detached themselves. I threw it into a bin and pulled out a magazine from the same bin. I placed it over my head like a house roof and made my way to the Oude Kerk, Amsterdam's oldest church. Rembrandt's wife Saskia van Uylenburgh lies at rest here. There's a story that every springtime, on a certain day at just after eight o'clock on a morning, her tomb is lit up by the sun coming through a stained glass window. Not much chance of seeing that on a wet Wednesday afternoon in autumn, but the Oude Kerk has some wonderful miserichords and from these I learnt three sayings that have stayed with me ever since.

'Don't pull too hard on a weak rope.'
'You can't yawn as wide as an oven door.'
'Money doesn't fall out of arseholes.'

On the ferry on the way back to Hull, I walked past a compere just as he was about to take the mike. He said, in that muffled voice that comperes in grubby suits on ferry boats adopt, 'Hi, I'm Dan, your entertainments manager. Get your bingo tickets from 9pm, eyes down at 9.45pm, you gotta be in it to win it! In the meantime we're going all the way back to the swingin' sixties.' He then pressed a button on a karaoke machine and started singing Tommy Roe's song 'Dizzy'.

I went back to my cabin and remembered another saying. It was one my grandfather often dusted off and brought out: 'There's never a bloody catapult handy when you want one.'

I started to chuckle at first, then I laughed out loud. My gran came into my mind, she was telling Hannah Pyatt, her next door neighbour, 'Our Ian would laugh if his arse was on fire. He takes after his father.'

Fading Away

On my birthday in September, our Andrew phoned to say that he couldn't cope with looking after my dad and his dog anymore. He let the dog go to a place that looks after strays. He said my dad was heartbroken, 'He loved that dog like it was a baby.' He then told me, 'He's going down fast now. I have to change his bedclothes twice in the night, it's a good job he's got a decent washing machine. He just keeps asking after his dog.'

I walk my dog down the same farm track every day and watch the seasons change. As summer turned to autumn and the fields were harvested and hedgerows trimmed, I found myself torn between thinking about my dad's last few breaths and a family holiday I wanted to go on with Edward and Heather.

One morning I watched leaves blowing across a field that had just been ploughed. Some people were out with metal detectors searching for anything that might have been unearthed. I shout across to the one nearest to me, 'Have you found owt?'

He walks across and takes something out of a shoulder bag. 'Here, what does tha make of this?' He shows me a rotting purse and inside are three old pennies, all with Queen Victoria's head on them. 'Makes you wonder doesn't it? Who walked on these fields? Where were they going and how did they come to leave this behind?'

'I suppose we all leave something behind whether we mean to or not.'

'Aye, lad, I suppose we do.'

He puts the purse back into his bag.

'Press on, lad, press on!'

After we lost Billie, I didn't want to go on holiday anymore. I came to associate going off and having a good time with accidents. It was almost as though I felt guilty for enjoying myself. But it was more than that, it was as if I didn't want to be away from home. I didn't even want to be working away from home and staying in hotels and boarding houses. Part of the anxiety about going to China was that as well – as though my not being near home would cause something to happen that I didn't want to happen.

I came to a stage where I didn't want anything to alter, change, move or be different. This even extended to leaving piles of stuff everywhere in parts of our house that I liked to call mine. I ended up where I didn't even want dust to move. This caused a lot of arguments with Heather and bizarre questions like, 'Why do we own a vacuum cleaner?', 'Why do we have dusters?' and 'Is that roof slate that blew off and smashed in the yard going to get replaced?'

We did manage to agree to some changes in routine. When Edward went to France on the First World War Battlefield trip we snook off to Florence and when he went on the school Spanish trip to Barcelona I booked the birthday treat to Paris. Yet, these were not 'proper' holidays, just quick sightseeing tours with a couple of nights in a convenient hotel, where you hardly bother to hang your clothes in the wardrobe.

China changed a lot of things. China forced me to focus on things that weren't turning to dust or decaying in front of my eyes. China was about making a journey, about moving out of my familiar space, disorientating myself on purpose. China was about fresh starts and building anew. When I got back Heather said, 'I don't want anymore excuses, me and Edward deserve a nice big holiday and we're bloody well having one and you're going to organise it and take us.' I feebly suggested that we go to Devon and stay with Heather's Auntie Val up on Exmoor.

'No! We want to go somewhere we haven't seen before.'

I gave in, 'Okay! You tell me!'

Edward said, 'America!'

We had two sets of American visitors in the space of a month just after I got back from China.

First came Susan and her partner Angela. They share a house in the woods in rural Indiana, about ten miles our of Indianapolis where Susan lectures in anthropology at the university. About twenty years ago, Susan was over here doing a project about the aftermath of the miners' strike. When we met her she was upset about living in rough lodgings owned by a seedy landlord, so we said she could have the back bedroom at our flat above a hardware shop in Station Lane. We took her to the theatre and to watch Featherstone Rovers. For the last twenty years she has been inviting us to come over to America so that she can repay our hospitality. On the day that Susan and Angela visited, we tentatively suggested that we might come over to America 'before Christmas'.

Not long after, Michael and Vanessa were over from a visit from San Diego. Michael who's from Bradford and Vanessa who's a Californian had studied together on the famous Peace Studies course at Bradford University. They fell in love and got married over in America and Michael applied for his Green Card; he'll proudly tell that he got it a lot faster than John Lennon got his. They set up home in San Diego and work together on a music project that enables people who suffer mental stress to tell their story through words and songs.

We had a boozy night in the Robin Hood pub and by the fourth round we were planning to visit them in the autumn. Vanessa told us that even in October and November the temperatures in Southern California can be in the eighties. Eddie was delighted, especially when Michael suggested that we could take a tram down to Tijuana in Mexico and eat shrimp burritos. Vanessa said, 'Hey, guys! You should come for Halloween, my mom makes great pumpkin pie.' Eddie smiled again.

It was indeed still in the eighties Fahrenheit at the end of October when we got to San Diego and Vanessa couldn't wait to drive us in her convertible Volkswagen to Ocean Beach. This is a small town that looks like a faded photograph of the 1960s. There are beach bums with filthy legs and matted beards laid on sea-view benches, thrift shops galore, back-pack hostels and surf shops and a fantastic record shop called Cow Records. I bought a Ventures CD and on the way back we put it on the car stereo and blasted out 'Hawaii Five-O,' Heather and Edward were in their glory.

I'm sitting on Vanessa and Michael's front porch watching a tiny hummingbird moving from flower to flower. I've never seen a hummingbird before and it fascinates me. My dad comes to my mind. He once asked me, 'What's the only bird that can fly backwards?' Before I could answer he said, 'Hummingbird!' And then, like he always did, he spoiled his information by adding, 'And if you ever see a magpie flying backwards over Heath Common, it's going to rain!'

On the Sunday before we set off to America our Andrew had phoned me.

'I'll just say it straight out,' he said.

'Has he died?' I replied.

'Yes, about ten minutes ago. I'm just waiting for the doctor to come to confirm it.'

'Are you alright?'

'No, I'm a bit frightened.'

'Why?'

'Well, I'm sat on my own on the settee and there's a dead body in the next room.'

'You've done a good job looking after him these past few months, just think about that.'

'He asked me to hold his hand this afternoon.'

I don't think I've had such a touching conversation with my brother before. I didn't know what to say and I don't think he did either.

The hummingbird moves to the garden next door.

My father followed me down to Mexico. We went on a tram, like we went on the tram from Blackpool to Fleetwood in the holidays of forty odd years ago. We arrived at Tijuana as they were preparing for the *Dia de Los Muertos* – the Day of the Dead – or as we call it, All Saints Day. There were photographs of relatives and loved ones in the shop windows.

Tijuana is strange, in the way that a lot of border towns are strange. On the borders between Poland, Germany and the Czech Republic, they sell gnomes and the prostitutes stand inside what look like bus shelters out of the rain. Here they sell Viagra and clenbuterol to American day trippers. They fix rotten teeth for far less than they do in LA. Here they paint donkeys to look like zebras and tourists have their photos taken alongside them, and the newspaper sellers wear red noses like Charlie Cairoli. My dad would have loved it in this town.

I spend a lot of the day thinking about what my dad liked; fresh air, allotments, wellingtons, bib-and-brace overalls, chips and duck eggs. He said that chips and duck eggs was one of the finest meals a man could have and if you 'got a plateful of that across your chest, you would ail nowt'.

On the way back Heather said, 'You've been quiet today, what's up?'

I looked through the window on the tram to see we were passing through the suburb of Chula Vista. I remembered the old Tom Waits song, so I started to sing: 'Once had a girl in Chula Vista, I fell in love with her sister, and the doctor says I'll be alright, But I feel blue.'

Heather said, 'Ignore him, everybody says he takes after his dad.'

By the time we got to Chicago, it was 'Day of the Dead'. We stayed in Pilsen, in the south side, once the place where Czech people settled, now a neighbourhood of Mexican and Latin American people. In the evening we watched a street parade of skeletons, witches, devils, zombies and children with painted on stitches and scars. Earlier on this day, at a crematorium in Hull, a vicar who my dad had never known and my two brothers said their last goodbyes.

We went for coffee in a lovely Mexican café called 'Kristofers'. Next door in the front window there was a photo of a young woman with some words about her life underneath it. She was the mother of two children who had been run over and killed outside the coffee shop by a hit-and-run driver a few years before. In the intervening time the local authority had named a nearby street after her. I can't ever see anything ever being named after my dad. In my mind I temporarily called the street our apartment was on, Sidney Street. As the band Was (Not Was) once sang, 'Somewhere in America, there's a street named after my dad.'

After Chicago we spent a week in the woods of Indiana. The autumn colours were out of this world. In Susan and Angela's garden there was a big old maple tree full of golden leaves when we got there, by our final day the last few leaves were spinning in the breeze.

At the airport in Chicago we sat waiting to check-in next to an old man and his son. The old man introduced himself to me. He said, 'My name is Edward Schawalski, sir, and I'm 92 years old.' He told me that he'd just been in California with his son and then started telling me about when he was a boy.

'I was raised on a farm on the border between Illinois and Indiana. We grew tomatoes and onions. My father drove a horse and buggy. When we saw a Ford Model T come by we threw tomatoes at it. Great fun! Did you ever throw tomatoes at a Ford Model T?'

Edward Schawalski's son sidled up and whispered, 'You'll have to excuse him, he has Alzheimer's.'

I ignored him and said to his dad, 'No, I never threw tomatoes at a Ford Model T, but I wish I had done.'

'Great fun, son!' said the old guy, 'Great fun.'

I said, 'My dad taught me a poem abut tomatoes when I was a lad, would you like to hear it?'

'Sure, son, go right ahead.'

'When I was walking with my uncle Jim, a boy came round a corner and chucked a tomato at him. Now, tomatoes don't hurt when they come in their skin, but this one did, 'cos it came in a tin.'

Heather and my lad Edward winced. Edward Schawalski's son moved to one side and a mixture of mine and the old man's laughter echoed across the waiting area of O'Hare Airport terminal one. Passers by looked across at us and then away. The old man winked, 'Yep! That's a good 'un, son!' Then he lowered his head onto his chest, his chin resting just above the waistband on his trousers. He looked up and twinkled. 'Did you ever throw tomatoes at a Ford Model T? When I was a boy on the farm we used to throw tomatoes when our neighbour came by in his Ford Model T. Great fun that was!'

The last time I saw my dad, on the day he shoved his wallet down the front of his underpants, we talked about where he wanted his ashes scattering. He said that he had been thinking about Heath Common. 'It's a place I've always gone back to. I've even been up there with my metal detector.'

Before I went to America I left word with Andrew for him to hold onto Dad's ashes. 'We'll have our own little remembrance service, just you, me and our Tony, and then we'll scatter his ashes on the wind up on Heath Common.' When I got back home from America, the first letter I opened was the bill from the funeral directors. I sent a cheque to an old-fashioned firm somewhere up Beverley Road. I phoned our Andrew.

'When you're ready, we'll set a day to scatter Dad's ashes.'

'I've buried them.'

'You've what!'

272

'I've buried them. I thought they ought to go in that bit of garden in front of his flat. He put a lot of work into that bit of land to make it look nice, so I thought it would be good for him to be in there.'

'So, our dad's last resting place is in a bloody flower bed next to a car park in front of a block of council flats in Hull?'

'It seemed the right thing to do. You were in America. Our Tony wasn't bothered either way and I had an urn full of ashes that needed something doing with them.'

I was a bit hurt. Having tried to make an effort to reconcile I thought I might have a bit more say on what happened with the ashes. Our Andrew reminded me about the last time he had been put in charge of ash scattering. When my dad's mother Joyce died, Dad decided he would find his father's grave and scatter them on the earth there. He and Andrew put the urn in a carrier bag and took the bus from Hull to Wakefield. They searched a cemetery at Outwood, but couldn't find a headstone. My dad remembered then that they probably hadn't been able to afford one at the time, so they poured out the contents of the urn at the back of a tree.

Happiness Cottage

Once upon a time there was a little girl called Pauline. When she was just one year old her father was called away to fight a war. This little girl was doted on by her mother and her aunts, they dressed her in little frilly frocks, they made her hair look nice and bought her lots of dollies to play with. This little girl's favourite book was one called *Heidi*, a book all about a simple little girl who grew up in the mountains in Switzerland and went to stay with her grumpy grandfather after her parents died. When Heidi grew up she went to be the companion of a disabled girl in the city, she looked after the disabled girl very well, but some people laughed at Heidi because of her simple country ways. Pauline loved reading her book about Heidi and when they made the book into a film starring Shirley Temple, Pauline's aunt took her to see it at the cinema. Pauline promised herself that one day when she grew up and married a handsome young man, she would have a beautiful princess daughter and she would christen her Heidi and they would all live happily together in a lovely little cottage with a wishing well and a bird table in the garden. Pauline was, of course, my mother.

When Pauline was just eighteen she met a man called Sid who span Waltzers round on the fairgrounds. He chewed chewing gum, wore a leather jacket with his name in studs on the back of it, combed his hair like a Teddy Boy and talked in riddles. Pauline's mam and dad really didn't like Sid, but one day when Pauline told them that she was having a baby, they said that she had made her bed, so now she should lie on it. One day in spring, Pauline got married in the church where, twenty years before, her parents had been wed. Pauline and Sid had their wedding reception in The Clock Café, a greasy spoon just two hundred yards from where they rented their first house. Pauline felt sick at the reception and started to cry. Sid put an extra spoon of sugar in her tea, told her to sup up and not to be so bloody soft. Pauline's dad took Sid to one side and said, 'If you ever do owt wrong to that lass, you'll have me to bloody answer to,' and he clenched his big coal miner's fist and said, 'And I'm not laughing.' Sid laughed, a shrill, nervous laugh and shrugged his shoulders. Pauline's dad said, 'I'm still not bloody laughing!'

Pauline carried her baby all through the red hot summer of 1959 and gave birth to a seven pound four ounce healthy boy in the September. That baby was me. By the beginning of the following spring she was pregnant again and before the year was out my brother Tony came along, a strapping lad of nine pounds. Pauline loved her two little boys, but yearned to have a little girl. The trouble was she had very quickly gone off Sid and went days, sometimes weeks, without even talking to him. Sid didn't seem too interested and spent his days cleaning windows for neighbours and feeding the hens and rabbits he kept on his allotment. Not long after Pauline had got her boys off to school she was carrying another baby. One of the old superstitious neighbours dangled a needle and cotton over the bump in her belly and when the needle turned in circles, the neighbour said, 'You will have a girl,' and then asked, 'Have you had a lot of heartburn?' When Pauline said she had, the neighbour said, 'A girl with a good head of hair.' Pauline had another boy, ten pounds this time and she called him Andrew David. And before Andrew was out of his terry nappies, Pauline started to be poorly. It was a hard time for her, she did her best to bring up three lads in a poky little terraced house that she didn't even own, without much help from a husband who told her he didn't give a bugger about anything and thought she ought to 'pull herself together'. Pauline daydreamed about the countryside and mountains in Switzerland and little girls running across meadows with wildflowers.

One day, Sid's youngest brother Jimmy paid a compliment to Pauline, smiled at her in a nice way and told her that she deserved better. And then every time Jimmy saw her he found something nice to say. Pauline looked forward to Jimmy popping in. One day when Sid was at work, Jimmy asked Pauline out and she put on her best coat and shoes and they did go out. This became a regular event until one day Sid, who was becoming suspicious about Pauline's many visits to town to meet 'a friend', decided to follow and found Pauline and Jimmy holding hands. On that day Jimmy decided he would leave his wife and Pauline would run away from her husband. They found a house together and before long Pauline was pregnant with Jimmy's child. This time she had the little girl that her heart desired and she called that little girl Heidi. Jimmy and Pauline doted on Heidi, they dressed her in lacy pinafore frocks and made garlands of flowers for her hair. They moved to the countryside and bought a little bungalow and, apart from an occasional visit to eat Sunday dinner with Pauline's ageing mother, they didn't socialise with many people apart from themselves.

I came to live back at my gran's not long after my dad found my mam holding hands with Jimmy. That was in 1975. I saw my mother just a few times after that, mostly at my gran's when she and Jimmy came over for visits. I left school the following year and, after I met Heather, we lived a very different life to the one I'd had. I heard the odd bit of news from time to time, but I never felt the urge to be part of my mother's new life and I'm sure she didn't see any need to be part of mine. Jimmy died of cancer when he was still in his sixties, Heidi had a daughter of her own and my mother's health declined. When my dad asked if I might go and see him before he died, I started to think that perhaps I ought to try and visit my mother as well. I'd heard that she had become confused and was suffering from developing senility. One day I came home from work and opened my e-mails. There was one from a man I didn't know that said, 'I have been given the task of informing you that your mother has died, I understand from your sister Heidi that due to a family rift, you have had little contact in nearly forty years, but Heidi wanted you to know. The funeral is at St Andrews church in Paull on Thursday at one pm.'

I phoned our Tony and Andrew. We decided that we would travel to the funeral together, to pay our respects, and that we would spend an hour or so with Heidi, the sister we hardly knew, and beyond that we didn't know what else we could do. We drove into Paull, the village where our mother had chosen to spend her retirement years, to look for a bungalow that none of us had ever seen. Paull must have been a pretty enough fishing village on the banks of the Humber at one time, but these days its gateway is a huge oil terminal in the flatlands that run out to the sea beyond Hull. We saw ornaments in a Walt Disney little garden and a sign that said 'Happiness Cottage'. Our Tony and me turned to each other and at the same time said, 'That'll be it.' The bungalow was damp and smelled strongly of Glade air fresheners and drying washing. Heidi came to the door head-to-toe in black, her daughter holding her hand. She told the girl, 'These are your uncles, Mary Lou.' The little girl skipped off to sit on the settee and picked up a colouring book. I didn't know what to say, I'd last seen Heidi for half an hour at my gran's funeral thirteen years before and maybe half a dozen times before that. I said, 'Your shoes are nice.' She said, 'I used to go line dancing in them.' On the shelf I noticed some videos of Loretta Lynn and there was a photo of Heidi on the wall in a cowboy hat.

There were about fifteen people at the funeral. The church was bonny, on a little hill at the edge of the village with its own graveyard. We filed in and sat on the front pew. The vicar waited for everyone to settle and then offered up his prayer. 'Lord you have been our refuge from generation to generation...' He obviously hadn't known our mother. He talked about her coming from West Yorkshire originally, that she had retired to this village and that she loved her daughter and granddaughter and fought bravely against the illness that blighted her recent life, and that was that. He announced that Heidi had chosen some music and we would hear Elvis Presley singing 'Love Me Tender'. There was too long a pause while the man at the organ fiddled with a portable CD player and half of the congregation started coughing. Elvis started to sing 'The Wonder of You' and the vicar looked up to his rafters or perhaps beyond. As the bearers picked up the coffin to carry it on its short journey to a plot by the wall, Elvis joined us again and this time he did sing 'Love Me Tender'. Our mother was buried in the same hole as Jimmy. I saw his name on a wooden stick that had been placed there by the gravedigger. We stayed to eat some egg-mayonnaise sandwiches and Bakewell tart, we met a jolly woman and her three friends. The jolly woman said, 'We were your mother's carers.' I met the man who had sent me the e-mail, he told me that he ran local karaoke sessions. Then we set off back. I said to our Tony, 'Do you feel sad?' He shook his head, 'No, not sad, just a bit strange.' I said, 'I'm the same.' I guess that not all stories that start 'Once upon a time…' end up with everybody living happily ever after.

Letting Go

My dad gave me the ring that our Tony found in the hole on the beach at Blackpool. I think he gave it to me when I came to live at my gran's. My first job after I left school was at a long-gone engineering works. I did bench fitting next to an El Alamein veteran called Ted who drove a powder-blue Volkswagen. Ted smoked one woodbine after another whilst filing the flashings off bottle moulds. I also learned to engrave with a hammer and a diamond-nosed chisel from a man with a brush moustache called Pat, who looked like he ought to have been in a third-division football team, either that or a working men's club glam rock band. One lunch break I decided to file off the initials on the ring and put my own name there. I engraved 'Ian' onto it under Pat's supervision. I wore that ring until my fingers became too fat for it. For the past thirty years it has been at the bottom of a drawer. It's one of the few things I have that came from my dad.

It's a bright, cold Sunday morning just before Christmas. I take my dad's ring out of its drawer and squeeze it onto my little finger. I phone Eleanor, Barry Hines' wife, and ask if she will pick me up at Elsecar railway station. I haven't seen Barry for a couple of months now and Eleanor says he's had a bad few weeks. He has some sores on his head and he's sleeping more than usual, though he's still eating well.

On the train I sit opposite a young boy who is being taken to Meadowhall shopping centre for a pre-Christmas treat.

'It's his first time on a train,' says Grandma.

'I used to go on steam trains when I was your age.' I say to the little lad, 'to the seaside at Blackpool.'

The little lad looks at his gran, she says, 'Me too!'

I pretend to be a train driver and say 'Choo! Choo!'

The little lad looks at me, looks at his grandma and then out of the window. I fiddle with the ring to see if it will slide off. I close my eyes and think of childhood visits to the seaside and trips on the train to see Auntie Laura; her back garden backed onto the railway line and she always came out to wave with her handkerchief as the train went by.

Barry comes into my mind. I don't know if he knows who I am and I never really know what to say to him. They say you should never meet your heroes don't they? I ponder on whether you should meet your heroes when they're in a nursing home. Then I wonder what Bob Dylan said to Woody Guthrie when he visited him in hospital when he got to New York.

I remember when Heather met her hero, the MP Claire Short. We were visiting the House of Commons and enjoying a drink in the bar. Someone had laid on plates of nibbles; sliced carrot batons with various dips and cocktail sausages spiked on wooden sticks. Claire Short walked in and Heather jumped up straightaway, 'Oooh! Claire Short,' she said 'I've got to say "Hello" to her.' She was only gone two minutes. When she came back to our table, I asked her what she had said. Heather laughed, 'Well I didn't know what to say, so I offered her a cold sausage.'

Perhaps that's what you do on meeting heroes.

Eleanor is waiting in her car at the station. It takes about twenty minutes to drive from here to the nursing home. I spend a fair part of the journey fiddling with the ring, when I slide it up my finger it leaves a white ridge. On the car stereo Jacques Brel is singing.

'Juliette Gréco has just done an album of Brel songs,' I say.

'Is she still alive?'

'Yep, though I don't think she much as sings these days as talks.'

As we come towards the home I show Eleanor the ring. I tell her the story about our Tony finding it on Blackpool beach all those years ago, about my dad claiming it and then about it coming to me.

Barry is sitting in a high-backed chair dozing with his chin on a charity shop shirt. Eleanor takes out his wedding ring and places it onto his finger, 'I like to bring it and put it on. When we got married I didn't expect him to buy a ring or anything, it wasn't a fussy wedding, just a registry office, because he'd been married before. Then he pulled out this ring that he'd bought. He was very proud of it.' She touches the ring with her own. 'I bought this one at an antique fair in Derbyshire. It's an American one. I made a little story up to go with it. I imagine it was worn by a GI who was over here during the war. He gave it to a young woman from Buxton or somewhere in return for a nice shag.' She laughs. Barry has his eyes closed, but a smile comes to his face. Eleanor kisses him and holds his hands. She notices a mark on his arm, 'I haven't seen that before, I wonder what it is.'

'We used to call them blood blisters,' I say 'Can you remember blood blisters, Barry?'

Barry opens his eyes momentarily, then shuts them again.

'I've just come back from America, Barry. I saw a lovely exhibition of Matisse's work at Indianapolis.'

Eleanor squeezes Barry's hands, 'You like Matisse don't you Barry?'

Barry keeps his eyes closed.

'He likes Matisse, but his favourite is Leger, he likes the ones he did of acrobats and miners.'

I can only stay for an hour today. I want to get back to Wakefield. Before I leave I go to give Barry a hug. He is surprised by the feel of my whiskers on his cheek. He opens his eyes and becomes animated.

'Fucking fart,' he says.

I get off the train at Wakefield Kirkgate on the way back. This is the station where nearly half a century ago I sat with my dad while he pondered on how he would bring my mother home after she left him. I look to where I thought the bench we sat on was, then I walk out of the city towards Heath Common. It's bitter cold now, the sun is still low and shining, but the wind is picking up. I pass the new Hepworth gallery and then Wakefield Trinity's rugby-league ground where Lindsay Anderson set the film of David Storey's book *This Sporting Life*. Somewhere on the grass at this ground, Richard Harris got his teeth kicked out, before he went to be a lodger at Rachel Robert's house.

On Heath Common a woman is pushing an old pram full of carrots across the grass. Gypsy ponies tied to stakes are grazing. This Common was never enclosed and the gypsies still take up their right to graze animals here.

I walk up the hill to the top of the Common and think about my dad. I find a stone to sit on and light a cigarette. In my mind I conjure my father. It's not a cold day like today, but a summer day a long time ago. My dad lays on the grass propped up on one arm, he has a nipped cigarette behind his ear and he's chewing on a spent match stalk. He looks over to me and calls me 'Narrow'.

'What's tha know then, Narrow?'

'How do you mean?'

'Well, what do people tell thee?'

'My Auntie Alice says that you should never eat the pips from an apple or else an apple tree will grow inside you.'

'She's right!'

'How can that be? Apple trees don't grow inside people.'

'No, I know. But you should never eat apple pips. What else do people tell thee?'

'My gran says that her bread and pastry and Yorkshire puddings never come out right when she's not feeling well.'

'Stands to reason, lad, so that's true an'all. You need cold hands for baking. When you're off it your hands get too warm. What does thi grandad tell thee?'

'He says you should always pick up a stone, because you never know what you might find underneath it.'

'Depends on how big the stone is, kid. There's no point in putting a lot of effort in to picking up a stone only to drop it on your feet.'

I look at my dad in this mind's eye. In his little red book, Chairman Mao quotes an old Chinese proverb that says 'The effort of picking up a heavy stone is only worth it if you can then hold up the stone to prevent it falling on your toes.'

My dad is disappearing now, but I can still hear his voice. 'Here's one from me. Some people *say* and other people *do*? And there's some that say they're going to do and then don't but the buggers you've got to watch your back with are them that say they're going to do what they say and then do something else.'

'I don't know about that.'

'I thought you were supposed to be educated!'

My dad spits out his match stalk. 'I'll tell thee this. A lot of the best stuff happens behind you and underneath. Always look underneath.'

High above my head some birds of prey hover like kites, I think they're buzzards, they circle like the ones in cowboy films.

My dad's voice echoes now. 'Tha can't ever kid a kidder kid, never pretend.'

I think about my recent visit to Indianapolis. I went to the Kurt Vonnegut library. On the wall there is a sign bearing one of his quotes, 'We are what we pretend to be, so we must be careful about what we pretend to be.'

The wind is whistling now over this Common. It brings water to my eyes. I start to twist the ring from my finger. It won't come off and my hands are so cold I rub my fingers together and spit on them like I'm about to make a deal. The ring slides off. I walk to the edge of the Common and dig a small hole. I put the ring into the damp, soft earth, press the ring down into it and cover it over. I pick up a big old stone and place it over where

I have dug. I hope that a metal detector of the future finds this ring and then makes up a story about it for their son or daughter.

I say 'Ta-ra' to my dad now, that's all.

I walk from the Common past the row of cottages where I once knocked on a door to ask for a glass of water on the day England played Brazil in the Mexico World Cup. Then on, up a country road that is called Hell Lane towards Sharlston Pit where my grandfather worked in a seam that was only twenty-two inches deep. The pit's all gone now and they've started building new detached houses here. Opposite the pit gates the 'Kibble' working men's club still stands, but its windows are boarded up. When these windows had glass in them I looked through once to see my grandad gambling away his wage on dominoes and cards.

I come past the Lin-Pac factory on Wakefield Road. This is where, on a windy day like this nearly half a century ago, my dad was hit by a falling roll of paper. I couldn't help but wonder, what if? What if that roll hadn't fallen, what if it hadn't hit my dad and fractured his pelvis, what if he hadn't got compensation and spent it on a crumby terraced house at Hull? What would have been different?

When I get home I sit at the kitchen table and draw a little map of where I have buried the ring. I fold it up like a pirate and place it in an old shoe box with other mementoes of life's passing; my dad's funeral bill and a copy of my dad's birth certificate which tells me that he was born on 7th January 1934. I start to write about what I have done.

If I have learned one thing over this last year or so, it's that he wasn't such a bad old stick. I won't wince the next time somebody says to me, 'You're like your bloody father!'

Acknowledgements

To Ian Daley and Isabel Galan for all they do at Route.
To Richard Jeffrey, Chris Johnson, Hui Xiao for commenting on the draft version.
To Pam Oxley for typing an early draft.
To Peter Wilson for proofreading.
To John Finch, Alice Nutter and Andy Kershaw and Eleanor Hines for kindness.
To Our Tony for giving me some of the best dialogue.

For further information on this book
and other titles please visit:
www.ianclaytoninfo.wordpress.com
www.route-online.com